ITALY IN
Small Bites

ITALY IN
Small Bites

CAROL FIELD

HarperCollins*Publishers*

HarperCollins books may be purchased for educational, business,
or sales promotional use. For information, please write:
Special Markets Department, HarperCollins Publishers Inc.,
10 East 53rd Street, New York, NY 10022.

Some of the biscotti recipes in this book
have been previously published in *Gourmet* magazine.

Originally published in 1993 by William Morrow and Company, Inc.

FIRST EDITION

BOOK DESIGN BY JOEL AVIROM
DESIGN ASSISTANT JIM COZZA
ILLUSTRATIONS BY MELANIE PARKS

Printed on acid-free paper

Library of Congress Cataloging in Publication Data
is available upon request.

ISBN 0-06-072279-7

04 05 06 07 08 ❖/RRD 10 9 8 7 6 5 4 3 2 1

This book is for
Alison and Matthew

C O N T

E N T S

Introduction to the 2004 Edition

*B*ruschetta drizzled with freshly pressed olive oil, a frittata of sweet spring onions, focaccia filled with creamy cheese, grilled eggplant, and sun-warmed tomatoes: I knew I had found a powerful idea for a book when I could establish an instant rapport with Italians merely by mentioning the centuries-old tradition of between-meal meals that they call *spuntini* and *merende*. These midmorning and midafternoon informal refreshments are located on the Italian culinary map somewhere between the nurturing tastes of home, a simple picnic, and a snack in its most exalted form. Hearing men and women speak with passion and reverence about food memories from their childhoods, I became convinced that *spuntini* and *merende* are the true "soul" food of Italy. Once I knew what these small tastes meant to them, I was hooked—I had to know more.

Now, more than ten years after this book was first published, I see the word *merenda* everywhere in Italy. It turns up in newspapers and magazines, crops up in casual conversations, and is sometimes used as it was in the past to denote a series of authentic local dishes made with the freshest and finest ingredients. Websites are devoted to it. Some feature food for children and others are focused on teaching children how to cook.

Italians are still attached to *merende*, but now they are adopting them in new ways. There are more and more wine bars that present tantalizing little dishes with which to make a meal. More *osterie* put out assorted bite-size tastes, *enoteche* offer slices of assorted salame and cheeses, and more bakeries make stunningly good *focacce* and *panini*. Smallish portions are now *molto di moda* as antipasti or *primi* or as a whole meal made by combining several. Served informally, they represent some of the best food Italy has to offer. Exalting the irresistible flavors of home and countryside, made from the best local products and fresh ingredients at the peak of their flavor—sweet tomatoes in season, artichokes with purple-tinged leaves, fava beans bursting in their pods, creamy young sheep's milk cheese or fennel-flecked salame—*merende* are eaten out of hand or with a piece of *focaccia*, with a sprinkling of cheese or a drizzle of the finest olive oil, seated at a table or standing.

From the beginning Italians could hardly believe my interest in *merende*, a phenomenon they took entirely for granted. Nor could they fathom an entire book on the subject, since each person assumed there was a single *merenda*—his or hers. I, in turn, was amazed that no one guessed that a child in Turin might eat differently from one in Sicily, or that men in the fields of Puglia ate differently from marble workers in Carrara. Now both Americans and Italians can realize that *merende* are as irresistible, numerous, and endlessly tempting as ingenuity and the endless regional culinary possibilities of Italy permit. Healthy and nutritious, these small meals fit into our lifestyles as well as they do into the Italians'. Revelations all around.

Acknowledgments

*T*his book would never have been written without the help of count-less Italians who responded with untold kindnesses and generosity, educating me about *spuntini* and *merende*, and making them for me. I hope they will forgive my taking a few liberties in including some wonderful dishes discovered during my research, which, while not technically true *merende*, were too delicious to leave out.

Invaluable help came from Professor Renato Bergonzini; Francesca Colombini Cinelli and Donatella Cinelli; June di Schino; Daniela Falini; Patience Gray; Camillo, Roberta, and Simona Guerra; Giovanna Iacopetti; Massimo Lorenzetti; Sonia Lorenzini; Andrea Luciani; Antonio Marella; Teresa and Antonio Mastroberardino; Ze Migliore; Teresio Montesi; Giorgio Onesti; Italo Pedroni; Lucio Pompili; Pasquale Porcelli; Angelo and Dora Ricci; Lamberto Ridolfi and his mother, Amalia Ceccarelli; Professor Luigi Sada, Margherita Simili, and Vanucci Venanzio.

Giovanni Minuccio Cappelli graciously permitted me to use recipes collected over many decades in ancient family ledgers. Maria Ferrante allowed me the use of some recipes from Puglia she had researched and published in Italy.

Thanks to my loyal testers Diane Dexter, Chris Engle, Jon Eldan, Carol Sinton, and Donata Magiapinto; to the International Olive Oil Council; and to the GRI, and Tony May, in particular, for the educational opportunities they provided me in Italy.

In America I could not have done without the help of Paola and Giuseppe Bagnatori, Rolando Beramendi, Sunnie Evers, Ridgely Evers, Corby Kummer, Carlo Middione, Maria Quinn, and Zanne Zakroff Stewart of *Gourmet*, who commissioned an article on biscotti.

Special thanks to Riccardo and Gianna Bertelli, Romana Bicocchi-Picchi, Shirley and Francois Caracciolo, Sammie Daniels, Nicoletta Peduzzi and her entire family, Antonio and Cynthia Piccinardi, Franco Santasilia, and Faith Willinger for their help and hospitality in Italy. I am always grateful to Carlo and Renato Veggetti for their knowledge of bread and bakers, and to Silene Veggetti for her warm friendship.

Special thanks to my editor, Ann Bramson, to copy editor Ann Cahn, to book designer Joel Avirom, and to my agent, Fred Hill.

I could not have done any of this without the enthusiastic encouragement of my family. John lived through all the travel with good humor and lots of helpful suggestions and then once again ate his way through the results. Matthew and Alison, who loved *merende* before any of us knew what they really were, are, as always, my greatest supporters.

Merende

Eating in Italy is such an immense pleasure that it should be no surprise to discover that Italians have a tradition of eating not three but five meals a day. Breakfast, lunch, and dinner may mark the beginning, middle, and end of the day, but for centuries two small informal meals have been tucked in between. These are *merende*, tasty, nourishing little bites eaten at midmorning and midafternoon.

These appetizing tastes are really food in its simplest form. They come from a world rooted in the cultivation of the earth and are based on a respect for natural ingredients. They take the products of the countryside and transform them into irresistible little meals: from fields and kitchen gardens come a myriad of greens and herbs, eggplant, tomatoes, sweet peppers, artichokes, garlic, and onions. Olives, one-third of the great Italian triumvirate that includes grapes and grain, are harvested from groves of silvery gray trees and pressed into fresh, fruity oil. From the seaside of Campania, where white sheets flap against cobalt skies and cliffs drop away sharply to the sea, come salty anchovies and sardines. The farmhouses and dairies of Lombardy, Tuscany, Campania, and Puglia send forth milky cheeses that are sliced and interwoven with tomatoes, tossed with toasted walnuts and slivers of crunchy celery, or roasted whole in the oven. From the Veneto and the arc of mountains west and south come steaming mounds of polenta, poured onto gigantic wooden boards. Cooled and cut into bite-size squares and rectangles, then fried or grilled, polenta becomes *crostini*, personal platters for wild mushrooms, fresh tomato sauces, quail, sausages, and buttery cheeses. From every part of the country comes homemade bread in all its glorious incarnations, the entire panoply of products of the pig, and always bottles and jugs and glasses of wine to be passed among friends.

If I were to choose the archetypal *merenda*, it would have to be *bruschetta*, slices of a chewy country bread grilled over an open fire, rubbed with a fat clove of garlic, and drizzled with the newly pressed pungent fresh green oil. I'd want to add cheeses flavored by herbs that the sheep have fed on and olives inflected with the scent of garlic or herbs. Necessity—another word for poverty, the mother of so much invention—respect for abundant local ingredients, and exuberant imagination have created these small informal meals.

I am not talking about food that is totally unknown here. In fact, a few of these dishes are so familiar in America that they have already become a part of our everyday lives—pizza, for example, or the olives, salami, and cold salads on antipasto platters—while others, like bruschetta and crostini, are newer passions that we are embracing with enthusiasm. Most of these little dishes partake of the unpretentious attitude about food that is at the heart of much Italian cooking. They have been taken for granted in their communities for so long that even in Italy no one has given them much thought, which is why many of them have never left home. Until recently they haven't appeared on menus except in the down-to-earth *osterie* and *trattorie* that serve a midafternoon snack to workers, to men playing cards or drinking wine and needing bites of tasty food to accompany their drinks.

Just as some of these dishes are familiar, others will be entirely new. Americans have already discovered Italian food with a passion: Pasta and pizza have conquered the New World, and rustic regional breads have made an auspicious appearance. The triumphant tastes that Italians create—so fresh, so bright—are one reason why Americans find their food so accessible and irresistible. Now here come *merende*, rustic tastes from the countryside that are meant to be shared with friends and family. As the foods of this ancient Italian custom find their way across the Atlantic, they may find yet another incarnation as we fit them easily into our daily lives.

If *merende* have any common denominator at all, it is the presence of bread dough. *Merende* may vary dramatically from region to region—the fig sausage of Le Marche would never be found in the Veneto, and Friuli's crunchy cheese *frico* is totally unknown in Calabria—but the people of every area care passionately about their rough country loaves and the crunchy crusted wheels that come out of the baker's oven. This deep attachment to traditional bread has inspired numerous specialties that begin with bread dough, the most accessible of ingredients in Italy. These simple inventions may be twists or rectangles of dough flavored with sausage and cracked black peppercorns, with dustings of cheese, or with sprinklings of fresh herbs or tangles of sweet peppers. They may be baked in the oven or fried in hot oil, they may be served with varying flavorings and fillings, but they all belong to the family tree of bread.

Merende descend from the rural past. They did not start out as antipasti or as little light dishes to open the way to a series of further courses. Rather, they were a necessity during the long, tiring days of work in fields and pastures that were too vast to allow men to return home for their meals. Workers needed hefty fare to fuel them in their labors, and they found recourse in quick meals that they could carry with them. The term *companatico*, a lovely word meaning "something to eat with bread," from the Latin *col pane*, was really born in this situation, where instead of a dining table there were pastures, fallow lands, the woods, the shoulder of a hill, or the shore of a riverbed. In those days, a *merenda* was thickly sliced crusty country bread and whatever products nature provided at that season: tomatoes still warm from the vine, a handful of home-cured olives, wild marjoram or oregano or basil, figs or persimmons just plucked from the tree, a hunk of cheese, a few walnuts, a couple of sardines, tuna, anchovies sprinkled with garlic, pepper, and a little oil, a spoonful of homemade preserves, mortadella or salame and prosciutto from the family pig. At *merenda* time, says Renato Bergonzini, an expert on regional foods and mores, "the soul is free." And the food is truly soul food. It is basic food with a connection to all that Italians hold most important: family, friends, and the products of the earth.

Merende are very simple: the two eating implements usually consist of one right hand and one left one. Often the bread is in one hand, the fruit or salame or cheese in the other, and the rhythm of the meal is to eat a bite of one, then a bite of the other. Or perhaps they are simply *bruschetta* or *crostini*, *focaccia* or *calzone*, forms of flavored bread as a portable plate dappled with flavoring, the container and the contained eaten all at the same time. In bygone days a bottle of mineral water always stood nearby, and there was abundant wine as well, cooled in the summertime in the waters of a stream or covered with moist fig leaves and left in the shade of a tree. Sometimes the wine was in special flasks made with a very fine neck so that, as with a boda, a thread of wine fell at a distance from the container, making it not only a fine accompaniment to a meal but also a tidy way around the need for glasses. *Merende* are the tastes of a world in which landscape, agriculture, and food all meet in harmony, where food has a clear connection to the earth from which it has been harvested. They satisfy the spirit as well as the stomach.

Everywhere I traveled, I asked people what they ate for their *merende*. Sometimes women dashed into their kitchens and came out carrying loaves of country bread and a jar of homemade preserves or spicy black olive paste, slices of zucchini tarts, or a ladle full of home-cured olives. They cut wedges of cornmeal focaccia fragrant with walnuts or slid a slice of raisin-studded cake into my hands. Sometimes they insisted on frying bread dough and stuffing it with soft creamy cheeses that literally melted in my mouth. Or they took me to friends' houses or to simple take-out shops, to wine bars and *locande* where the food that everyone eats is so taken for granted that it doesn't even appear on the menu.

If I worried aloud that I was putting them to trouble, they laughed and insisted I eat more. These simple foods are a way of locating themselves in childhood or in the embrace of family, friends, and the countryside in which many of them once worked. My questions often triggered intense nostalgia, images of generous fireplaces and hearths as well as taste memories of earlier times.

Today Italians are often nostalgic for the *merende* of their childhoods, especially since most contemporary versions are commercially prepackaged. Leisurely moments in midmorning and midafternoon are fast disappearing even in Italy, where simple *merende* are being replaced by fast food, microwaved food, and multiple kinds of *panini* that have been described as "the tombs of taste." I have seen a bite-size bar of aged Parmesan cheese individually wrapped and sealed in vacuum-packed pop-top tins. There is an instant cheese product destined for the microwave called Zappetite. The current ubiquitous *merenda* is Nutella, a chocolate hazelnut paste in a jar, to be scooped out and spread on a slab of bread.

Often when I asked people about their *merende*, I got no reply at all—just a blank look and quizzical silence. It was only when I asked what they had eaten as children, or what their grandmothers and mothers had made, that the puzzlement lifted and they embarked on an exhilarating remembrance of dishes that still made their eyes light up. They recalled the vendors who used to sell crisp fritters filled with apples, chestnuts, or fresh melting ricotta, and told of wives and mothers arriving in the fields bearing fritters of hot *baccalà*. They remembered buying thick slices of *pizza rustica*, an envelope of dough filled with cheeses, prosciutto, even tangles of the sunny vegetables of the south. In Palermo, children rushed out with cupped hands to greet the mulberry vendor, waiting for their ration of the delicate fruit that stained their fingers and mouths a deep blue-black.

Merende were an inherent part of country life until the end of World War II and the consequent phenomenon called *il boom*, whose prosperity brought dramatic changes in the Italian way of life. It coincided with the phasing out of the *mezzadria*, the sharecropping system in which the farmers lived in farmhouses around the villa of the wealthy proprietor, cultivating his fields and sharing in his profits. By the 1960s, as the system was being dismantled, huge numbers of families had already begun to move off the land, having discovered there was more money to be made in the cities. The prosperity of the postwar years and the abandonment of the countryside eroded the tradition of the *merenda*, since no one really needed the little meals and the food once associated with them.

Now, in one of those lovely twists of fortune, the breads and polentas, the rustic tortes and light vegetable mixtures, the focacce and pizze and crunchy little bites of cheese, are all reappearing in Italy, for they have become chic, full of rustic charm and appeal, a way of remembering all that has been lost in modern life.

Perhaps the same thing will happen here. *Merende* are perfect for contemporary eating, for they fit easily into the relaxed way we live now. Small plates with many little tastes can become a meal—any meal—and they are healthy, inexpensive, casual. Put several together and you have a light lunch, a brunch, an informal dinner. This food brings people together to celebrate the rich pleasures of family, friends, and everyday life.

The term *merenda* comes from the classical Latin verb *merere* (*meritare* in Italian), to earn or deserve, because the meal was given as a reward for work done beyond what was expected. Plautus, the Latin author of comedy, used the term *merenda* with the same meaning that we use it today: a little break which then was the classical Romans' lunch, for *merenda* comes also from the Latin *meridies*, midday, to signify the midday meal. It was a quick meal which they ate for the most part between eleven and noon, on their feet, wherever they worked, without going home—a roll, fruit, eggs, perhaps vegetables, mushrooms. In the later Roman vocabulary *m'renda* became synonymous with *panberia*, *pane e bevanda* in Italian, meaning bread and something to drink, and it was food given only to workers.

Spuntino, the word Italians now use for the midmorning meal or snack in Italy, is a more recent term from the nineteenth century. Some purists look down upon it for its lack of precision and historical roots and prefer to stick with the term *merenda*, just as they refuse to countenance the idea of the *merenda* as a picnic, another recent departure. Yet *spuntino* is a perfectly good Italian word; it means a little something to nibble that takes the edge off the appetite, or just something to lessen the first twinges of hunger.

Similar customs exist in other Mediterranean countries. Spanish *tapas* and Greek *mezes* are usually a prelude to lunch or dinner, while the French midafternoon *goûté*, Spanish *meriende*, and Catalan *refrigeris* are similar nourishing little bites but with less diverse offerings.

High tea in England occurs at the hour of *merenda*, but it is a highly ritualized encounter presupposing knives and forks, plates holding little crustless sandwiches and tea cakes, and sometimes even a silver tea service. In Italy the tradition of *merende* is deep and rich, and the vast variety of the casual food served depends on season, region, and social class. This is the unpretentious cooking at the heart of much of Italian life.

The choice of food for a *merenda* always depends on the season and its produce, and of course the menu of every *merenda* varies from region to region. On cold and foggy days in Emilia-Romagna only thirty or forty years ago, for example, *frittelle di baccalà, frittelle di riso, frittelle di castagne* (crispy fritters made with salt cod, rice, or chestnut flour), even polenta with sardines stoked workers' energy and warmed them against the chill of the day. In the heat of summer, people escaped to the cool pleasure of the shade to munch a puffy diamond-shaped pillow of fried dough called *gnocco fritto*, eating it alone or with figs or prosciutto. They might pull bread and walnuts out of their sacks, or pluck a leek-like wild onion with red striations and extremely long leaves from the fields and eat it raw with a little salt, or grill it until it was charred on the outside and still creamy inside. Often there was only what Renato Bergonzini calls the "rosy smile of a piece of watermelon."

I have watched workers at the arduous labor of harvesting grapes during the warm autumn days in Piedmont and Tuscany. Their *merenda* might be as simple as some chunks of bread and a handful of grapes, or a glass of the sweet free-running grape juices. I've seen bakers in the Chianti region of Tuscany fill their arms with ripe Sangiovese grapes (they don't *all* find their way into Chianti Classico wine) and sprinkle them with abandon on *schiacciata dell'uva*, a seasonal dessert made of sweetened bread dough densely carpeted with grapes and finished with a crunchy blizzard of sugar. The fragrance of grapes hangs in the air not only in the vineyards of Tuscany but in little towns all over Italy where the grapes are harvested; their perfume pervades the stone cellars where they are taken to be pressed, and the fruits and juices find their way into many rustic sweets. In colder northern regions, for instance, workers share generous mounds of polenta spread with *mosto cotto,* a thick sauce made by cooking the freshly pressed grape juice to a concentrate.

Today many of these *merende* have become part of the rebirth of traditional Italian food. After flirtations with chic *nuova cucina* and the food of other countries and regions, Italians are looking again to their roots, to the simple foods they remember from their childhoods, the tastes that sustained their parents and grandparents. Rustic foods like *farinata,* a flat garbanzo bean pancake from Liguria, *l'erbazzone,* a spinach tart in Emilia, *piadina,* the tender tortilla-like bread of Romagna that is folded around prosciutto or buttery cheeses, *polenta dolce,* chestnut polenta served with ricotta in Tuscany, or *fave e foglie* from Puglia, fave bean purée served with wild greens and drizzled with oil, are being rediscovered and are even now beginning to appear on the menus of *osterie* and *trattorie.* Every region, practically every village, still has its individual *merenda* food (or at least a memory of it), which has been part of the culture since long ago, when *merende* were offered to the poor, to the traveler, to the wandering storyteller and ballad singer as they came through the towns and villages.

It is still possible to find memories of *merende* in all regions of Italy. In the ancient Etruscan area of Tuscany around Montepulciano, the tradition of *merenducce* continues to this day. For San Lazzaro, the third to last Sunday before Easter, people go into the countryside and choose silent spots—forested areas and great fields open to the first sunshine of spring—where they stay to *far merenducce.* The menu is simple: good Tuscan bread with *capocollo,* lean boned and rolled pork shoulder, *prosciutto,* and very salty *lombino,* which is like an extremely fine prosciutto.

Until the end of World War II, people living in towns in the plain of Lombardy, which is split by the river Po, always had meals and *merende* to match their work. Hard labor in the fields and the extremes of temperature obliged men to stop for a break once in the morning and again in the afternoon, and the food they ate was almost always tasty, highly caloric, practical. Between the Po and the city of Modena, people ate *torta degli Ebrei* or *sfujada,* a savory tart that tradition says was brought out of the Jewish community of Finale Emilia. During the foggy season, hot slices of this substantial dish were sold at counters in the streets and piazze to be washed down with homemade wine or anise-flavored liqueur. Nearer Modena, which sits in the center of Emilia-Romagna's fertile plain, the *merende* were slices of polenta with various flavorings, and on the hills farther from the banks of the river they were *crescentine*, little grilled breads the size of a sand dollar, served with prosciutto or a pesto of *lardo*, rosemary, and a light sprinkling of grated Parmesan.

Every city and town, every tiny fraction of the landscape, is nourished by the special breads of the countryside, so it is hardly surprising that many *merende* are made of a simple bread dough. It may be flattened, drizzled with olive oil, sprinkled with salt and cooked as soon as the oven is hot enough to bake it; it may become *focaccia* topped with a tangle of summer vegetables or chunks of fresh tomatoes, it may be fried like *frittelle* or cooked on a grill like the *piadina romagnola,* but for the most part the breads are as round as the sun. They may be baked to a crunchy hardness so they will keep for a very long time, like the *gallette* and *friselle* of soldiers and shepherds, or they may be made for immediate consumption, like the famous pizza of Naples.

"The more fortunate ones, like me," writes Giuseppe Bonaviri of *merende* in his novel *L'incominciamento,* "could eat, when we were children, bread and cheese, bread and apples, or jujubes with their faded purple-pink colors, olives in oil, or roasted in the coals. Or soak our bread in honeyed *vino cotto,* or in the juice of black mulberries come to Sicily from the southern shores of the Caucausus, from Persia and from Greece. At other times we ate bread to which our mothers would add thin slices of more bread, telling us, 'You can pretend that the thinner bread is the thigh of a pheasant, a stewed hen's ventricle or *biscotti regina.'* "

I remember driving in Tuscany late one November, when the leaves had turned yellow and the nets were on the ground for collecting the olives. Chestnuts had begun to fall, leaving prickly shells under the trees and on the roadways. I saw old women pushing wheelbarrows along the country roads, collecting the chestnuts for sustenance in the dark days ahead. A chill was in the air, the melancholy presence of winter hovered, and it was clearly time for an invigorating slice of *calda-calda,* a golden garbanzo bean pancake baked in the scalding heat of a wood-burning oven. In Tuscan and nearby Ligurian towns, I stopped for *pasta fritta* or *panzanelle* or *sgabei*, all names for simple tasty bread dough stretched out as long as a grissino and as fat as a wand, fried in hot oil and sprinkled with lots of sea salt, sometimes filled with salame or buttery stracchino cheese, sometimes eaten plain. Sometimes I couldn't resist *pizza bianca*, bumpy pockmarked crispy dough with a drizzling of olive oil, and *focaccia farcita*, a plate of dough baked in the wood-burning oven, slit open, and filled with prosciutto or mozzarella—hot, appetite-quenching, simple, nourishing food. In winter especially, *merende* may be just such simple fare or they may be leftovers that can be reheated, such as cooked greens, or soup, or pasta in its innumerable forms.

There are still some places where workers interrupt their labors to open packets of food wrapped at home. A marble quarryman's wintertime *spuntino* in Carrara, for instance, might be a salt herring wrapped in thick brown butcher paper. When it is time to break off work in the early morning, the quarryman simply strikes a match, lights the wrapping, and creates a meal of the hot salty contents, which he eats with bread, of course, and wine. In Puglia workers picking the olives in the fields still plunge spoons into *pancotto*, a thick fava bean soup cooked with fiery peperoncini, topped with chicory, and drizzled with oil. If this sounds like an ordinary dish, it may help to know that Hercules is said to have made this his meal after he finished his labors.

In the south of Italy, even though laborers went into the fields at dawn and worked all day, many were too poor to afford an extra meal. A midmorning *merenda* might be a glass of wine or grappa, or bread eaten with greens or tomatoes picked on the spot. Fishermen in Puglia or Campania might eat anchovies "cooked" in lemon juice. In the old days sailors ate *gallette*, small rings of bread that had been cooked three times (*triscotti*, baked even harder than the popular biscotti we all eat today) to evaporate all the water so that the breads would not go stale. Shepherds took *friselle*, rings of bread twice cooked to the same purpose, to last through their long voyages across the landscape as they tended their sheep.

Merende were always more intense during great moments of the agricultural year, such as the threshing of grain and the harvesting of grapes and olives, when workers might be in the fields for a full eighteen hours. Sauro Sagradini, an Italian writer, remembers collecting hay in the fields with three men and two women when his grandmother arrived with two baskets hanging from her arms. From one she took a tablecloth that she spread in the shade of a long line of elms, and then she dealt the plates out as if they were cards from a deck. A bottle of wine, wrapped in a cloth, marked the spot where the head of the family would sit. From the other basket came *coniglio al pomodori*, rabbit with tomatoes, eggplant fried with cheese, and *spezzatino con patate*, stew with potatoes, an onion *frittata*, even eggs poached in a dense mixture of vegetables and tomatoes. His grandmother sliced the rustic country bread, made in a wood-burning oven on the farm, and served it from beginning to end, for the *merenda* always ended with slices of bread and pieces of fresh cheese or salame.

Merende* can be celebratory as well as restorative. A melon festival in Venice in 1789 included an elaborate parade that ended at the Campo Santa Maria Formosa, where fruit vendors brought the Doge enormous numbers of melons. In return the Doge was obliged to offer a *merenda* that consisted of two casks of wine, six prosciutti and various salami, six wheels of pecorino cheese, twenty-four smaller cheeses, one hundred breads, and sizable sweet dessert rings called *bussolai*.

People still eat *merende*, but rarely as they did in the past. As life in Italy changes, there is less time—women have gone to work, many people have two jobs—and customs are changing, especially in the north. But *merende* haven't entirely disappeared; they have simply been transformed. People still snatch moments midmorning and midafternoon for informal small meals, but they are more likely to find themselves at coffee bars, *osterie*, or *trattorie* than at home, in the woods, or on the mountainsides where traditional *merende* were once shared. Morning snacks, sometimes called *spuntini*, may be little packets of food children take for recess at school, or they may be the steaming slices of crunchy pizza bought when they surge en masse into bakeries during the midmorning break. They are uncomplicated foods eaten sitting around with friends, standing at a counter, and sometimes just strolling along the street during a break from work.

The generation of people who knew how to make the traditional dishes is departing this world and often taking their knowledge with them. Their children and grandchildren have less time for making the familiar little meals and in some cases wouldn't know how, because they have never even tasted them. In Italy as elsewhere, these ancient snacks, rooted in history, region, and family, are being lost as ancient customs meet modern technology in fast and packaged foods.

But all is not lost. The best place to find authentic *merende* (besides people's homes) is in the countryside. Look for hand-lettered signs for *piadina* in Romagna, go to *osterie* in Emilia in search of *gnocco fritto* or *crescentina*. Venture up to Colonnata, a tiny town high above the marble quarries in Carrara where marble workers have always eaten *lardo*, silky slices of the preserved hind of the pig, as white and as finely sliced as prosciutto but saltier, silkier, richer of flavor. Stop at the *friggitorie* in Genoa for *farinata*, *frittelle*, and *paniccia*, little fried bites of garbanzo bean dough; then pick up fingers of *focaccia* to munch as you wander. Eat the true *pizza* of Naples, search for *pizza rustica* in Puglia, and make your way to stands in central Florence for warm tripe, ready to be tucked in a crunchy roll. In the wintertime comb the hills of Tuscany for *necci*, ricotta-filled chestnut flour crepes, then head for Friuli and its crunchy *frico*. Take yourself off to wine bars or an *enoteca*, especially in Venice, where *cicchetti*, authentic bite-size tastes of the region, are often served along with the wine. If you see a sign by the side of the road or posted on a tree mentioning a *sagra*, a rural festival, follow the arrow to a celebration devoted to genuine country food.

Merende still exist all over Italy, but they take a bit of searching out. It is time now to try them here, to let them nourish us in big bites or small, to let their simple and informal tastes bring the warmth of Italy to our everyday lives.

A Little History

Merende may be comfort food eaten at home, in caffès, in wine bars, or while strolling in the streets, but no one should assume that they have sprung up recently in response to the demands of modern life. *Al contrario,* as the Italians would say. The tradition of eating rustic appetizers from street stalls, from little shops that fry food on the spot, or from wine bars where people nibble on salty tidbits while spending time with friends has roots deep in Italian history and can be traced through various eras and cities.

Although the ancient Romans ate three meals a day, breakfast was minimal, if it was eaten at all, and lunch might consist of only bread and cheese or a bite of fruit or legumes. No wonder people often stopped for a break during the morning, eating bread spread with an anchovy sauce or a paste made from olives too ripe to be pressed into oil, or filled with whatever greens or figs they could pick in the countryside.

Not everyone could leave the crowded, noisy streets of the city and return home to eat during the day, so those early Romans passed many hours in taverns, wine shops, country *osterie*, and a variety of what could only be called "dives." Many were dark and smoky, frequented by a promiscuous population that consequently gave them a questionable reputation, but a large number of them were definitely places to eat. Some, in fact, were attractive parts of the urban landscape. There were taverns that had one side open to the street, with a stone counter in which five or six wine jars were embedded next to a little stovetop where cooking took place. Other counters opened onto the street in front of bakeries, where bread, fresh out of the oven, was sold to people who lined up, lured by the fragrance that drifted through the air. There were cookshops with counters, and stands set up in arcades and in piazze. Some offered food ready to eat, some specialized in take-out food—sausages, boiled meats, *lardo* and prosciutto, cheese and milk—and others offered seats at a counter as well as tables where people could eat.

The foods they ate were more than slightly reminiscent of what Italians still eat today. Virgil wrote of *moretum*, an herb, cheese, and garlic topping made with oil and a little vinegar, which was spread on bread or cooked as a kind of focaccia; and Cato was enthusiastic about *libum*, a popular cheese focaccia that was baked on a bed of aromatic bay leaves. People in Pompeii ate *scriblita*, a rustic savory tart in which layers of fresh feta-like cheese alternated with fine, thin pastry, while Romans snapped up garbanzo bean fritters and schiacciata that may be similar to the *farinata* eaten today in Genoa. Cicero was crazy about *il tirotarico*, a frittata in which a little of everything was cooked—his favorite incorporated cheese and salted fish. There were flatbreads,

risen breads, both flavored and plain, and a kind of hard baked *biscotto*, some of which were eaten with a variety of sauces and raw or cooked vegetables, others with delicacies like dried meat. There were even Roman flatbreads made of pastry-like dough, possibly the ancestor of the pizza that, two millennia later, itinerant pizza sellers were hawking in the crowded streets and lanes of Naples.

Taverns were so numerous that a single street in Pompeii boasted twenty within one third of a mile. Tavern keepers served little salty tidbits to encourage people to drink a lot, much as *rosticcerie* in Rome and Sicily still offer numerous traditional snacks like *arancine* or *suppli*, crispy little deep-fried rice croquettes filled with meat and peas or with molten mozzarella.

The tradition continued in the Middle Ages and Renaissance, when the Tuscans, who were busily rediscovering the classical tradition of arts and architecture, also found time to spend in *osterie* where salty snacks and spice-and-pepper-filled sweets were offered with just the same purpose in mind. *Merende* are twice mentioned in the *Decameron*, and Lorenzo de' Medici wrote in verse of extemporaneous *merende* when he invited friends into the rustic *osterie* to taste *cialdoni, confortini, berlingozzi,* and *berricuozzoli,* all accompanied by good wine.

Today wine bars in Venice operate on much the same premise, offering salty *cicchetti* with a great variety of wines. The first such thirst-provoking tidbit was an anchovy surrounded by two pickled onions and impaled on a toothpick. The choice of tasty tidbits in Venice is considerably larger these days—fried olives, prosciutto wrapped around grissini, smoked herring and herring spreads, whipped baccalà and baccalà with herbs, fried octopus and calamaretti, sole or sardines *in saor,* hard-boiled eggs with *sottaceti,* vegetables preserved in vinegar—but the original intention hasn't changed: keep the client happy (and thirsty). Things have changed, however, since the seventeenth century, when wine sellers provided a piece of fennel to innocent buyers who had no idea that the fennel bulb improves the taste of bad wine!

Dinners in ancient Rome, served around twilight, were divided into three courses, of which the first, the *antecoena,* was essentially made up of antipasti. Much of the food that appeared at table were what we consider *merende:* raw vegetables, olives, eggs cooked under hot embers, thinly sliced leeks and lettuces—sometimes served with *allec,* which was very like an anchovy sauce with vinegar—tuna covered with slices of hard-boiled egg, radishes, anchovies on a bed of the penetrating bitter herb rue, and fine cheeses. The *antecoena* must have been plentiful because Cicero kidded a friend that he could no longer get away with serving antipasti to fill him up before the meal.

Shops selling cooked food were common in the Middle Ages and Renaissance, when Italian towns had almost as few places for ordinary people to cook their meals as the ancient Romans had. Masses of people routinely bought ready-cooked food at public cookshops, at open-air markets, and at rosticcerie and outdoor friers.

Of the many such shops where people have stopped from Roman times on, perhaps the best known were the *friggitorie,* snack bars where food was deep-fried and sold hot from the pan. Classical Romans ate *globi,* cheese fritters that puffed up into golden balls when they were fried in lard, and they feasted on a sweet made by funneling the same dough into the hot oil—it assumed a spiral shape—frying it, and covering it with honey and a veil of poppy seeds.

Pezzetti, a famous specialty of much later Roman *friggitorie*, continued the tradition with small pieces of broccoli, potato, cauliflower, artichokes, pumpkin, cardoons, baccalà, and all kinds of small fish that were dipped into a batter, fried on the spot, sprinkled with salt, and slipped into a cone of paper for easy munching. In the pantheon of much-loved portable fried foods were (and still are) *suppli* stuffed with *provatura*, a mozzarella-like cheese that melts inside as the balls of rice cook, creating *suppli al telefono*, named for the cheese strands that stretch out fine and thin like phone wires.

The tradition of frying received the seal of approval when a Papal Bull granted Tuscans permission to fry foods everywhere, and fry they did. In the early nineteenth century the numerous *friggitorie* around the Mercato Vecchio in Florence were turning out pans full of fried frogs and little fish, *frittelle*, and lozenges of fried cream, leaving their aromas to perfume the air. Today in Genoa, *friggitorie* are open only between eleven and one at midday and six and eight in the evening, perfect times for a *spuntino* and a *merenda*. Out of their frying pans come fried baccalà, fritters of tiny white fish, of cauliflower and of artichokes, *farinata*, a simple garbanzo bean polenta, and *paniccia*, a kind of garbanzo bean polenta seasoned with oil, lemon, and pepper, cut in thin strips and fried or sautéed with onion and parsley.

Itinerant vendors who cook and sell food on the street have been a feature of city life since classical Rome. Seneca left a lively picture of these men who hawked drinks, sweets, biscotti, and sausages. Visitors to Rome in the seventeenth and eighteenth centuries were treated to spectacularly lively urban scenes, with any number of musicians and literally hundreds of such vendors. They strolled with their wares threaded on long rods that hung across their shoulders, in baskets on their arms, or on little tables that hung from around their necks. Some foods were for eating on the spot and others for taking home. They ranged from *bruschetta* to fresh milky cheeses, live eels and many little fish, golden pears and honeyed figs, tripe and kid and even oysters, *cialdone* and anise-flavored *ciambelle* and wine to go with them, *porchetta* roasted and sliced on the spot, wheels of bread and salted meat, slices of melon and hot *frittelle*, roasted chestnuts and many savory fried treats.

For their *merende* many Romans, who became known as *fagottari*, bought such food or carried their own bundles from home to eat in an *osteria*, where they bought wine from the nearby Castelli Romani. Even today a very few *osterie* keep the tradition alive, although they are fast disappearing. I recently saw a sign at one such place in Grottaferrata that makes clear that the tradition no longer applies: "*Non si accetano clienti con cibi propri*" ("We don't serve people who bring their own food").

Itinerant vendors did not neglect the famous Roman sweet tooth. They sold monumental *bigne* filled with sweetened cream and *croccante*, a nut brittle made with hazelnuts and honey, both of which remain favorites today, although sugar has taken the place of honey. Early Roman sweets included a *placenta* made with sheets of pastry dough filled with honey-sweetened ricotta and *savillum*, perhaps an ancestor of today's cheesecake. Most Roman *dolci* were made with honey and flour, and some, like the chewy, spicy, nut-filled cookies called *mostaccioli*, are still eaten in southern Italy. Definitely memorable and still made today in the wine country of the Castelli Romani is a gingerbread-like cookie in the shape of a three-breasted woman. Two breasts, they say, are for water, while the middle one is for wine. All this was explained to me by the baker, a young boy who proceeded to demonstrate with complete nonchalance the technique for making the very three-dimensional breasts and the particular flourish with which he created the nipples.

If life in Rome was lively, noisy, and full of the sounds and smells of food, Naples was more intense by an exponential factor. In the

seventeenth and eighteenth centuries, vendors of everything from watermelon to mussels and shellfish sang out their wares, tempting inhabitants and passers-by with their lusty descriptions. Each seller had his own cry and his own chant about the food and wares that varied by season; many tied animals to their stands or to an adjacent door. In the crushing heat of summer, the water seller's seductive cries lured people to a stand decorated with Corinthian columns, paintings and highly polished bronzes, garlands of olive branches and heaps of oranges and lemons. With the spring waters he sold little peppery rings called *taralli*, whose bite made his customers thirsty and encouraged them to keep drinking. The sorbet seller proffered lemon sorbets, economic thirst quenchers, and drinks that, as culinary historian June di Schino points out, were sometimes cooled with snow in caves just as they had been in Roman times. Heady aromas floated from *zeppole* friers, who usually fried outside their front doors although some wandered through the streets, selling their wares from a copper tray. What wares they were—*frittelle di riso*, plump rice balls filled with meat, anchovies, or eggplant; potato croquettes; puffy golden yeast-based *zeppole*; and *mozzarella in carozza*, a mozzarella sandwich fried to a crispy golden turn. When Goethe went to Naples in 1787, he wrote that "at almost every corner of the main streets, there are pastry-cooks with their frying pans of sizzling oil, busy, especially on feast days, preparing pastry and fish on the spot for anyone who wants it. Their sales are fabulous."

Most characteristic were the stalls where pasta was prepared and hung to dry, then cooked, and consumed right in the city streets. In these stands gaily decorated with gaudy drapes, the *maccaronaro* would set strands of pasta into boiling water in a large copper cauldron, and then he would pull out a tangle of them and toss it with the traditional topping of *cacio e pepe*, grated cheese and pepper. The eater was charged by how much he took from the mountain of pasta—one price for two fingers full, more if he took three. For a fee, Neapolitans showed foreigners how to eat the macaroni. June di Schino describes the picture: "In a ritual fashion, eyes cast upwards, the maccaroni eater would lift the strands with two fingers just above the head which tipped back. With a deft twist of the wrist and a rapid movement of three fingers, the *maccheroni* would disappear instantly, never leaving a trace or stain.

" '*I maccarune se magna guardanno o'cielo*' (*Maccheroni* is eaten looking at the sky). This probably indicates the state of seventh heaven of the eater and his thanks to the gods." Everyone came—street urchins, merchants, nuns—and they all ate with their hands. From that time on, pasta took on different shapes and became the food not just of Naples but of all of Italy. But not until the mid-nineteenth century did pots of tomato sauce bubble alongside the strands of pasta.

Polenta, the equivalent of pasta in the northern part of Italy, was also eaten with the hands. Finely ground corn was sifted into a big cauldron of boiling water, cooked and cooled, cut with a string or a wire, sometimes grilled or baked, and served with whatever food was available. Romans ate its porridge-like equivalent made of grains like farro or spelt, sometimes combined with legumes to make an even thicker mixture, according to Plautus, who noted that "for a long time the Romans lived not on bread but on gruel." Polenta goes back so far that the inhabitants of southern Italy were called *pultifaghe*, just as northern Italians today are known as *polentoni*, big polenta eaters. (The Latin word for gruel is *puls*, *pultis*, an obvious ancestor of Italian *polenta*.) Northern Italians stirred herbs or sausage or bits of tomato into the creamy mass; they would make a sauce of mushrooms or tomatoes and spread it on top of the wedges and squares. They would serve it with baccalà and with stockfish, and in cases of extreme want, a family would have a single herring which each member would slap against the polenta to catch a bit of the flavor. Polenta was also served as a sweetmeat, flavored with raisins and cut into a diamond shape, just as people today eat *zalletti*, the popular raisin-studded cornmeal cookies still made in Venice.

Roving vendors and fry shops provided the *merende* of many cities. Glowing braziers of chestnuts roasting in the streets were a cheering sight in the dreary winter, while food stalls in Tuscany offered *pattona*, chestnut flour polenta, and *necci*, chestnut crepes filled with lightly sweetened ricotta. Shops in the area around Lucca sold chestnuts boiled with fennel in copper cauldrons, while vendors from enterprising cookshops in much of Tuscany carried huge pans of *castagnaccio*, a deep chocolate-colored chestnut cake flavored with rosemary and pine nuts, into the streets while it was still hot, sliced it, and sold it to hungry passersby. In summer, instead, they sold a cooling barley water and a lemon *granita* that was the Tuscan equivalent of lemonade.

On the first three Sundays of springtime in Florence, men made *brigidini*, crisp anise-flavored wafers, by cooking little balls of dough flattened in a waffle iron–like device with two long handles, which cooked over the fire until they turned into thin and crunchy cookies. Some vendors shaped the same dough in the form of a glass into which they poured *rosolio*, an extremely sweet strawberry-colored liqueur, thereby making a snack called *mangiabei*, which means to eat and drink at the same time. In summertime roving vendors called out their wares—little fish freshly plucked from the Arno, peperoncini, radishes to eat with tuna, ricotta and *marzolino*, young sheep's-milk cheese made in March, marinated eel and tench and salad greens.

Some of the traditions still remain. Mobile wagons sell fried tripe and doughnut-like *bomboloni* in the center of Florence. Counters with *porchetta*, the large roast pigs stuffed with herbs from the hillside, still dot the streets of Rome and the surrounding countryside, offering people the opportunity to eat *panini* filled with slices of the meat and a heaping spoonful of the spicy herb stuffing. Street markets in Rome and Sicily sell *passatempi*, little snacks to eat while passing the time. They include nuts, lupini beans, and grass-green olives that sit in water, not brine, which gives them such a sweet taste (they make a wonderful pasta sauce), along with ceci beans, roasted favas, and salted pumpkin seeds.

The people of Sicily have bought their snacks from vendors, cook-shops, and street stalls for centuries. In the crowded bazaar-like atmosphere of the Vucciria, Capo, and Ballaro markets, men grill *stigghiole* that look like translucent ribbons wrapped around a mysterious smoky packet but are actually caul fat enclosing veal or lamb heart, a much tastier biteful than the description suggests. Vendors proffer deep pink octopus boiled to a silky tenderness for people to eat as they stroll among pyramids of glossy green and black olives, gigantic squashes, sacks of dried beans, ovals of yellow citron with bumpy rinds, and the entire panoply of Mediterranean fish hanging in nets and resting on chunks of ice. Some vendors cook on the truck they have parked at a city curb, turning out little flavored garbanzo bean snacks called *panelle* and tucking them between slices of golden durum bread. Other street food uses parts of the animal not normally encountered in butcher shops. Soft focacce called *guasteddi* or *guastella* are filled with ricotta and calf's spleen and dipped in lard, while *sfincioni*, thick pizzas covered with tomato sauce, anchovies, and cheese, are walk-about food. During the steamy heat of summer, the ubiquitous water seller, a much-sought-after figure, offers *zammu*, water flavored with a splash of anise extract. All morning long, no matter what the season, the people of Palermo seem to be eating big brioche stuffed with scoops of Sicilian ice cream.

The informal improvised tastes of these *spuntini* and *merende* are every bit as delicious as they sound, but behind the romance of the products of an informal country culture lies the necessity of invention. These tastes of the countryside and city are a creative response of people who have little but the sea, the sky, tiny plots of earth (perhaps), endless imagination, and a passion for improvisation. Many homes in ancient Rome, and much later in Naples, simply had no kitchens or cooking facilities. Rooms were small and dark, set on extremely crowded streets and lanes. "The house is far less the refuge into which people retreat than the inexhaustible reservoir from which they flood out," writes the celebrated critic Walter Benjamin. "Life bursts not only from doors, not only into front yards, where people on chairs do their work (for they have the facility of making their bodies tables). Housekeeping utensils hang from balconies like potted plants. From the windows of the top two floors come baskets on ropes for mail, fruit, and cabbage." It took the virtuosity of the citizens, and in the case of Naples an unmatched flair for theater, to create not only a source of food supply but a way of eating that was extremely economical. Life was in the streets.

"True laboratories of this great process of intermingling are the cafes," says Benjamin, describing Naples in the early part of this century. "The poorer the quarter, the more numerous the eating houses. From stoves in the open street, those who can do so fetch what they need. The same foods taste different at each stall; things are not done randomly but by proven recipes. . . . In the fish market this seafaring people has created a marine sanctuary as grandiose as those of the Netherlands. Starfish, crayfish, cuttlefish from the gulf waters, which teem with creatures, cover the benches and are often devoured raw with a little lemon."

The small meals called *spuntini* and *merende* were born in the meeting of Italian gregariousness, ingenuity, hunger, and an unqualified pleasure in eating. If prosperity and the demands of modern life have jeopardized the continuity of this Italian soul food, a romantic nostalgia for the past may be bringing it back, for many of these rustic dishes are being appreciated again. Italians are returning to dishes once spurned as emblems of a poverty they wanted to forget. Nostalgia for a time when the earthy, simple tastes of the countryside were part of their daily lives, and an unspoken yearning for communion with the past, are reinforced by fragrances that release powerful memories: pungent rosemary, brilliant basil, tomatoes slowly simmering with garlic, the startling bite of edible wild greens, the soothing smoothness of mounds of golden polenta. Eating these simple dishes is a way back to a world rooted in grain, olive, and vine, where a loaf of bread, some herbs from the fields, and produce from the vines nourish the spirit as well as the body. "Poverty rather than wealth gives the good things of life their true significance," says Patience Gray, author of *Honey from a Weed*, an extraordinary book on the food of the Mediterranean. Now dishes from simple ingredients seasoned with imagination are exerting a powerful pull, and the flavors of a poorer, more basic time are returning. After all, if polenta has been elevated in the pantheon of Italian eating, can fava beans be far behind?

In the Beginning
There Is Bread

In the beginning there was fire, and in its wake came the rudimentary ovens in which man baked bread, the primordial food that has nourished humanity for millennia. Bread in its myriad incarnations finds its true fulfillment in *merende*, and *merende* are an ode to bread. Certainly the key to many *merende* is having great bread on hand. This is not a problem if you live in Italy, but it can present difficulties in America.

Making your own bread is a simple, life-enhancing process. It is my passion in life to convince everyone to bake bread, but of course that isn't always possible. There are other solutions: If you're lucky, there's an old-fashioned bakery in your neighborhood or you can stock up on country breads at a weekend farmer's market. Wrap each loaf in foil, slip it into a self-sealing plastic bag, and pop it in the freezer, where it will keep well for up to 3 months. When you're ready to use the bread, remove it from the plastic bag and put the frozen loaf, still wrapped in foil, in a preheated 350°F oven for about 30 minutes.

Another possibility is to make friends with your favorite local baker and convince him or her to sell you a little dough for use at home. Italians of course can go to the bakery and ask for bread dough that has already risen once. That dough becomes the point of departure for innumerable simple *merende*: flavored, enriched, scented with everything from herbs to crumblings of sausage, and baked, grilled, or fried.

If you can't convince the neighborhood bakery to sell you some dough, try your favorite pizzeria. Many pizza makers are more than happy to sell a few balls of their dough. You can buy them for use later in the day or carefully wrap them first in foil, then in a self-sealing plastic bag, and freeze them for up to 4 months. Pizza dough can be used for bread as well. Like pizza, the bread used in *merende* is a portable plate that holds as many flavors as you wish to put on it.

If you are persuaded that making bread (or focaccia or pizza) is one of the great pleasures in life, please read the instructions in "Merende di Pane."

Once you have your bread, you have a universe of tastes at your fingertips. *Merende* often begin (and sometimes end) with bread and something to eat with it, for even the poorest people have a chunk of bread, a small bottle of olive oil, and herbs and wild greens from the fields. For generations workers have cut off a chunk of bread with a large penknife, dipped it into water and squeezed it dry, then spread it with tomato, garlic, oregano, and salt and pepper. Simple, basic, nourishing: what the earth renders is set upon a slice of bread.

If your bread is stale, all the better. Most of these *merende* were originally dreamed up as ways of using bread that was a day or two old. When grilled, slices of stale bread become bruschette to be drizzled with olive oil or crostini ready for toppings; moistened with water they absorb toppings of vegetables and herbs or become fillings for tarts; toasted they become croutons for salads; ground into crumbs they give flavor and texture to soups and country desserts.

Merende can be almost too simple to need a recipe. Over the years I have eaten or heard about:

- golden Sicilian country bread brushed with olive oil and grilled, then sprinkled with salt and oregano, and topped with sardines or slices of fresh pecorino cheese

- saltless Tuscan bread covered with slices of flavorful salame, prosciutto, pancetta, or any number of the various multi-nuanced products of the pig

- bread spread with butter and topped with thinly sliced speck, smoked prosciutto, or bresaola, delicate salt-cured, air-dried beef

- bread dipped in water, squeezed dry, and tossed with salt, pepper, olive oil, garlic, and wild mint—panzanella without the tomatoes

- stale bread sprinkled well with bottled water, then seasoned with vinegar, olive oil, salt, pepper, and finely chopped parsley

- big slices of country bread grilled, rubbed with garlic, topped with chunks of fresh tomato, sprinkled with bits of sea salt, and drizzled with olive oil

- bread with a caramel-colored crust, spread with butter and dotted with sardines or anchovies

- focaccia filled with slices of cheese and salami and heated until the cheese melts

- Tuscan finocchiona (fennel-flavored salame) eaten with fresh fava beans, bread, and a glass of red wine

- hot chile peppers tossed whole into a pan of warm olive oil, stirred with crushed tomatoes, salt, and a mint leaf, and spread on bread

- bread with thin slices of lardo, the purest white fat from the pig's back or rump, rubbed with herbs and spices, layered with dry salt, and preserved in marble basins covered with a simple brine

- a whole-wheat roll cut in half, much of the interior removed, then both halves rubbed with garlic, flavored with extra-virgin olive oil, salt, and freshly ground pepper, and given a chance to rest before being sprinkled with drops of white wine vinegar; the interior flavored the same way and restored to its original position; and the roll closed up and served forth

- bread drizzled with olive oil and salt and topped with hot peppers

- bread and wedges of local cheese (a chef in the countryside near Crema in Lombardy described the *merenda* he took on bicycle outings as a local cheese called *salva*, which he diced, drizzled with olive oil, and ate with bread and green peppers preserved in vinegar)

- crusty Pugliese bread and a red onion that has been soaked in water for half a day to mellow its pungent flavor

- wild salad greens from the fields eaten with hard-boiled eggs, young salame, and chunks of bread

- finely sliced spring onions, soaked in water, and anchovies dressed in olive oil, vinegar, and pepper eaten with lots of bread

- bread spread with butter and jam, the classic middle-class *merenda* for children

- crostini spread with marrow, which melted on the grilled bread in the oven; Roman mothers and grandmothers sprinkled them with salt and served them immediately

- bread eaten with a dried fig filled with a walnut, almond, or anise seeds

- bread spread with fruit-filled preserves, such as the deep-colored Tuscan mostarda made of apples and pears

- bread spread with honey often made from the honeycombs of bees raised by the family

- bread that has been buttered and sprinkled with sugar

- bread eaten along with raisins and toasted walnuts

- bread topped with sliced strawberries sprinkled with droplets of balsamic vinegar—a countrified version of strawberry shortcake

- bread and a sweet ripe persimmon

- lightly toasted bread spread with ricotta, sweetened with preserves

- grilled bread spritzed with red wine and a light veiling of sugar (a grandmother's after-school *merenda* that often gave children their introduction to wine)

- fresh ricotta cheese with a sprinkling of cinnamon on country bread

Some *merende* are as elemental as the sun and the moon. Giuseppe di Lampedusa, the author of *The Leopard*, knew the sacredness of such food: "From then on until my school days, I spent all my afternoons in my grandparents' apartments at Via Lampedusa, reading behind a screen. At five o'clock my grandfather would call me into his study to give me my afternoon refreshment—a hunk of bread and a large glass of cold water. It has remained my favorite drink ever since."

Bocconcini

Nibble on spiced black olives or sun-dried tomatoes with a wash of herb-scented olive oil, pop a crispy wafer of cheese into your mouth as you sip a glass of white wine—as simple as they are satisfying, these little bites are the pure tastes of Italy. They feature the cheeses, the olives, the cured meats, and the beans that have sustained people over time, and they are served in such a way as to preserve their essence.

What most of these small bites share is simplicity. Some are so elemental that a recipe seems redundant. Who can say how many fresh fava beans should be served with a wedge of pecorino cheese? How many green onions should be set out with anchovies or sardines?

This is finger food, walk-around food, bites to eat in the most informal situations. Indulge in a few of these morsels with a glass of wine and they should have a calming effect, for this is food for the soul as well as the body. Of course you can serve them as antipasti or put a few together to make a small plate. Or you can just let them be the tempting beginning, the little tastes that you eat with friends as you sit with a cooling drink in the heat of the afternoon, laze under a grape-shaded arbor in the country, or settle down at the end of the day, ready to talk and laugh and be enfolded by family and the heat of a warm fire. Let them be satisfying in themselves or a prelude to more.

Calda Calda

GARBANZO BEAN PANCAKE

The chick-pea flour used to make this crispy pancake is very powdery and light. Sift it gradually into the water, whisking so the mixture doesn't become lumpy. Be sure to use Italian chick-pea flour, not the Indian variety, which has Indian spices incorporated in it.

Slice the thin, lightly crispy pancake into wedges and eat it like a piece of pizza. The Genoese call it *farinata* and eat it out of hand, while Tuscans along the coast call it anything from *calda calda* (hot-hot) to *cecina* and tuck it inside a slice of focaccia. Sip some white wine flavored with a few drops of bitters while you nibble on this wonderful appetizer.

1½ cups water
1 cup, tightly packed (100 grams) Italian garbanzo bean (chick-pea) flour
½ teaspoon sea salt
4½ tablespoons olive oil
1 tablespoon finely chopped fresh rosemary
Lots of freshly ground pepper

Pour the water into a large mixing bowl and gradually sift the flour into it, whisking it in well and being careful to smooth out any lumps. Let sit for 3 to 4 hours.

Preheat the oven to 500°F.

Skim any froth off the batter, and whisk in the salt. Oil a 12-inch pizza pan with 1½ tablespoons of the olive oil and a 9-inch shallow metal baking pan with 1 tablespoon of the oil. Pour into each a very thin layer—no more than ¼ inch—of the batter. Scatter the rosemary leaves and drizzle the remaining olive oil over the tops.

Bake in the upper third of the oven until the top is golden and bubbly. Start checking at 20 minutes; it may be ready then, or it may take a bit longer. Cut into wedges, season abundantly with pepper, and serve immediately.

VARIATION

Farinata Eliminate the rosemary and scatter a handful of sliced green onions over the surface of the batter after it has baked for 10 minutes.

SERVES 4 TO 6

Bocconcini di Mozzarella Marinata

LITTLE BITES OF MARINATED MOZZARELLA

Whenever I am in Italy, I eat shamelessly huge quantities of mozzarella cheese, never being able to get enough of its milky fresh flavor. The grocer in the little Ligurian town where we once lived adamantly refused to sell me mozzarella that was more than a few hours old because he was certain that it was already losing its flavor. Since we cannot hope for such a mozzarella here, I take an entirely different approach. I marinate mozzarella and use it for antipasti (thanks to Joyce Goldstein for the inspiration) or toss it in a salad with celery and toasted walnuts (see the following recipe).

1 cup olive oil
3/8 to 1/2 teaspoon red pepper flakes
2 medium cloves garlic, minced
About 20 grindings of fresh pepper
Pinch salt
1 pound mozzarella, scooped into melon-ball-size rounds or cut into 1½-inch cubes

Heat the olive oil in a small sauté pan over low heat. Add the red pepper flakes, garlic, and grindings of black pepper, and leave over very low heat for about 5 minutes. Cool and add salt.

Pour the marinade over the cheese and toss to coat well. Let the cheese marinate at room temperature for several hours. (Or let it marinate in the refrigerator, where it will keep well for several days; bring to room temperature before serving.) Serve with toothpicks.

SERVES 10 TO 12

Insalata di Mozzarella, Noci, e Sedano

MARINATED MOZZARELLA, WALNUT, AND CELERY SALAD

This particular *merenda* is my own fantasy. I just love the combination of the crunch of the celery, the toastiness of the walnuts, and the softness of the mozzarella.

Little Bites of Marinated
　　Mozzarella (page 37)
6 ribs celery, cut into ½-inch
　　diagonal slices
8 ounces walnut pieces, toasted

Toss the mozzarella, celery, and walnuts together in a bowl, using the mozzarella marinade to bind the salad together. Let rest at room temperature for 1 hour before serving.

SERVES 6 TO 8

Pancetta e Mozzarella

PANCETTA WRAPPED AROUND A BITE
OF MOZZARELLA

A discovery from Locorotundo in Puglia, this antipasto is simplicity itself. Just scoop a small round of mozzarella cheese, wrap it in finely sliced pancetta, and broil until it is crispy on the outside and the cheese is just beginning to melt inside.

18 slices pancetta, sliced as thin as prosciutto

8 ounces fresh mozzarella cheese or 8 ounces mozzarella balls in water

Using a melon baller, scoop out 18 balls of mozzarella. Wrap a slice of pancetta around each ball of mozzarella, secure with wooden toothpick, and set on a broiler pan. Continue until you have used all the pancetta and cheese. Broil on a rack 4 to 6 inches from the heat until the pancetta begins to crisp on one side, about 5 minutes. Turn them over and broil on the other side until the pancetta is somewhat crisp and the cheese has begun to melt, another 3 to 4 minutes. Serve hot.

SERVES 6 TO 8

Pomodori Secchi Imbottiti

SUN-DRIED TOMATO "SANDWICHES"

I discovered this simple and delicious appetizer in Puglia, at a trattoria deep in the countryside near Martina Franca. It stood near many *trulli*, the indigenous whitewashed round stone buildings with conical roofs that look like so many shuttlecocks that have landed on the earth. Trulli are built entirely of stone without mortar. Beside providing shelter, they once turned out to be a clever way around property taxes, since their owners could reduce them to rubble when the tax collector came by, then build them right back up again as soon as he'd gone on his way.

Taste your sun-dried tomatoes to be sure that they are not overly salty, and look them over to be certain they have no holes.

30 sun-dried tomatoes
1 tablespoon olive oil
2 to 3 teaspoons finely minced garlic
Scant ⅛ teaspoon red pepper flakes
¼ teaspoon dried oregano
Salt and pepper

*R*efresh the sun-dried tomatoes in warm water to cover for about 10 minutes. Soak them just long enough to soften them, but be careful they don't become soggy. Drain and pat dry.

Warm the olive oil in a small sauté pan over very low heat. Add the garlic, red pepper flakes, and oregano and warm for 5 to 8 minutes, being careful not to let the garlic burn. Season with salt and pepper to taste.

Make the "sandwiches" by laying one sun-dried tomato face down, drizzling a bit of the herb-infused olive oil on it, and covering with a second sun-dried tomato. Serve at room temperature.

MAKES 15

Salame dei Fichi

FIG SALAME

This singular "salame" is made of figs. It was once comfort food in the Marches, the lovely mountainous green area of Italy to the east of Umbria. In those rare places in the countryside where fig salami are still made, sun-dried white figs are chopped and bound with *sapa*, grape juices reduced to a syrupy consistency, and Mistrà, an anise-flavored liqueur. Currant jelly cooked to a thick syrup and Sambuca liqueur are available substitutes. If you want to be authentic, roll the mixture into the shape of a salame, wrap it in fig leaves, and serve it with shards of pecorino cheese. It keeps for months in the refrigerator.

8½ ounces dried figs, preferably Calmyrna
2½ teaspoons Sapa (page 265) or currant jelly reduced to a thick syrup
1 to 1¼ teaspoons Sambuca liqueur
2 tablespoons walnut pieces, in large chunks
¼ teaspoon anise seeds

Chop the figs into very small pieces by hand; do not use the food processor even though the idea is tempting. Put all the ingredients in a mixer or a food processor and pulse, mixing only until they begin to clump together. Set on a piece of aluminum foil and form into the shape of a sausage. Leave uncovered at room temperature for 3 to 4 days or until a skin has formed. In Italy they roll the sausage inside a fig leaf, tie it with fine string, and then set it inside a wood cask for a month of aging. Aluminum foil works as well as the fig leaf, even if it isn't quite as pretty. Refrigerate, but serve at room temperature.

SERVES 4 TO 6

Frico

CRISP LACY CHEESE CHIPS

A saying in Friuli has it that *"frico fa respirare i morti,"* meaning that a frico is so delicious that it even makes the dead breathe again. Shepherds and woodsmen traditionally took frico along as a *merenda* on their long treks. Once you've made these delicate crunchy cheese chips, you'll understand why.

Frico come in two sizes: shaped like small discs or like ruffled cups. The trick to making them is to use a nonstick pan and the right kind of cheese, and to cook them until they become lacy, deep golden pancakes. Spread the finest possible layer of grated cheese in the bottom of the pan and cook it over very low heat. Don't rush the process; at midpoint it looks unpromising, but it really works. As with all pancakes, the first one may stick and pleat up. Don't worry; just go on to the next one. You can shape each warm frico over the bottom of a drinking glass or a Pyrex measuring cup, or you can let it cool flat.

Resist the temptation to eat these when they are warm; frico develop their true crunchiness as they cool to room temperature. You can make frico ahead; be sure to make a lot, because everyone will want seconds and thirds. Serve with chilled white wine.

1 to 1½ teaspoons unsalted butter, or as needed to keep the first frico from sticking
1 pound aged Montasio or aged Italian Asiago cheese, rind removed, grated

B efore you begin cooking, set out a small cup into which you can pour off the oil that is produced as the cheese cooks. If you plan to shape the frico, set out an inverted drinking glass or Pyrex measuring cup, and cover it with a paper towel to absorb any oil. Have a second paper towel nearby to pat the other side.

Melt the butter in a 6- or 7-inch nonstick skillet. Pour off any excess; the butter should just film the bottom. Spread a very fine layer of grated cheese over the skillet surface, and cook over medium-low heat until it has completely melted and formed a crunchy crust, about 4 to 5 minutes. The cheese will melt, bubble, and spread out like a very liquid crepe. Press the frico firmly with the back of a fork, pour off any oil that oozes from the cheese, and wait for golden crisp edges to develop. Once the bottom and edges have definitely set, turn up the heat and cook to a light golden brown. Use a spatula to gently turn over the frico; cook it briefly on the second side until golden. Remove the frico immediately, and shape it over the inverted glass, or lay it flat on a paper towel. Blot the top with another paper towel. Cool to room temperature before serving. Continue making all the rest of the frico.

MAKES ABOUT 20

Suppli al Telefono

DEEP-FRIED RICE AND MOZZARELLA BALLS

Here's my idea of an unbeatable appetizer. If you have ever been in Rome and bitten into these little crispy balls of rice to discover the creamy core of molten mozzarella, you'll want to leap up and make some for yourself. These Roman specialties are called *suppli al telefono* because the hot mozzarella in the center pulls into a mass of thin strings, like telephone wires. The trick to making suppli is having prepared risotto on hand. I often make a double risotto recipe, serving some for dinner and keeping the leftover portion for making *suppli* the next day.

TO PREPARE RISOTTO

4 to 5 cups chicken broth, preferably homemade

¼ cup olive oil

4 tablespoons unsalted butter

1 medium onion, diced

2 cups Arborio, Carnaroli, or Vialone Nano rice

½ cup freshly grated Parmigiano-Reggiano or pecorino cheese

Salt

Bring the broth to a boil in a medium-size saucepan and keep it at a simmer. Heat the oil and butter in a large saucepan. Add the diced onion and sauté over medium heat until translucent, 4 to 5 minutes. Stir in the rice and cook just long enough to coat the grains thoroughly, 1 to 2 minutes. Add ⅓ cup of the boiling broth and cook, stirring, until the liquid has been absorbed. Continue adding the broth, ⅓ cup at a time, and stirring constantly over medium heat until it has all been absorbed, about 16 minutes in all. Add the cheese at the end, and season with salt. Serve risotto now, or set it aside to cool for about 2 hours before making *suppli*. You may also cover and refrigerate the risotto for use the next day.

TO PREPARE SUPPLI

3 large eggs

4 ounces mozzarella, diced

4 ounces sliced prosciutto, diced

½ cup freshly grated Parmigiano-
  Reggiano cheese

2 tablespoons minced flat-leaf
  parsley

Salt and pepper

2 cups fine dried bread crumbs

Oil for deep-frying, preferably
  olive or peanut

Beat 1 of the eggs, add it to the cooled risotto, and mix well. Combine the mozzarella, prosciutto, Parmesan, parsley, and salt and pepper, and mix well. Scoop up a large egg-size spoonful of the risotto mixture (about 1½ tablespoons), and lay it in the palm of your hand. The rice should be no more than ½ inch deep. Make an indentation in the center, fill the hollow with some stuffing, add a little extra rice to close the cavity, and close up your hand to envelop it. Shape into an oval about 2 to 3 inches long, and lay it on a baking sheet lined with parchment paper. Continue forming the balls until the mozzarella and rice are used up.

Beat the remaining eggs with a little salt in a small bowl. Set the bread crumbs on a small baking sheet. Dip each ball first into the eggs, rolling it around to coat it thoroughly, then into the bread crumbs. Set on the parchment paper–lined baking sheet. You may refrigerate for a few minutes to allow the rice balls to become firm.

Heat 3 inches of oil in a deep pan to 375°F. Test the oil by dropping a few bread crumbs into it; if the oil bubbles and the bread crumbs turn golden almost instantly, the oil is ready. Using a slotted spoon, lower the rice balls, one at a time, into the hot oil and fry until golden brown, about 2 minutes. Do not overcrowd the pan. Repeat until all the *suppli* are cooked. Remove the *suppli* with the slotted spoon, and drain them on paper towels. Serve immediately. Eat with your hands, breaking them open so that the threads of mozzarella pull into long strands.

MAKES 20 TO 24

Olive Fritte all'Ascolana

STUFFED FRIED OLIVES

*F*or generations these stuffed green olives with their crisp crumb coating have been the *merenda* of Ascoli Piceno, the southernmost city in the Marches, where the market is held in a spectacular rectangular piazza. I would be hesitant to tell anyone to go to the trouble of stuffing olives if I hadn't been totally captivated by their glorious taste. They are so popular in Italy that you can now buy them frozen there, stuffed and ready to cook. Here's an option: In other parts of Italy, people skip the stuffing and simply fry the olives.

The enormous, meaty round green Ascolane olives that once grew in profusion outside the city walls are hard to find these days (even in Italy), although they are available in some specialty stores (see the Source Guide at the back of the book). If you can't find them, use another large meaty green olive from Italy, Spain, or Greece. Paula Wolfert's technique of cutting and pitting olives is a big help!

No one knows who invented this delicious specialty, but it must have been someone of great wealth, since it calls for leftover scraps of meat, which were rare indeed. Use the leftover filling as a delicious topping for Crostini or Polenta Crostini (pages 155, 161).

½ onion, diced
½ carrot, diced
½ celery rib, diced
3 to 4 tablespoons olive oil
⅓ pound lean pork, diced
1 pound 2 ounces lean veal, diced
2 ounces chicken breast, diced or ground
2 ounces white turkey meat, diced or ground
⅓ cup white wine
1 large egg, room temperature
½ cup plus 2 tablespoons grated Parmigiano-Reggiano cheese
Substantial grating of nutmeg
1 teaspoon sea salt
100 huge green olives in brine, preferably Ascolane, rinsed
1 cup unbleached all-purpose flour
1 cup dried bread crumbs
1 egg
Olive oil for deep-frying

Sauté the onion, carrot, and celery in the olive oil over medium heat until they are limp and lightly golden, about 5 to 7 minutes. Add the meats and sauté until they are lightly browned. Pour in the wine and cook over medium heat until it has evaporated. Transfer the mixture to the bowl of a food processor, and pulse until it is chopped as fine as a ravioli filling. Stir in the egg, cheese, nutmeg, and salt.

Using a sharp paring knife, cut the olives in an S curve and free them from their pits. They are large, so it is not as daunting as it sounds. Fill them with the stuffing mixture, being careful not to break them open. (The recipe can be prepared ahead to this point. You may leave the stuffed olives in the refrigerator for a day or freeze them for a month.)

Set the flour and bread crumbs on separate plates or sheets of aluminum foil, and beat the egg in a bowl. Roll the stuffed olives in the flour, shaking off any excess, then in the beaten egg, and finally in the bread crumbs.

Pour olive oil to the depth of 1½ inches in a heavy saucepan or deep Dutch oven, and heat it to about 350°F or until a tiny pinch of the bread crumbs sizzles immediately. Fry the stuffed olives, a few at a time, until they are golden brown and crisp. Using a slotted spoon, remove them from the pan and set them to drain on a platter lined with paper towels. Serve immediately with a glass of wine.

SERVES 12 TO 16, WITH 1 CUP FILLING LEFT OVER

Pecorino con le Fave

PECORINO CHEESE AND
FRESH FAVA BEANS

*I*t isn't exactly a recipe, but no book on *merende* would be complete without this Tuscan specialty. The combination is especially prized in springtime, when the skins of the new fava beans are silky and tender and the young sheep's-milk cheese is made with the first milk of March and so is called *marzolino*. Open a bottle of red Chianti, and feast on the food of the countryside.

1 pound pecorino dolce (young
sheep's-milk cheese), preferably
Tuscan or Sardinian
4 pounds raw fava beans in the
shell

*C*ut the cheese into small slices or wedges, and arrange them on a plate. Put the fava beans in a bowl, and serve them together. Let everyone pop the beans out of the pods and nibble them with the cheese. If you can't find very young fresh favas, rub the skins off before setting them out.

SERVES 4 TO 6

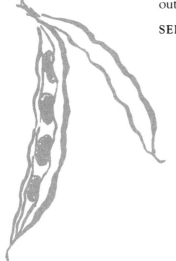

Olive Profumate

FENNEL- AND ORANGE-SCENTED OLIVES

"What do you eat for *merende?*" I asked a woman in Abruzzo, who promptly dashed to her kitchen and returned bearing these. You can make them with black olives from Italy, France, or Greece, but avoid Kalamata olives, which are too salty, and California black ripe olives, which are too bland. Serve them with bruschetta, with focacce, or with shards of cheese and toasted walnuts—but always with a glass of wine.

1 clove garlic, finely sliced
Zest of 1 orange, cut into small pieces
½ tablespoon fennel seeds
2 cups oil-cured black olives

At least several hours before you plan to serve them, mix the garlic, orange zest, and fennel seeds with the olives. Leave them at room temperature for several hours, or cover and store in the refrigerator for up to 2 weeks. Serve at room temperature by themselves or as part of an antipasto.

MAKES 2 CUPS

Olive Marinate

MARINATED OLIVES

Heat the olive oil and change the taste.

2 tablespoons extra-virgin olive oil
4 cloves garlic, peeled and crushed
Zest of 1 orange, cut into small
  pieces
½ tablespoon fennel seeds
2 cups oil-cured or brined black
  olives, rinsed and drained
Olive oil

Heat the olive oil in a small saucepan over low heat. Add the garlic, orange zest, and fennel seeds, and simmer for 3 to 5 minutes.

Combine all the ingredients in a glass or ceramic container. Let stand at room temperature for several hours before serving, or store in a covered container in the refrigerator. Bring back to room temperature before serving.

MAKES 2 CUPS

Condimenti

These are tastes of home that have made Italians happy for centuries. More than half of these toppings were originally spread on crostini, but as I made them, ate them, and served them to friends, I discovered that they are amazingly versatile. I am using them here in a somewhat unconventional way, but why not? They make wonderful sauces for pasta and polenta and are easily turned into fabulous salads or antipasti. Simple to make, delicious to eat, many of these *condimenti* will keep in the refrigerator for a week or more.

Most of these recipes are so uncomplicated that even non-cooks can make them. Whip up a couple of the toppings and put them in the refrigerator—they offer triumphant spontaneity. When it's time to feed yourself or your friends, you'll be ready to spread them on crostini, toss them with pasta, swirl them in risotto, spoon them over polenta, even to add broth and produce a sensational soup.

Pesto

BASIL SAUCE

Basil, with its brilliant green leaves and a fragrance as heady as anything in nature, is the star of pesto sauce, the aromatic specialty of Liguria. Its name (from *pestare*, to pestle or pound) comes from the method of pounding the basil, garlic, salt, and nuts together in a stone mortar, before the cheese and light Ligurian olive oil are beaten in. Pesto can also be made in a blender or food processor in a matter of seconds. Slide a single spoonful into Minestrone Genovese (page 180); toss it with pasta (page 69). To store pesto for several days, cover it with a fine layer of olive oil and refrigerate it in a tightly sealed jar; or omit the cheese and freeze the pesto, adding the cheese after you defrost it.

1 cup firmly packed fresh basil leaves
2 teaspoons minced garlic
½ cup extra-virgin olive oil, preferably Ligurian
½ cup grated Parmigiano-Reggiano cheese, or 6 tablespoons Parmigiano-Reggiano and 4 tablespoons pecorino sardo
2 tablespoons pine nuts or chopped walnuts
⅛ teaspoon sea salt
Freshly ground pepper

Purée all the ingredients in a blender or in a food processor outfitted with the steel blade.

MAKES 2 CUPS

Pesto Toscano

TUSCAN PESTO

My friend Faith Willinger lives in Florence, where she invented this witty Tuscan take-off on Ligurian pesto. Instead of basil she uses kale, the Tuscan vegetable par excellence. While Faith blanches it, I leave it raw and in a minute turn it into a thick deep green topping for crostini. It makes a delicious pasta sauce when mixed with a few spoonfuls of mascarpone cheese, and it can also be a great salsa verde to serve with roasts and boiled meats.

1 pound 2 ounces fresh kale
2 cloves garlic, minced
¾ to 1 teaspoon sea salt
¾ cup extra-virgin olive oil

Wash the kale well in cold water and pat it dry. Cut away the ribs and stems, leaving only the leafy greens. Combine all the ingredients in a food processor outfitted with the steel blade, and process to form a thick paste.

The mixture can be made ahead and kept covered in the refrigerator for 5 or 6 days. Bring it to room temperature before serving.

VARIATION

For a mellower, less robust flavor, blanch the kale in boiling water for 3 to 5 minutes.

SERVES 12 AS AN APPETIZER ON CROSTINI, 6 TO 8 AS A PASTA SAUCE

Condimento Pugliese
SWEET PEPPER SPREAD

The people of Puglia think this delicious sweet pepper spread is wonderful spread on slices of bread at *merenda* time—and so do I, but I can never resist using it as a pasta sauce as well. Just cook whatever shape pasta you choose, drain, toss with Parmesan cheese, and add the sweet pepper mixture; you'll have a sensational dinner.

2 large sweet red or yellow
    peppers
5 anchovy fillets in oil, drained
    and mashed
1 tablespoon extra-virgin olive oil
Scant ⅛ teaspoon red pepper
    flakes or minced peperoncino
    (dried red chile)
Pinch salt
8 to 10 grindings pepper

Roast the peppers over a direct flame or under the broiler. Turn them so they char evenly, and then transfer them to a bowl or paper bag, cover or close up tightly, and leave for about 30 minutes, or until they are cool enough to handle. The skin will peel off easily; remove the seeds, cores, and ribs, and slice them into thin strips. (You may roast the peppers 2 to 3 days in advance and refrigerate them.)

Chop the peppers roughly. Set them in the bowl of a food processor outfitted with the steel blade, and add the anchovies, oil, red pepper flakes, and salt and pepper. Pulse until you have a slightly chunky mixture. Do not purée or the mixture will be too fine. (You can also finely dice the ingredients and mix them together by hand.) Taste for seasonings and spread on grilled bread or use as a pasta sauce.

SERVES 6 AS AN APPETIZER ON CROSTINI, 4 AS A PASTA SAUCE

Le Cozze

MUSSEL TOPPING

This topping should taste as though the mussels have just been fished from the sea. Only the slightest cooking is required: garlic and anchovies are warmed in olive oil, then the glossy black mussels are tossed with parsley and warmed briefly in the pan before being served. This is a perfect topping to spoon onto crusty country bread for crostini or to toss with strands of pasta.

2 pounds live mussels
1 cup water
1 cup white wine
3 tablespoons extra-virgin olive oil
2 cloves garlic, finely chopped
5 anchovy fillets, chopped
    very fine
10 to 12 drops wine vinegar
¼ cup finely chopped flat-leaf
    parsley
Salt and pepper

Soak the mussels in a sink or large tub of cold water for 15 minutes. Grasp their beards with your fingers, and with a paring knife cut each one away. Scrub the mussels thoroughly with a stiff brush under cold running water to remove all the grit. Discard any that have cracked or open shells.

Set the cleaned mussels in a large saucepan, add the water and wine, and cook over high heat until they open, about 2 to 4 minutes. As soon as they open, use a slotted spoon to transfer the mussels to a large platter. Discard any that haven't opened, and as soon as they are cool enough to handle, detach the meat from each shell.

Warm the olive oil in a saucepan over medium-high heat, add the garlic and the anchovies, and sauté gently for about 2 minutes. As soon as the garlic is a very pale golden color, add the vinegar and cook for 2 minutes. Then add the mussels and parsley, stir once or twice, and taste for salt and pepper. Turn off the heat and serve immediately.

SERVES 6 TO 8 AS A CROSTINI TOPPING, 4 AS AN ANTIPASTO

Puré di Olive Nere

BLACK OLIVE PASTE

Olives grow everywhere in Italy, from the steep corniches of the Ligurian coast to the interior flatlands of Sicily. Bright and deep green, dark purple and black, some are as small as a baby's fingernail, others as big as a walnut. The greatest number of them are pressed into service as olive oil, but many are preserved under brine with garlic and local herbs and become antipasti or *merende*, or are incorporated into a vast number of dishes.

Ligurians, who live in the boomerang-shaped coastal region that extends from the French border past Genoa all the way to the northern edge of Tuscany, press olives into an olive paste they call "poor man's caviar." They spread it on squares of bread for crostini, they smooth it on focaccia, they bake it in bread doughs, and they toss it with pasta as a wonderful sauce. Although you can buy any number of imported purées from Italy, olive paste is simple to make, and this particular recipe has an exceptionally fresh taste. Be careful not to use extremely salty Greek Kalamatas or bland pitted California black olives.

1 pound 2 ounces black olives in brine, such as Italian Gaeta or Vall'Aurea, or French Niçoise, pitted
½ cup extra-virgin olive oil
Grated zest and juice of 1 lemon
10 grindings pepper
1 heaping tablespoon very fresh bread crumbs
Pinch salt

MAKES ABOUT 2 CUPS

Put all the ingredients in a blender or in a food processor outfitted with the steel blade, and blend. You may leave the texture slightly chunky or proceed to make a smooth, rather soft paste. Leave to mellow for several hours before serving. The olive paste will keep for weeks under a ¼-inch layer of olive oil in a tightly covered container in the refrigerator.

Puré di Olive Nere Liguriane

SPICY LIGURIAN ''CAVIAR''

If you don't have time to make your own olive paste, you can buy one of the many varieties on the market, sprinkle in a few capers, add the bite of red pepper flakes, and *ecco*: a spread for crostini just made to accompany a glass of white wine.

½ cup good-quality olive paste
⅛ teaspoon red pepper flakes
1 tablespoon capers
Salt to taste

In a small bowl or in a food processor outfitted with the steel blade, blend the olive paste, red pepper flakes, and capers to make a moist spreadable mixture. Season with salt. Use the purée immediately, or transfer it to a jar, cover with a thin layer of oil, and refrigerate. It will keep for weeks.

MAKES ½ CUP

Acquasale

SWEET PEPPER SAUCE

Acquasale is the answer to every course: It can be an antipasto, a salad, a sauce for pasta or polenta, and with the addition of chicken broth, it becomes a delicious soup. It started as a simple country dish in Basilicata, where people simply pluck onions, tomatoes, and sweet peppers from the garden, slice and drizzle them with olive oil, sprinkle them with salt, and set the mixture on top of softened stale bread.

To make splendid crostini, spread the mixture on pieces of grilled country bread, top with a bit of arugula, drizzle with olive oil, and serve.

3 to 4 tablespoons olive oil
1 red onion, finely sliced
½ clove garlic, finely minced
3 sweet red peppers, roasted (see page 56), ribs, membranes, and seeds removed, cut into ½-inch slices
2 or 3 medium tomatoes, seeded and cut into chunks
¼ to ½ teaspoon sea salt
¼ to ⅓ cup fresh bread crumbs (optional)

Warm the olive oil in a large heavy sauté pan. Add the red onion and sauté over low heat until the onion begins to become limp and translucent. Add the garlic and sauté briefly. Then stir in the pepper strips, and sweat them over low heat for 20 to 25 minutes. Add the tomatoes and salt, and cook another 2 or 3 minutes. Cool to room temperature.

Put the mixture in a food processor outfitted with the steel blade, and pulse about 30 times. *Do not purée*; the mixture should be chunky in texture. If it seems too moist, add the bread crumbs.

MAKES 3 CUPS

Condimento alle Verdure

COOL SUMMER VEGETABLE TOPPING

I love the versatility of this summery vegetable mixture from Puglia. It can be spooned onto grilled slices of country bread or friselle, it can double as a delicious antipasto salad, or it can be tossed into cooled curls of pasta to become a summer salad.

1 small red onion, diced
½ cucumber, peeled and diced
2 full-flavored ripe tomatoes
1¼ teaspoons sea salt
⅛ teaspoon dried oregano
¹/₄ cup finely chopped flat-leaf parsley
¹/₄ cup finely shredded basil
Scant ⅛ teaspoon red pepper flakes
1½ tablespoons extra-virgin olive oil
Salt and pepper

*S*et the diced onion and cucumber in a bowl. Bring a pot of water to the boil, drop in the tomatoes for a minute, remove, and slide off the skins. Seed and dice the tomatoes, and add to the bowl. Sprinkle with the salt and leave for 2 hours.

Drain any liquid from the vegetables, and stir in the oregano, parsley, basil, and red pepper flakes. Toss with the olive oil, and season with salt and pepper.

**SERVES 6 AS AN APPETIZER,
4 AS AN ANTIPASTO SALAD**

Condimento ai Funghi

WILD MUSHROOM TOPPING

There is no cooking involved in this elegant and easy topping; it is simply mixed and left to marinate for a day. If you can't get brown cremini or portobello mushrooms, try mixing an ounce of musky-flavored dried wild mushrooms with a pound of cultivated white ones. Use this topping in many incarnations: It is wonderful as a salad, as a spread for grilled bread, and if you leave out the lemon, as a delicious pasta sauce.

To make crostini, brush olive oil lightly over ½-inch-thick slices of Italian whole-wheat country bread, and grill or toast until the slices are lightly browned. Spread the mushroom mixture on top.

1 ounce dried porcini mushrooms

1 pound fresh brown mushrooms, such as cremini or portobello

1 pound (about 2 medium) ripe tomatoes, peeled, seeded, and finely chopped

1½ teaspoons finely minced fresh rosemary

8 sage leaves, finely chopped

2 cloves garlic, finely minced

Freshly ground pepper

Juice of 1 lemon

¼ cup olive oil

1¼ teaspoons sea salt

Soak the porcini mushrooms in 1½ cups warm water for at least 30 minutes. Drain in a sieve lined with cheesecloth or two layers of paper towels, reserving the liquid for use elsewhere. Squeeze the porcini, letting any extra moisture fall into the water in which they soaked. Wash them in several changes of cold water and cut them in very fine pieces.

Clean whatever fresh mushrooms you are using with a damp paper towel, dice them, and put them in a medium-size bowl. Add the porcini, the tomatoes, rosemary, sage, garlic, and pepper, and mix together well. Toss well with the lemon juice and oil, cover, and leave for 24 hours.

Add the salt just before you are ready to serve the topping. If the mixture seems moist, drain it.

SERVES 10 TO 12 AS AN APPETIZER, 6 AS AN ANTIPASTO SALAD

Pistada

EMILIAN PESTO

I never quite know how to explain this delicious Italian topping because it uses *lardo*, a word whose very mention is alarming to Americans. If only I could introduce them to the wonders of this silky, fragrant, highly flavorful specialty of Colonnata in northern Italy, I know it would win masses of converts. Lardo is nothing other than chunks of the choicest white pork back fat layered with handfuls of salt, pepper, cinnamon, cloves, coriander, sage, rosemary, and other local spices and herbs and then preserved in marble basins that have been rubbed with garlic. The lardo is enclosed in the basin for a week, then covered with a salty brine and left for 8 to 12 months. What results is ambrosial. The lucky people who live near Carrara eat it sliced as fine as prosciutto on crostini or warm bread. For this topping, however, it is minced so that it can be spread. To make the recipe as authentic as possible, I use the white part of pancetta and chop or pestle it well. Serve it with Gnocco Fritto (page 232) or with any of the warm breads in "Merende di Pane."

4 ounces white part of pancetta, (don't worry if you include some streaks of the meat)
Scant 2 teaspoons minced garlic
½ cup minced flat-leaf parsley
Pinch salt and freshly ground pepper

*R*oughly chop the white part of the pancetta and place it in a food processor outfitted with the steel blade. Process to make a smooth paste. Add the garlic, parsley, salt, and pepper, and process again to blend all the ingredients into the paste.

MAKES ⅔ CUP

Pistada II

SPREAD FOR GNOCCO FRITTO

The crunchy golden fritter known as *gnocco fritto* in Modena may change its name from town to town (ask for *torta fritta* in nearby Parma and *crescentina fritta* in Bologna), but it is always a hot puffy pillow of dough served with this *condimento* melting on its crispy surface. Don't worry if there is a little meat mixed in with the pancetta fat.

4 ounces white part of pancetta or high-quality lard
½ teaspoon minced fresh rosemary leaves
2 teaspoons minced garlic
Pinch salt and freshly ground pepper
¼ cup freshly grated Parmigiano-Reggiano cheese (optional)

Roughly chop the white part of the pancetta with a sharp knife, and place it in a food processor outfitted with the steel blade. Process to form a smooth paste. Add the rosemary leaves, garlic, salt, pepper, and cheese if you are using it, and process again to blend the ingredients together.

MAKES 1 SCANT CUP

Pomodori Sott'Olio

MARINATED SUN-DRIED TOMATO TOPPING

This delicious *merenda* comes from southern Italy, where drying tomatoes in the sun is part of country life. Most of us don't leave clusters of tomatoes to cure on our roofs since others conveniently sun-dry them for us, but we can certainly make this delicious topping. It's a perfect example of what Italians call a *companatico*—something to eat with bread. It keeps in the refrigerator for months and can be used as a delicious pasta sauce as well as an antipasto.

A word of caution: Look for tomatoes that have been dried by the sun, not by the oven, and beware of overly salty dried tomatoes. This recipe is not for sun-dried tomatoes already preserved in olive oil.

4 ounces sun-dried tomatoes

³/₄ cup red wine vinegar

1 cup (or slightly more) firmly packed fresh basil leaves

¹/₈ teaspoon red pepper flakes

1 teaspoon sliced garlic

Pinch salt

1 cup extra-virgin olive oil, or more as needed

Soak the sun-dried tomatoes in ¾ cup warm water and ¾ cup warm vinegar for 2 to 3 hours. Drain, set on a kitchen towel, and pat dry.

Stir together the basil, red pepper flakes, garlic, and salt.

In a 12-ounce glass jar, alternate layers of the tomatoes with the basil mixture. Pour in the olive oil, making sure that it covers the top layer. To eliminate any air bubbles that may be trapped between the layers, slide a metal spatula or kitchen knife down the sides of the jar. Screw on the jar lid tightly to seal well. Marinate for 1 day before using.

VARIATION

Use mint leaves instead of basil.

SERVES 10 TO 12

Agliata per Pasta

GARLIC AND WALNUT SAUCE FOR PASTA

I have to admit that I dreamed up this sauce when I decided to cross *agliata*, the garlicky condiment of Modena, with my adaptation of a sauce that sailors probably brought to Liguria from Marseilles. The sailors' original consists of only garlic, bread crumbs, oil, and a splash of vinegar—fine for serving with whitefish but definitely too strong for pasta. With a little license, here's a sauce made of ingredients that you probably have around the house all the time.

2 slices stale country-style bread, crusts removed

2 tablespoons chicken or beef broth, warmed

1 cup plus 2 tablespoons chopped walnuts, toasted

½ cup densely packed flat-leaf parsley, stems trimmed

3 medium cloves garlic, chopped

½ teaspoon sea salt

⅛ teaspoon freshly ground pepper

6 tablespoons olive oil

*S*oak the bread in the broth for 15 minutes, and then squeeze out any excess moisture. Combine the bread with the walnuts, parsley, garlic, sea salt, and pepper in a food processor outfitted with the steel blade. Process, adding the olive oil in a very slow stream as for mayonnaise, until you have a thick paste. (You can also pound the mixture by hand in a pestle until it forms a paste.) Toss with your favorite pasta, and serve hot.

SERVES 4

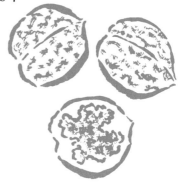

Salsina di Salsiccia e Pecorino

SAUSAGE AND PECORINO SAUCE

One recipe, three possibilities: sensational crostini, a delicious pasta sauce, or a filling for ravioli or tortelli. The salsina may be made a day ahead and refrigerated, covered.

2 tablespoons olive oil

3 tablespoons minced red onion

5 or 6 (about 1 pound) small smooth-textured Italian pork sausages flavored with garlic and pepper

Scant 8 ounces young pecorino cheese, grated

½ cup minced flat-leaf parsley

4 to 6 large fresh sage leaves, torn into small pieces

Substantial grindings of fresh pepper

Salt

Heat the olive oil in a heavy sauté pan over medium heat and sauté the onions until soft and translucent, 10 to 15 minutes. Peel off the sausage casings and crumble the meat as fine as possible. Add the sausage meat to the pan with the onions and herbs and cook for 10 minutes. Stir in the grated cheese, the parsley and torn sage leaves, grind the pepper, taste for salt, and mix well.

SERVES 6 TO 8 AS CROSTINI OR PASTA SAUCE, 10 TO 12 FOR TORTELLI OR RAVIOLI FILLING

Condimenti Combinations

PASTA AND CONDIMENTI

Here are marriages made in Italian heaven: *condimenti* that you have on hand, pasta in a package. Warm the first, cook the second, toss them together, and you'll have a meal in a matter of minutes.

Pasta ai Peperoni
PASTA WITH SWEET PEPPER SAUCE

Two sweet pepper spreads—one with tomato, Condimento Pugliese (page 56), and one without, Acquasale (page 60)—are delicious as fresh and delicate pasta sauces. Even when kept in the refrigerator for 3 to 4 days, these sauces taste of the sweetness of late summer and the mellowness of fall. Toss the sauce with 12 ounces of a long thin pasta such as spaghetti, linguine, or bavette, or a short tubular type such as penne or rigatoni.

Pasta ai Funghi Porcini
PASTA WITH MUSHROOM SAUCE

Prepare Condimento ai Funghi (page 62), but omit the lemon. Toss with a short tubular pasta such as penne or rigatoni, and serve with lots of freshly grated Parmigiano-Reggiano cheese.

Lasagne ai Funghi Porcini
WILD MUSHROOM–FILLED LASAGNE

Have 1½ cups grated Parmigiano-Reggiano cheese on hand. Cook 12 ounces dried lasagne according to the directions on the package. Arrange the lasagne layers in a shallow baking pan, spreading each layer with Condimento ai Funghi (page 62) and sprinkling with a handful of cheese. Finish with a layer of cheese. Bake at 350° F for 30 to 40 minutes, until bubbly and lightly golden.

Pasta al Pesto
PASTA WITH PESTO

Bring the Pesto (page 54) to room temperature and toss it with 1 pound of a long flat pasta, such as trenette or lingue di passero, with wide flat lasagna noodles, or with spiral pasta such as trofie or fusilli, which capture the sauce in their whorls.

Pasta al Pesto Toscano
PASTA WITH TUSCAN PESTO

Deep green Pesto Toscano (page 55) makes an irresistible pasta sauce. Simply beat in ½ to 1 cup mascarpone cheese and warm the sauce over a low flame. Toss with a long thin pasta such as tagliatelle, fettucini, or fettucelle.

Pasta alle Olive
PASTA WITH BLACK OLIVE SAUCE

Gently mix Puré di Olive Nere (page 58) with a simple thin pasta such as tagliarini, spaghettini, or vermicelli.

Pasta alla Marinara
PASTA WITH TOMATO SAUCE

Warm sweet, fresh-tasting Sugo di Pomodoro (page 193), add a handful of basil leaves just before serving, and pour the sauce over 1 pound of a long thin pasta such as spaghetti or spaghettini or a short tubular pasta like penne or rigatoni. Serve with Parmigiano-Reggiano cheese.

Pasta alle Cozze
PASTA WITH MUSSEL SAUCE

Warm Le Cozze (page 57) and toss it immediately with 12 ounces thin spaghettini.

Pasta all'Agliata
PASTA WITH GARLIC AND WALNUT SAUCE

Warm Agliata per Pasta (page 66) in a saucepan with a little chicken or beef broth, and toss it with tagliatelle.

Pasta alla Salsiccia
PASTA WITH SAUSAGE SAUCE

Prepare Salsina di Salsiccia e Pecorino and toss it with conchiglie, fusilli, or spaghetti. The sausage and pecorino topping, Salsiccia e Pecorino (page 67), and the stuffing for Olive Fritte all'Ascolana (page 46) also make excellent stuffings for tortelli, ravioli, and other stuffed pastas.

PASTA SALAD AND CONDIMENTI

Insalata di Verdure e Pasta
SUMMERY VEGETABLE PASTA SALAD

Combine the summery vegetable mixture Condimento alle Verdure (page 61) with short tubular pasta such as ditalone, gramigna, sedanini, or maccherone.

VARIATION

Make a pasta salad of the Insalata di Mozzarella, Noci, e Sedano (page 38) by cooking and draining 8 ounces of spaghetti, bucatini, or any pasta cut in short tubes, such as ditalini or penne. Immediately toss with ¼ cup of the marinade. Blend well and let cool completely. Half an hour before serving, add the cheese, celery, and walnut mixture to the pasta and mix thoroughly. Serve at room temperature.

RISOTTO AND CONDIMENTI

Risotto e Peperoni
SWEET PEPPER RISOTTO

Make Risotto (page 44), and during the last 10 minutes of cooking, stir in the sweet peppers of Peperoni Arrostiti (page 86) or Acquasale prepared without bread crumbs (page 60).

POLENTA AND CONDIMENTI

Make a giant mound of Polenta (page 155), and spoon one of these sauces over the top to make a one-dish meal.

Polenta ai Peperoni
POLENTA WITH SWEET PEPPERS

Glossy ribbons of red sweet peppers (Peperoni Arrostiti, page 86) tumble over a steaming golden circle of polenta: a perfect one-dish meal for a cold winter evening.

Polenta ai Funghi
POLENTA WITH WILD MUSHROOMS

Prepare Condimento ai Funghi (page 62) without the lemon, and pour the rich dark sauce over a smooth, velvety mound of Polenta.

Polenta ai Salsiccia e Pecorino
POLENTA WITH SAUSAGES AND PECORINO CHEESE

Polenta topped with sausages and pecorino cheese (page 67): a hearty, rib-sticking dish.

RICE SALAD AND CONDIMENTI

Insalata di Riso
RICE SALAD

For an irresistible hot summer day's salad, combine the Verdure topping (page 61), 2 cups cooled cooked Italian rice, a handful of black olives, a few well-rinsed capers and cornichons, and some fresh basil leaves. Toss with about ½ cup extra-virgin olive oil and 3 tablespoons lemon juice, and serve at room temperature.

Insalata di Riso ai Peperoni
RICE SALAD WITH SWEET PEPPERS

Mix Peperoni Arrostiti (page 86) with 2 cups cooled cooked Italian rice and some torn fresh basil leaves or a handful of meaty small black olives. Toss with olive oil, salt, and freshly ground pepper.

SOUP AND CONDIMENTI

Zuppa di Acquasale
SWEET PEPPER SOUP

Pour 3 cups of Acquasale (page 60) into a heavy saucepan, stir in 3 cups chicken broth, simmer for 3 to 4 minutes, and serve it forth.

Zuppa alle Verdure
COOL SUMMER VEGETABLE SOUP

Mix 3 tablespoons chicken broth and 1½ tablespoons olive oil into 1 recipe Condimento alle Verdure (page 61). Omit the two-hour rest and proceed without draining the liquid. Serve as a cool summer soup.

ANTIPASTO SALADS AND CONDIMENTI

What could be simpler? Scoop up these toppings and serve as main course salads or as delicious little bites on an antipasto platter. Serve them singly or in combination; you're bound only by the season and what you can find in your market.

Antipasto di Verdure
VEGETABLE ANTIPASTO

Arrange roasted or grilled summery vegetables on a platter and spoon Condimento alle Verdure (page 61) over them, or serve Condimento di Verdure as a salad.

Antipasto di Cozze
MUSSEL ANTIPASTO

Serve Le Cozze (page 57) as a salad.

Antipasto di Peperoni
SWEET PEPPER ANTIPASTO

Serve Acquasale or Peperoni Arrostiti (pages 60, 86) as a salad.

Antipasto di Pomodori, Arugula, e Olive
TOMATOES, ARUGULA, AND BLACK OLIVES

Serve Ciaredda (page 82) as a salad.

Antipasto di Granchio, Arugula, e Uova Soda
CRAB, ARUGULA, AND HARD-BOILED EGGS

Serve a Cicchetti filling (pages 94, 95) as a tasty salad.

Antipasto di Funghi
WILD MUSHROOM ANTIPASTO

Serve the Condimento ai Funghi (page 62) as a salad.

Antipasto di Peperoni, Porri, Olive, e Pomodoro
SWEET PEPPERS, LEEKS, OLIVES, AND TOMATOES

Serve the Focaccia filling (page 135) as an antipasto salad.

Antipasto ai Pomodori Secchi
SUN-DRIED TOMATO ANTIPASTO

Serve as part of any antipasto plate or with slices of fresh mozzarella.

Bruschetta e Crostini

What could be more elemental than slices of bread from a country loaf that have been grilled over a fire (*abbrustolito*, toasted, hence *bruschetta*), rubbed with a clove of garlic, sprinkled with crystals of sea salt and freshly ground pepper, and permeated with extra-virgin olive oil? This deeply satisfying rustic food reaches its greatest moment during the olive harvest, when the fresh, fruity extra-virgin oil from the first pressing is collected and drizzled on the bread so that it oozes into the pores of each slice and then onto your tongue. In Tuscany this deceptively simple dish is called *fettunta* (oiled slice), while it is known as *soma d'ai* (brushed with garlic) in Piedmont and as *panunta* (*pane unta*, oiled bread) elsewhere. It may be topped with tiny bits of tomato, the crunchy bite of fresh fennel, or a spoonful of cooked white beans. All over Italy, different regions add different tastes and combinations of herbs and greens to their bruschetta.

Crostini (which simply means little toasts) also begin with slices of country bread, but the toppings tend to be more refined. In Italy, where wasting bread is a cardinal sin, crostini and bruschetta are two ingenious ways to make use of bread that may be slightly stale. The bread for crostini may be grilled or toasted, fried in oil, or even cut into cubes and strung, alternating with cheese, on skewers. Bruschetta and crostini are extremely versatile. Put several on a plate and you have a light lunch, a brunch, a picnic, or a Sunday night supper. They make excellent antipasti and hors d'oeuvres, and are wonderful with an aperitif before any meal.

Many of the crostini in this chapter, as well as the toppings in "Condimenti," come from Giovanni Minuccio Cappelli, a passionate lover of good food who owns the wonderful trattoria Montagliari in Panzano, between Florence and Chianti. This rare man raises his own geese to make goose salame and has an *acetaia* where he makes balsamic vinegar, products that require a very long and consistent commitment to quality and care. Signor Cappelli has collected family recipes that stretch back into the nineteenth century. Many of the toppings and crostini—those with particularly compelling and unusual flavors—come from his collection.

Use chewy, crusty country bread for both bruschetta and crostini. For bruschetta, cut large country loaves into ½- to ¾-inch-thick slices, and then cut those pieces in half or in thirds. Use baguettes for crostini, and slice them ½ inch thick on the diagonal.

Bruschetta

TOASTED GARLIC BREAD

A dish as simple and down to earth as bruschetta is only as good as its ingredients. The bread should be a chewy, porous-textured country loaf with a crackly crust, and the olive oil should be the finest-quality extra-virgin. Serve this as an appetizer or as part of an antipasto plate, or set it on the bottom of a minestrone, such as the one on page 180.

6 slices rustic country-style bread,
cut ½ to ¾ inch thick and
halved
2 cloves garlic, lightly crushed
¼ cup extra-virgin olive oil
Sea salt

Grill or broil the bread on each side by setting the slices 4 to 6 inches from the heat source.

Rub each slice with a crushed garlic clove, letting it release its fragrance and juices into the bread. Drizzle the bread with the olive oil and then sprinkle with the salt. Serve warm, if you can.

VARIATION

Bruschetta delle Marche Sprinkle bits of fresh marjoram and grind fresh pepper over the garlic bread. This is particularly tasty served with a slice of young sheep's-milk cheese, such as caciotta, pecorino sardo, or a comparable Spanish, Greek, or French cheese.

SERVES 4 TO 6

Fettunta Toscana

GRILLED COUNTRY BREAD WITH TOMATOES AND BASIL

Country tradition at its finest: grilled bread topped with chunks of juicy ripe tomatoes and shreds of fresh basil. Serve it with slices of fresh mozzarella cheese for a summery first course.

4 large firm, ripe tomatoes

¼ cup torn fresh basil leaves

6 slices crusty Italian bread, cut ½ inch thick, halved

2 to 3 large cloves garlic, lightly crushed

Salt and freshly ground pepper

3 to 4 tablespoons extra-virgin Tuscan olive oil

Wash the tomatoes, cut them in half, remove as many seeds as possible, and dice them. Set them in a small mixing bowl and combine with the torn basil leaves.

Grill or broil the bread slices by setting them 4 to 6 inches from the heat source; turn them over so both sides are light brown.

Rub each slice with a crushed garlic clove. Spoon some of the tomato mixture over each slice, sprinkle with salt and pepper, and drizzle the olive oil liberally over the top. Serve at once.

VARIATION

Fettunta con Rucola Substitute 1 small bunch of arugula, stems removed and leaves finely sliced, for the basil.

SERVES 4 TO 6

Bruschetta Romana Piccante

SPICY ROMAN BRUSCHETTA

Roman *panzanella*, a "primordial" dish once used for children's afternoon snacks, began simply as slices of moistened bread flavored with oil, vinegar, salt, and parsley or basil. Add anchovies, garlic, vinegar, and a bit of hot red pepper, and it becomes something spicy and tantalizing, very much for the grown-ups. This recipe is based on a description of the dish by Ada Boni, author of *La Cucina Romana* and *Il Talismano della Felicità*, perhaps the most famous Italian cookbook published in the past fifty years.

¾ teaspoon red wine vinegar

¼ cup olive oil

6 tablespoons finely chopped flat-leaf parsley

3 tablespoons finely chopped fresh basil

4 to 5 anchovies, minced

½ teaspoon minced garlic

⅛ teaspoon red pepper flakes or minced peperoncino (dried red chile)

1 to 2 tablespoons freshly ground bread crumbs, if needed

6 to 8 slices Italian country-style bread, cut ¾ to 1 inch thick, halved

1 tablespoon olive oil, preferably extra-virgin

Whisk together the vinegar and oil, and then stir in the parsley and basil. Set the anchovies, garlic, and red pepper flakes or peperoncino in a food processor fitted with the steel blade, and process well. Add to the oil and vinegar mixture, and leave for 2 hours to allow the flavors to meld. If the mixture seems too thin, stir in a tablespoon or two of the fresh bread crumbs.

Grill or toast the bread slices. While they are still warm, brush them with a little olive oil, spread with the mixture, and serve.

SERVES 4 TO 6

Ciaredda

BRUSCHETTA WITH FRESH TOMATOES,
ARUGULA, AND BLACK OLIVES

This rustic bruschetta from Lecce has it all: the sweetness of juicy ripe tomatoes, the bite of field greens, and the saltiness of olives. The mixture makes a wonderful antipasto salad as well.

6 slices crusty Italian country-style bread, cut ½ inch thick, halved

3 to 4 tablespoons olive oil, preferably extra-virgin

Salt and freshly ground pepper

½ cup peeled, seeded, diced ripe tomatoes

¼ to ⅓ cup densely packed torn arugula leaves

16 to 20 small black olives in brine—Italian, French, Greek, or Moroccan—pitted

Broil or grill the bread on both sides, and set the slices on a platter. While they are still warm, drizzle one side well with the olive oil, and sprinkle with salt and a dusting of pepper. Dapple with the tomatoes and arugula, taste for salt, and tuck in the olives.

SERVES 6

Bruschetta con Pancetta

BACON BRUSCHETTA

Here's proof that *cucina povera* can nourish us all. Four elemental ingredients are all it takes for an ambrosial bruschetta, food Italians have been making since they first lit fires on a hearth: *pancetta*, the unsmoked Italian bacon flavored with black pepper and cloves, garlic, slices of rustic bread, and olive oil. Simplicity itself. Eat the bruschetta immediately—let nothing interrupt you.

8 slices crusty country-style bread, cut ½ inch thick, halved

1 large clove garlic, halved

3 to 4 tablespoons extra-virgin olive oil

8 ounces very thinly sliced pancetta

Rub the slices of bread with garlic, brush with olive oil, and grill or toast them. Arrange the pancetta on top of the grilled bread, and slide under the broiler until the pancetta begins to melt slightly and the edges start to crisp. Serve immediately.

SERVES 4 TO 6

Friselle alle Verdure

BRUSCHETTA WITH COOL SUMMER VEGETABLES

*B*ruschetta made with the ring-shaped double-baked bread of Puglia.

1 recipe Condimento alle Verdure (page 61)
6 small Friselle (page 216) or 6 ½-inch-thick slices country bread

*I*f you are using friselle, moisten by dipping them briefly in water. Grill or toast the friselle or slices of country bread. Taste the vegetable mixture and correct the seasonings. Spoon it onto the friselle or toasted bread and let stand for 1 hour before serving.

SERVES 6

Crostini

TOASTS FOR APPETIZERS

Kitchens in Tuscany and Umbria have wood-burning fireplaces in which cooks can place a simple grill a few inches above the fire. It's the obvious and easy way to grill the bread for bruschetta and crostini. Most of us, however, must be content with using the oven, the broiler, or even a toaster.

These crostini can be made a day or two ahead and kept in an airtight container or self-sealing plastic bag. Use them for all manner of crostini or cut them into cubes for croutons. The only consideration is the size of the bread. If you choose a large country loaf, cut the slices in half or even quarters.

1 loaf good-quality Italian
    baguette cut into ½ inch thick
    diagonal slices, or 8 slices
    Italian country-style bread cut
    into 3- × 3-inch slices, ½ inch
    thick
Olive oil

Preheat the oven to 400°F. Brush the slices of bread with olive oil, set them on a baking pan, and bake until lightly browned on both sides, turning once, about 8 to 10 minutes. (You may also set the slices under a heated broiler and broil until lightly browned on both sides, or brown them over a grill.)

SERVES 8 TO 10

Crostini ai Peperoni Arrostiti

CROSTINI WITH RIBBONS OF SWEET PEPPERS

The name says it all, but the choice is yours: Scoop the ribbons of pepper onto the crostini, or first purée them into a smooth paste.

3 sweet red or yellow peppers
3 to 4 tablespoons extra-virgin olive oil
1½ cloves garlic, minced
Salt and freshly ground pepper
3 tablespoons finely chopped flat-leaf parsley
6 to 8 slices Italian country-style crostini, cut ½ inch thick, grilled

Roast, seed, and slice the peppers as described on page 173.

Warm the olive oil in a large sauté pan. Add the sliced peppers and garlic, and cook over low heat for 5 to 10 minutes, being careful not to let the garlic burn. Add the salt, pepper, and parsley, and cook another 2 to 3 minutes.

Either ladle the mixture onto the grilled bread, or purée the mixture and then spoon it over the crostini.

SERVES 6 TO 8

Crostini Rossi

SPICY RED CROSTINI

*I*nfusing the bread with vinegar creates the tantalizing spiciness that makes this topping so irresistible. Although it is completely unconventional, I'd serve this on a sandwich with slices of cold chicken or rabbit; I'd eat it as a spicy bread salad like *panzanella*. This spread is even better the next day and keeps well for a week.

4 thick slices Italian country-style
   bread, crusts trimmed, roughly
   chopped
¼ cup red wine vinegar
1½ tablespoons minced garlic
2 tablespoons capers, drained, rinsed,
   and chopped
3 tablespoons tomato paste diluted in
   ½ cup warm water
¼ cup finely chopped flat-leaf parsley
⅓ cup extra-virgin olive oil
Salt and freshly ground pepper
1 recipe Crostini (page 85)

*S*et the bread chunks in a bowl, moisten them with the vinegar, and leave them for 10 to 15 minutes. Then squeeze the bread with your hands to remove any excess liquid, and return to the bowl. Mix in the garlic, capers, tomato paste, parsley, and olive oil; stir well to make a soft paste. Taste for salt and pepper. Let rest for at least 2 hours so the flavors can mingle. Spread on crostini.

SERVES 6 TO 8

Crostini Gialli

GOLDEN CROSTINI

There's nothing rustic about these crostini, which come from earlier times in Tuscany. Butter and hard-boiled egg yolks give them their golden color, and the anchovy paste their slightly biting edge.

7 tablespoons unsalted butter, room temperature
3½ hard-boiled egg yolks
½ cup flat-leaf parsley
1 ounce anchovy paste
Freshly grated pepper
Salt
12 slices Italian whole-wheat bread, cut ½ inch thick, lightly toasted, broiled, or grilled

Put the butter, egg yolks, parsley, and anchovy paste in a food processor or blender, and whirl to make a smooth paste. Add the freshly grated pepper, and taste for salt. Spread on the whole-wheat crostini.

MAKES 12

Crostini Piccanti

IRRESISTIBLE SPICY CROSTINI

When Giovanni Minuccio Cappelli brought out his large ledgers of old family recipes written in fine loops and swirls, he marked several that he considered particularly outstanding. A number came from two women who began cooking for the family in the late nineteenth century and who both lived long lives, feeding several generations of Cappellis. "Ottimo" ("the best") says the note scrawled in the margin of this one. Who could disagree? The many ingredients of this smooth and spicy topping blend so well that everyone always wants seconds, not only to eat more (they always do that), but also to guess what could possibly be in it.

2 large slices country-style bread,
    cut 1 inch thick, crusts removed
3 tablespoons red wine vinegar
6 anchovy fillets in oil, or 3 anchovies
    preserved in salt, rinsed very well in
    cold water and boned
3 tablespoons flat-leaf parsley
3 cloves garlic, roughly chopped
¾ cup plus 1 tablespoon pine nuts
4 teaspoons capers, drained and rinsed
4½ hard-boiled egg yolks
12 large green olives, pitted
½ cup olive oil, preferably extra-virgin
Salt and freshly ground pepper
1 recipe Crostini (page 85)

Set the bread slices on a plate, drizzle the vinegar over them, and leave for 10 to 15 minutes. Then squeeze the bread with your hands to remove any excess vinegar.

Set all the ingredients except the crostini in a food processor outfitted with the steel blade, and process to a fine paste. Spread over the crostini, and serve.

MAKES 25

Crostini alla Mozzarella e Alici

SKEWERS OF MELTING CHEESE AND CRUNCHY BREAD CUBES

This traditional Roman snack is a form of crostini, although the bread and cheese are layered side by side instead of one on top of the other, and are then impaled on skewers and toasted together. This biteful of lightly melted cheese was originally made with *provatura*, a close relative of fresh mozzarella. Since no provatura is to be found in this country, buy the best quality mozzarella that you can find, avoiding the familiar rubbery balls that have minimal taste or texture. Reading the recipe doesn't give any sense of the wonders of this simple dish, whose subtle flavor comes from the delicate anchovy sauce that is spooned over the creamy cheese and crunchy bread cubes.

12 ounces finest-quality mozzarella cheese, preferably fresh buffalo mozzarella

4 slices Italian country-style bread, cut ½ inch thick

6 tablespoons unsalted butter

4 anchovy fillets in oil, rinsed, boned, and mashed

2 tablespoons milk, warmed

Salt and freshly ground pepper

Preheat the oven to 400°F.

Cut the cheese into ½-inch cubes. Broil or toast the bread slices until lightly golden on both sides, and cut them into ½-inch cubes. Alternate chunks of bread and cheese on skewers, starting and ending with bread. Suspend the skewers over a shallow pan, making sure that the bread and cheese don't touch the bottom.

Melt 3 tablespoons of the butter, and brush it over the bread and cheese cubes. Bake for 10 minutes, until the bread is golden and crunchy and the cheese is beginning to melt.

Warm the remaining 3 tablespoons butter with the anchovies, stirring with a wooden spoon to crush the anchovies and mix them in well, about 3 minutes. Stir in the hot milk. Season with salt and pepper.

Remove the skewers from the oven. Slip the bread and cheese cubes off the skewers onto a warm platter, pour the anchovy sauce over the top, and serve immediately.

SERVES 4

Crostini alla Mozzarella, Alici, e Pomodori

CROSTINI WITH MOZZARELLA, ANCHOVIES, AND TOMATOES

These are crostini to celebrate with. They were once made in Foggia only on the days when fresh mozzarella came to the cities of Puglia, the sun-drenched region that occupies the heel and spur of the Italian boot. The Pugliese are famous for their own outstanding cheeses, but true creamy mozzarella is made in Campania from the milk of water buffalo, those somewhat sinister-looking animals that inhabit only the plain outside Naples. The individual cheeses are usually shaped into balls that sit in their own milky whey. Their slightly provocative lactic tang and somewhat shredding texture are what make them unique. If you don't want to spend the large sum necessary (after all, the cheese has to be shipped air express to remain fresh), do look for the finest American alternatives and stay away from those hard rubbery yellow rounds on supermarket shelves.

4 ripe tomatoes
4 anchovy fillets in oil, rinsed, boned, and mashed
¼ cup minced flat-leaf parsley
4 slices Italian country-style bread, cut ½ inch thick, halved and grilled or toasted
⅓ pound finest-quality mozzarella cheese, sliced ½ inch thick

Preheat the broiler.

Peel and seed the tomatoes, cut them into strips, and put them in a small bowl. Add the anchovies and parsley, and mix well. Cover the crostini with the mozzarella slices, and top with the tomato mixture. Set on a broiler pan, and broil about 4 inches from the heat source until the cheese melts.

SERVES 4

Crostini con Crema di Olive e Melanzane

CROSTINI WITH OLIVE AND EGGPLANT SPREAD

This unusual and highly appealing spread comes from Piedmont, where olives are more likely to be encountered whole or in pastes than transformed into oil. Reserve some of the olive paste when you initially blend it with the eggplant; taste carefully to be sure that its strong flavor doesn't overwhelm the eggplant.

1 medium eggplant (about
   1 pound)
Salt
3 to 4 tablespoons olive oil
3 tablespoons Black Olive Paste
   (store-bought or see page 58)
1 recipe Crostini (page 85)

Peel the eggplant, removing the root and blossom ends. Cut it crosswise into ½-inch-thick slices. Sprinkle them with salt, set them in a colander, and let stand for about 1 hour to draw out their bitter juices.

Preheat the broiler or outdoor grill.

Pat the eggplant slices dry with absorbent paper towels. Pour the olive oil into a shallow dish, and dip both sides of each eggplant slice into it. On an outdoor grill, cook the slices on both sides until grill marks are clearly visible; in the oven, broil them until they are soft and lightly golden on both sides. Set aside and allow to cool briefly.

Place the eggplant and 2 tablespoons of the olive paste in a food processor outfitted with the steel blade, and blend. Taste to be sure that the olive paste doesn't overwhelm the eggplant; if it doesn't, add the final tablespoon of paste and process. Serve on crostini.

SERVES 6

Crostini con le Olive Nere e Tonno

CROSTINI WITH BLACK OLIVE PASTE AND TUNA

This paste may look like a chicken liver pâté, but the resemblance ends there. The color comes from the surprisingly delicious combination of tuna and black olive paste: simple, tasty, and amazingly light.

2 slices country-style bread, crusts
   trimmed
¼ cup milk
6 ounces best-quality tuna in oil
7 tablespoons unsalted butter, room
   temperature
2 heaping tablespoons Black Olive
   Paste (store-bought or see page 58)
1 tablespoon capers, preferably
   preserved under salt and
   rinsed well
⅓ cup chopped flat-leaf parsley
⅓ cup chopped fresh basil
1 anchovy fillet, rinsed well
Zest of 1 lemon
Freshly grated pepper
18 Crostini (page 85)
1 clove garlic, lightly crushed

Soak the 2 slices bread in the milk, and squeeze dry. Put them in a food processor outfitted with the steel blade, and add all the remaining ingredients except the crostini and garlic. Process to a paste. Transfer the paste to a piece of aluminum foil, shape it into a log like a salame (about 8 inches long and 2 inches wide), and roll it up in the foil. Refrigerate overnight, until well set.

Rub the garlic over the crostini, and spread the tuna and olive paste on top.

VARIATION

For a coarser texture and less cholesterol, use only 3 tablespoons unsalted butter.

MAKES 18 TO 20

Cicchetti di Granseola

OPEN-FACE SANDWICH OF CRAB,
ARUGULA, AND EGGS

*C*icchetti are "pick-me-ups," delicious little bites to munch upon while drinking a glass of wine. Venice is dotted with special wine bars that serve the venerable combination of cicchetti and a glass of wine, called *l'ombra* (the shadow), a name that comes from the tradition of gondoliers seeking shade from the hot summer sun in the shadow of the campanile in the Piazza San Marco. When I am in Venice, I often make lunch or dinner of a few cicchetti, and now I do the same at home, serving two or three as the centerpiece of lunch, brunch, or part of a buffet. Serve them as elegant antipasti, as a salad, or make them your Sunday night supper.

12 ounces fresh crabmeat
2 hard-boiled eggs, roughly chopped
1½ bunches arugula, washed, trimmed, leaves chopped to roughly the size of watercress leaves
6 to 8 tablespoons olive oil
1½ to 2 tablespoons lemon juice
Salt and freshly ground pepper
10 slices Italian country-style bread, cut ½ inch thick

*S*et the crabmeat, eggs, and arugula in a medium-size mixing bowl. In a separate bowl, beat together the olive oil and lemon juice. Mix with the crab mixture, tasting as you blend, and season with salt and pepper.

Serve on the slices of country bread. To make appetizers, grill or broil the bread, cut each slice in half, and top with the crab mixture.

MAKES 10

Cicchetti di Carciofi e Prosciutto

OPEN-FACE SANDWICH OF ARTICHOKES, EGGS, AND PROSCIUTTO

5 artichokes

2 hard-boiled eggs, coarsely chopped

3 tablespoons finely chopped flat-leaf parsley

Salt and freshly ground pepper

2 teaspoons lemon juice

5 to 6 tablespoons olive oil

8 slices prosciutto, sliced just slightly thicker than the usual paper-thin

8 slices country-style bread

Clean and cook the artichokes as for Torta di Carciofi (page 194). Reserve the leaves for another purpose. Throw away the choke and any thistle-like leaves. Place the artichoke bottoms on a board, and chop them roughly. Transfer them to a bowl, add the eggs and parsley, and mix together well. Season with salt and pepper. Beat the lemon juice and olive oil together, and toss with the artichokes to bind the mixture.

Lay a slice of prosciutto over each slice of bread. Heap a bit of the artichoke and egg filling on top of it, and serve.

MAKES 8

Cicchetti di Funghi

MUSHROOM, ARUGULA, AND HARD-BOILED EGG
OPEN-FACE SANDWICHES

From nine in the morning until late at night, the Cantin Do Mori in Venice is jammed with people who come to drink wine and Prosecco, both sparkling and still. Copper cauldrons pave the ceiling, racks of wine bottles cover the back wall, and the counter and glass cases are full of the delicious, often thirst-provoking, snacks called *cicchetti*. This peppery arugula, egg, and mushroom open-face sandwich is another winning Venetian combination.

2 hard-boiled eggs
1½ cups fresh brown mushrooms, preferably cremini or portobello
¾ cup rinsed and trimmed arugula leaves
2 tablespoons lemon juice
5 tablespoons extra-virgin olive oil
Salt and freshly ground pepper
8 slices dark bread, such as Valentino's Casareccio (page 214) or any country whole wheat

Cut the hard-boiled eggs into rough chunks. Wipe the mushrooms clean with a damp paper towel, and cut them into large dice. Tear or cut the arugula leaves roughly into strips. Mix the three together in a serving bowl. Beat the lemon juice and oil together, add salt, and pour over the prepared mixture. Taste for seasoning before grinding any fresh pepper, since arugula can be very peppery tasting. Spoon the mixture onto the bread slices, and serve.

SERVES 8

Focacce e Pizze

*F*ocaccia and *pizza*: two members of the same family, one from Genoa and the north, the other native to Naples and the south, both baked in wood-burning ovens. They can be thin or thick, round or square, as small as a saucer or so gigantic that a tall man must hoist one on his shoulder to carry it aloft through the city streets. Their flavorings can be as simple as sea salt or as complicated as Sicilian *sfincione*, in which everything from anchovies to tomatoes is laid in a dense paving across the top. Crusts can be crisp or chewy, delicate or sturdy. Pizze and focacce can be one fine layer or two, may be thick or thin, or may be wrapped around full-flavored fillings. Eat them hot out of the oven or at room temperature.

I have chosen a few of my favorites from all over Italy: a crunchy focaccia with toasted walnuts, another topped with ribbons of sweet peppers, an especially moist example made with oat flour, and several fabulous fine-crusted pizze. Signora Sada's golden durum focaccia and the onion and escarole pies are three irresistible discoveries from southern Italy.

The rustic double-crust pizze in this section are also from the south. Their fillings are often addictive: leeks and olives; tomatoes and sweet peppers; frisée and black olives; even tender, sweet onions combined with the sauciness of olives and the saltiness of anchovies. If these spectacular filled pizze look daunting, don't believe it. Most doughs can be refrigerated after they are made or after they have risen the first time. All doughs keep at least 24 hours in the refrigerator, and some pizza doughs keep up to 3 days. Just bring them back to room temperature before you shape or roll them.

Short-Cuts. If you just aren't prepared to make dough, try persuading your favorite pizzeria to sell you a few balls of theirs. Buy them for use later in the day or to freeze for up to 4 months. Flatten them into discs and carefully enclose them in self-sealing plastic bags. You can defrost them quickly in a warm spot (75° to 80°F) for 2 hours, or slowly in the refrigerator for 24 hours; then allow the dough to come to room temperature in a warm, draft-free place. Use the dough as soon as it is warm enough to stretch and shape. You can do the same with pizza doughs from the freezer case of your grocery or specialty store.

If doughs are more than you want to tangle with, you might decide to skip making them altogether and turn some of the fillings into first-course antipasti, salads for a light meal, or a vegetable combination.

Pizza and focaccia have been around for millennia. When the Greeks occupied the south of Italy, they were baking flavored flatbreads. Ancient Romans expanded on the possibilities, and centuries later Neapolitans made pizza their emblematic dish, flavoring bread dough with anchovies from the sea, mozzarella from the milk of buffalo that lived on nearby hillsides, and tomatoes that arrived from the New World and established their hold in the eighteenth century. The Neapolitans made pizza the impromptu food that it remains today.

In northern Italy, focaccia plays much the same role as a fast food. It is served at caffès, bakeries, tiny specialty shops, and stands where pans of the dimpled dough are slid into roaring-hot ovens and then brought out to be sliced into squares and eaten out of hand. In many places it is common to slice a hot focaccia horizontally and fill it with fresh cheese and prosciutto, or to slather the interior with ricotta that has been lightly salted and peppered, then put it back into the oven for a few minutes. Deeply fingerprinted focacce sprinkled with olive oil and crystals of sea salt are traditionally served with sweet prosciutto. Country people in northern Italy may press a single basil leaf in each indentation, while cooks in Puglia drop slivers of tomato and garlic into the hollows.

Before beginning, please read the tips about making doughs and baking them on page 209, especially if you have chosen one of the doughs that uses a *biga*, or starter.

Since everyone measures flour differently, I strongly recommend measuring by weight so nothing is left to chance.

Durum flour is glorious for golden pizza crusts as well as for doughs that enclose moist fillings because it resists getting gummy or sticky. If you can't find it easily, it can be ordered by mail (see the Source Guide on page 282). Durum is different from durum integrale (whole wheat) and from semolina flour. Semolina, also called pasta flour, is more granular than durum. It requires more water and more rolling to be turned into a successful dough. You can sprinkle semolina on your baking stone just before sliding pizze, focacce, or breads in the oven, but please don't try using it to make these recipes.

Making Dough in a Food Processor.   I have not given instructions in each recipe on how to make these doughs in the food processor, so here are the general rules. Have all your ingredients at hand before you begin. Set the steel or plastic dough blade in the work bowl of your processor. Measure the warm water into a container with a spout, such as a Pyrex measuring cup, sprinkle the yeast over the top, and whisk it in. Let stand until foamy and creamy, about 5 to 10 minutes. Add the optional oil. Place the flour and salt in the bowl of the processor, and process with several pulses to sift. With the machine running, pour the dissolved yeast and the oil down the feed tube as quickly as the flour can absorb it, and process only until a rough ball masses over or around the blade. Remove the dough from the processor, and knead it briefly on a lightly floured work surface.

Making pizza and focaccia doesn't require much in the way of special equipment, but there are two or three things I would strongly recommend. For baking all doughs, porous baking stones laid on an oven shelf replicate the inside of a baker's oven and produce crisper crusts than would otherwise be possible. Be certain to set the stones in the oven and preheat for 30 minutes.

The pizza can be shaped free-form and baked directly on the stones, but you will find that spreading the dough to the right shape and controlling it in the oven is infinitely easier when you use a pizza pan with a perforated bottom.

Focaccia Versiliese

CRISPY OLIVE-AND-HERB-FILLED FOCACCIA

This focaccia is as thin as a cracker and as addictive as peanuts. Once I start eating it, I can't stop. It is found only along a small stretch of the Tuscan coast, and while it is sold like focaccia in Viareggio, in nearby Camaiore it is made without olives and used as bread for sandwiches filled with slices of prosciutto and tomato, lettuce, a little oregano, and oil.

2 teaspoons active dry yeast

1 cup plus 2 tablespoons warm water (105° to 115°F)

1 tablespoon olive oil

1 tablespoon chopped fresh rosemary

4 leaves fresh sage, torn into small pieces

3½ ounces olives, preferably black Tuscan variety, pitted

2 tablespoons minced garlic

Scant 2 cups (250 grams) unbleached all-purpose flour

1 cup plus 2 tablespoons (150 grams) corn flour

2 teaspoons sea salt plus extra for sprinkling

About 2 teaspoons olive oil

Stir the yeast into the warm water in a large mixing bowl; leave until creamy, about 10 minutes. Then stir in the tablespoon of olive oil, rosemary, sage, olives, and garlic. Using a wooden spoon or the paddle attachment of a heavy duty mixer, mix in the flours and the 2 teaspoons salt, stirring until a smooth dough is formed. Knead the dough for 8 to 10 minutes by hand on a lightly floured work surface or for 3 minutes at medium speed in a heavy-duty mixer with the dough hook, until the dough is firm, elastic, and a bit gritty.

First rise. Set the dough in a lightly oiled container, cover with plastic wrap, and let rise until just doubled, 1 hour.

Shaping and second rise. Turn the dough onto an oiled 10½- × 15½-inch baking pan and stretch it to fit. If it won't cover the pan entirely, let it rest for 10 minutes and then stretch it again. Cover it with a towel and leave until half risen, about 30 minutes.

Baking. Thirty minutes before you plan to bake the foccacia, set a baking stone, if you have one, in the oven and preheat to 400°F. Just before baking, dimple the top of the dough with your fingertips and sprinkle it with some extra sea salt and the 2 teaspoons oil. Bake for 25 to 30 minutes, until golden. Slide the foccacia off the baking sheet onto a rack, and let it cool briefly. Eat warm or at room temperature.

VARIATION

Focaccia Dolce To transform this into a sweet focaccia, substitute 2 ounces raisins and 1 ounce pine nuts for the olives, herbs, and garlic. First soak the raisins in warm water for 30 minutes and then squeeze them dry.

Pine nuts always taste best when they have been heated in a 350°F oven for 5 minutes, or when toasted very briefly in a heavy cast-iron frying pan over the fire. Toast only until they begin to color.

Note: This dough can be prepared in a food processor. See page 211 for instructions.

MAKES ONE 10½- × 15½-INCH FOCACCIA

Fitascetta

ONION-COVERED BREAD RING

This delicious rustic *merenda* from the area around Lake Como is really a wreath-shaped focaccia covered with masses of sautéed red onions. The onions are sautéed slowly over very low heat to bring out their extraordinary sweetness, then cooled and piled on top of the ring just before it goes into the oven. Sprinkle them with a tiny bit of salt or sugar, depending on your preference.

Eat the fitascetta hot or at room temperature. For an especially splendid treat, add some shredded creamy cheese during the last few minutes in the oven. No one can explain how this focaccia got its mysterious name, although some natives of the area point to the fact that when local taleggio or stracchino cheese is added, it pulls into threads (*fila*) as it heats up.

¾ teaspoon active dry yeast

1 cup warm water (105° to 115°F)

¼ cup olive oil

Scant 2½ cups (340 grams) unbleached all-purpose flour

1½ teaspoons sea salt

1½ pounds (about 3 medium-size) red onions, sliced very fine

4 tablespoons unsalted butter

Salt and freshly ground pepper, or a pinch of sugar, to taste

Olive oil

½ cup shredded stracchino or taleggio cheese (optional)

Stir the yeast into the water in a large mixing bowl and let stand until creamy, about 10 minutes. With a wooden spoon or the paddle attachment of a heavy-duty mixer, stir in the olive oil, and then the flour and salt, stirring until the dough comes together. Knead by hand on a floured surface until moist, velvety, and slightly sticky, about 8 to 10 minutes; or knead in a heavy-duty mixer with the dough hook attachment at medium speed for 3 minutes.

First rise. Place the dough in a lightly oiled bowl, cover well with plastic wrap, and let rise until doubled, 2½ to 3 hours. The dough should be soft and velvety.

Meanwhile, sauté the onions in the butter over the lowest possible heat until they are soft and transparent, about 40 minutes. Season with salt and pepper or a pinch of sugar and leave to cool. You may want to drain any excess butter.

Shaping and second rise. When the dough is ready, turn it out onto a lightly floured work surface and shape it into a long log. Transfer the dough to a greased or parchment-paper-lined baking sheet, and join the two ends to make a ring 6 to 8 inches in diameter, keeping the hole in the center as open as possible. Pinch the ends together firmly. Cover with a moist towel and let rise until doubled, about 2 hours.

Baking. Thirty minutes before you are ready to bake the focaccia, set the baking stone, if you are using it, in the oven and preheat to 400°F. When the dough is fully risen, scoop up the onions in a slotted spoon, pile them on top of the ring, and set it in the oven. Bake for 15 minutes. Then reduce the heat to 375°F, brush the exposed surface with some more olive oil, and bake for another 15 to 20 minutes, until golden and slightly crispy. Add the optional cheese 8 to 10 minutes before you plan to take the fitascetta out of the oven. Remove and immediately slide off the baking sheet to cool on a rack.

MAKES 1 LARGE RING

Crescia

ONION-FLAVORED FOCACCIA FROM LE MARCHE

San Lorenzo in Campo is a lovely little town in one of the inland valleys of the Marches. Its attractions, beyond the truly delicious food at the Restaurant Il Giardino, are manifold: the old men in their undershirts who gather in the darkness of the cobbler's shop, entertaining each other with stories of the old days; a widow's huge garden overflowing with the tomatoes, squashes, and herbs that find their way to the restaurant and the market; a stamp "museum" that consists of a single room with four enormous murals made entirely of Italian postage stamps; and several bakeries making bread, sweets, and *crescia*. In the morning people are busily buying sheets and squares of the local focaccia, and come mid-afternoon, everyone in San Lorenzo in Campo is eating crescia, either the one flavored with little bits of onion (here) or the one with rosemary dappling the top (see Variation).

2½ teaspoons (1 package) active
   dry yeast
½ cup warm water (105° to 115°F)
1½ cups plus 2 tablespoons water,
   room temperature
6 tablespoons olive oil
5 cups (700 grams) unbleached
   all-purpose flour
1 tablespoon plus 1 teaspoon sea
   salt

TOPPING
2 tablespoons olive oil
1 cup finely chopped onions
1½ tablespoons olive oil
½ teaspoon sea salt

If you are making this by hand, stir the yeast into the warm water in a large mixing bowl; let it stand until creamy, about 10 minutes. Stir in the rest of the water and the oil. Whisk in 2 cups of the flour and stir until smooth. Then stir in the salt and the remaining flour, 1 cup at a time, until the dough comes together. Knead on a floured surface until velvety, soft, and sticky, about 8 to 10 minutes.

If you are making this in a heavy-duty electric mixer, stir the yeast into the warm water in the mixer bowl; let stand until creamy, about 10 minutes. Stir in the remaining water and the oil with the paddle; then add the flour and salt and mix until the dough comes together. Change to the dough hook and knead on medium speed for 3 minutes, until the dough is velvety, soft, and sticky. Finish by kneading briefly on a work table sprinkled with 1 tablespoon flour.

First rise. Put the dough in a lightly oiled bowl, cover tightly with plastic wrap, and let rise until doubled, about 1½ hours.

While the dough is rising, prepare the topping: Warm the 2 tablespoons olive oil over very low heat, and sauté the onions until they are limp and translucent, about 20 minutes. Cool to room temperature.

Shaping and second rise. Cut the dough into two pieces, one twice as large as the other. Shape the smaller one to fit an oiled 10-inch round pie plate and the larger one to fit an oiled 10½- × 15½-inch baking pan. Cover with towels and let rise for 45 minutes to 1 hour, until bubbles appear in the dough; it will have not quite doubled.

Baking. Preheat the oven to 400°F.

If you are using baking stones, set them in the oven and heat them for 30 minutes. Sprinkle the onions evenly over the dough, drizzle with the 1½ tablespoons oil, and finish with the salt. Place the pans directly on the preheated stones and bake for 25 minutes, until the tops are golden. Unmold onto a rack and serve warm or at room temperature.

VARIATION

Crescia al Rosmarino Substitute 2 tablespoons finely chopped fresh rosemary for the sautéed onions, and proceed as above.

MAKES ONE 10½- × 15½-INCH AND ONE 10-INCH ROUND FOCACCIA

Schiacciata con Noci

CORNMEAL FLATBREAD WITH WALNUTS

This unusual Tuscan flatbread, which is crunchy with walnuts and crispy cracklings, is a perfect example of country people taking whatever they had on hand—a handful of walnuts, a bit of coarse-ground golden cornmeal—and making a delicious treat. You have to search far these days to find someone who remembers, much less makes, this splendid schiacciata, so it truly qualifies as a taste from another way of life.

Of course almost everyone in Tuscany once had a pig, the source of the cracklings, but you may either use cracklings or bits of crispy fried pancetta—or leave them out entirely. Serve this as a wonderful snack anytime during the day, as an hors d'oeuvre, as part of an antipasto, or in place of bread at a rustic meal.

2½ teaspoons (1 package) active dry yeast

1⅓ cups plus 1 tablespoon warm water (105° to 115°F)

1 tablespoon olive oil (optional)

2½ tablespoons diced pancetta (optional)

¾ cup cornmeal, preferably stone-ground

Scant 3 cups (400 grams) unbleached all-purpose flour

1½ teaspoons sea salt

¾ cup walnuts, toasted and roughly chopped

Olive oil

Sea salt

Stir the yeast into the water in a large mixing bowl; let it stand until creamy, about 10 minutes. Meanwhile, if you are using the pancetta, heat the olive oil in a small heavy skillet and cook the pancetta until it is crispy. Let the oil and the pancetta cool separately. Once the yeast is creamy, stir in the cooled oil (if you are not using the pancetta, simply stir in the oil now).

Combine the cornmeal, flour, and salt. If you are making this by hand, whisk the first 2 cups of the flour mixture, 1 cup at a time, into the bowl. Then stir in the remainder with a wooden spoon. Knead by hand on a lightly floured surface until firm, about 4 to 5 minutes. Then knead in the walnuts, and the pancetta bits if you are using them, in two additions, resting the dough briefly in between.

Using a heavy-duty electric mixer, add the cornmeal, flour, salt, walnuts, and optional pancetta all at once, and mix with the paddle to produce a dough. Change to the dough hook and knead until the dough is firm, slightly sticky, and gritty, about 3 minutes. Knead briefly by hand on a lightly floured surface to eliminate any stickiness.

First rise. Place the dough in a lightly oiled bowl, cover tightly with plastic wrap, and let rise until doubled, about 45 minutes.

Second rise. Stretch or roll out the dough to fit an oiled 10½- × 15½-inch pan. Cover with a towel and let rise until doubled, 45 to 50 minutes.

Baking. Preheat the oven to 400°F 30 minutes before baking.

If you are using a baking stone, set it in the oven at that time. Just before baking, make little dimples in the top of the dough with your knuckles, and then drizzle them with a light wash of olive oil and sprinkle them with sea salt. Place the pan directly on the preheated stone and bake for 22 to 25 minutes, until golden. Serve hot or cool on a rack to room temperature.

Note: This dough can be prepared in a food processor. See page 211 for instructions.

MAKES ONE 10½- × 15½-INCH SCHIACCIATA

Focaccia Pugliese
FOCACCIA FROM PUGLIA

This focaccia gets its beautiful golden color from durum flour and the accents of red tomatoes that dapple the top. If you use unbleached flour, reduce the water by 2 tablespoons.

DOUGH
8 ounces potatoes, preferably yellow Finnish

1¼ teaspoons active dry yeast

1½ cups plus 2 tablespoons warm water (105° to 115°F)

3¾ cups (500 grams) durum flour or unbleached all-purpose flour

2 teaspoons sea salt

TOPPING

2 to 3 tablespoons olive oil

1 large ripe tomato, cut into small pieces

2 teaspoons capers packed in salt, rinsed

½ teaspoon sea salt

¼ to ½ teaspoon dried oregano

About 20 minutes before you are ready to make the dough, peel the potatoes and boil them until tender; drain, and mash or press them through a ricer. Use the potatoes while they are still warm but not so hot as to kill the yeast; they should be about the same temperature as the yeast water.

Stir the yeast into the warm water in a large mixing bowl. Add the flour, mashed potatoes, and salt in two additions and mix until the dough comes together. If you are making this by hand, knead for 10 minutes until the dough is velvety, firm, and slightly sticky. You may want to spread 1 to 2 tablespoons flour on the board to reduce the stickiness.

If you are using a heavy-duty electric mixer, use the dough hook to knead about 4 minutes on medium speed for the durum flour, 3 minutes for the unbleached flour, until the dough is soft and elastic. You may want to knead by hand for 1 minute longer on a lightly floured board to reduce the stickiness.

First rise. Place the dough in a lightly oiled bowl, cover tightly with plastic wrap, and leave to rise until doubled, about 1½ hours.

Shaping and second rise. Divide the dough in half on a lightly floured surface, and shape each into a ball. Place each ball in a well-oiled 9-inch round baking pan, and stretch the dough toward the edges. Cover with a damp towel, let sit for 10 minutes, and then stretch a bit farther to the edges. Cover again and leave until doubled, about 45 minutes.

Baking. Preheat the oven to 400°F. If you are using baking stones, preheat them for 30 minutes. Just before you are ready to bake the focacce, dimple the dough with your fingertips. Sprinkle the olive oil and distribute the tomatoes, capers, salt, and oregano over the dough. Bake the focacce for 25 to 30 minutes until golden. Remove the focacce from their pans, and let them cool to room temperature on racks.

MAKES TWO 9-INCH ROUND FOCACCE

Focaccia con la Ricotta

FOCACCIA FILLED WITH SALAME
AND CHEESE

In Puglia they call this a focaccia, but it is really a savory pie filled with a delicious combination of salame and cheeses.

DOUGH

2½ teaspoons (1 package) active dry yeast

1¼ cups warm water (105° to 115°F)

¼ cup olive oil

Scant 3 cups (400 grams) unbleached all-purpose flour

2 teaspoons sea salt

Whisk the yeast into the warm water in a large mixing bowl; let stand until creamy, about 10 minutes. Stir in the olive oil, then the flour and salt, and mix with a wooden spoon or the paddle attachment of a heavy-duty mixer until the dough comes together. You may need to add another tablespoon of flour. Knead for 4 minutes by hand on a lightly floured work surface, or for about 1 minute with the dough hook in a heavy-duty mixer. Transfer the dough to an oiled bowl, cover with plastic wrap, and leave for 30 minutes.

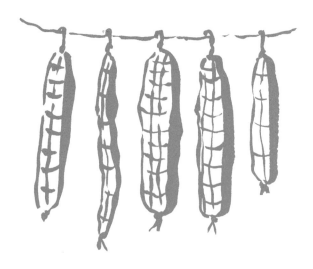

FILLING

11 ounces ricotta cheese, as fresh
   as possible
2 large eggs, room temperature
1/3 cup (2 ounces) diced spicy
   salame
6 ounces mozzarella cheese, diced
1/3 cup (scant 2 ounces) grated
   Parmigiano-Reggiano cheese
Generous grating of nutmeg (about
   1/8 teaspoon)
Salt and pepper
2 to 3 tablespoons olive oil

While the dough is rising, preheat the oven to 450°F.

Press the ricotta through a sieve, or whirl it in a food processor to aerate and lighten it. Set it in a large bowl, add the eggs, and mix well. Stir in the salame, mozzarella, Parmesan, nutmeg, salt, and pepper.

Divide the dough into two pieces, one twice the size of the other. Roll out the larger one to form a circle about 13 or 14 inches in diameter, and lay it gently in an oiled 9-inch springform, high-sided quiche or baking pan with removable bottom, so that it covers the bottom of the pan and slightly overlaps the sides. Lightly oil its surface, and spread the filling over it. Roll the second piece of dough out to form a 10-inch circle, and set it on top of the filling. Trim the overhanging dough, and with your fingers carefully press the two layers of dough together to close the focaccia. Prick the top crust with a fork and brush with olive oil.

Bake until golden, about 30 minutes. Cut into wedges, and serve.

SERVES 6 AS A LIGHT MEAL, 10 TO 12 AS AN ANTIPASTO

Puddhica

PUGLIESE FOCACCIA WITH SEAFOOD

Puddhica, one of the oldest and most loved *merende* in the coastal towns of Puglia, is simply a soft focaccia with shreds of tomato, slivers of garlic, and sprinklings of oregano filling every dimple on the surface. You may bake it any time during the day on which you plan to serve it.

This *merenda* is a seafood lover's dream since it is often served with a mixture of mussels, clams, octopus, and sea urchin. Octopus, already cleaned, is available at some ethnic markets, but sea urchins are a much rarer commodity. They are a familiar feature at the seashore in Puglia, where they are heaped on platters ready to be opened and eaten on the spot like oysters. Simple eating establishments serve bread on which to spread their deep orange pulp.

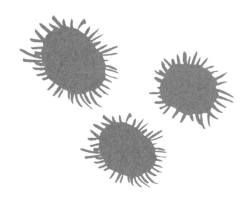

1 recipe Focaccia Pugliese (page 110) made with unbleached all-purpose flour; substitute 2 to 3 cloves garlic, slivered, for the capers
1 pound mussels
1 pound clams
1 small octopus (optional)
6 tablespoons extra-virgin olive oil
2 cloves garlic, crushed
Juice of 2 lemons
Salt and pepper
¼ cup finely chopped flat-leaf parsley

Clean the mussels as directed on page 57. Scrub the clam shells well and rinse them under cold running water. Set the mussels in a large saucepan with 2 cups water. Put the clams in a heavy pan over high heat to cook in their own liquid. Cover, and steam each open over high heat. Transfer the mussels and clams to a bowl, discarding any that haven't opened, and as soon as they are cool enough to handle, detach the meat from the shells. Save the cooking water and strain it.

Clean the octopus if necessary, removing the eyes with a sharp knife; then beat the tentacles with a mallet until they feel tender and relaxed. Wash well under cold running water. Place the octopus in a saucepan with the clam and mussel cooking liquid, add water as needed to partially cover, and simmer until tender, about 30 minutes. As soon as it is cool enough to handle, cut into small pieces.

Warm the olive oil in a sauté pan over medium heat. Add the garlic and sauté gently until it is a pale golden color and its fragrance infuses the oil, 2 to 3 minutes. Arrange the mussels, clams, and octopus if you are using it, on a serving platter. Stir together the infused olive oil, lemon juice, salt, pepper, and parsley. Pour this dressing over the seafood and leave to marinate for 30 minutes to 1 hour. Serve with the focaccia, at room temperature.

SERVES 4 TO 6

Focaccia Rustica

COUNTRY FOCACCIA WITH RED PEPPER TOPPING

A delicious focaccia that actually stays moist for a day or two. By itself the red pepper topping makes a delicious antipasto, pasta sauce, or vegetable dish.

DOUGH

2 medium-size cloves garlic, lightly crushed

2 tablespoons plus 1 teaspoon olive oil

2½ teaspoons (1 package) active dry yeast

1⅓ cups warm water (105° to 115°F)

3¾ cups (500 grams) unbleached all-purpose flour

1½ teaspoons sea salt

20 fresh sage leaves, roughly chopped, or 2 teaspoons chopped fresh rosemary leaves

Warm the garlic cloves in the olive oil over very low heat just until the garlic begins to brown. Discard the garlic and cool the oil to room temperature. Meanwhile whisk the yeast into the warm water and leave until creamy, about 10 minutes. Add the cooled olive oil. Stir in the flour, salt, and herbs, and mix until the dough comes together; you may need to add 1 more tablespoon of water. Knead by hand on a lightly floured work surface for 6 to 8 minutes, or if you are using a heavy-duty mixer, change to the dough hook and knead on medium speed for 3 minutes. The dough will be silky and elastic.

First rise. Place the dough in a lightly oiled bowl, cover tightly with plastic wrap, and let rise until doubled, 1 hour.

While the shaped dough is rising, roast, peel, and slice the peppers into thin strips (see page 173). Sauté the onions in the ¼ cup olive oil over very low heat for 25 to 30 minutes, until they are soft and limp.

Shaping and second rise. Set the dough in an oiled 10½- × 15-inch pan. Stretch the dough to cover as much of the bottom as possible; the dough will be very springy and cooperative. Cover with a towel and let it relax for 15 minutes. Then dimple and stretch the dough some more, until it covers the bottom in a very thin layer. Leave to rise until puffy, about 50 minutes.

Baking. Preheat the oven to 400°F. If you are using baking stones, set them in the oven and preheat for 30 minutes. When the dough is ready, lightly dip your fingertips into the remaining 3 tablespoons olive oil and dimple the tops of the dough. Divide the vegetables evenly and distribute them over the surface of the two focacce; sprinkle with the basil and salt; and finish by drizzling the remaining oil over the tops. Bake for 25 to 30 minutes, until the dough is crispy at the edges and the vegetables are soft but still very slightly crisp. Let cool briefly, then remove from the baking pans and let cool on racks. Serve tepid or at room temperature.

Note: This dough can be prepared in a food processor. See page 211 for instructions.

MAKES ONE 10½- × 15½-INCH FOCACCE

Focaccia di Maddalena Carella Sada

MADDALENA CARELLA SADA'S FOCACCIA

While I was talking with Professor Sada, a great scholar and expert on the foods of Puglia, about the *merende* of the region, his wife appeared with a tray bearing glasses of local wine and this glorious, moist tomato-covered focaccia. She made it with a combination of durum and *farro* flours, two grains indigenous to Puglia. Golden durum flour, the grain that grows across the wide Tavoliere plain, is available here (see the Source Guide, page 282), but farro has barely reached these shores, so with her permission, I have substituted unbleached all-purpose flour. This focaccia gets its crispiness from the generous amount of olive oil on the bottom of the baking pans.

⅘ cup (200 grams) Durum Flour Biga
  (page 213)

2½ teaspoons (1 package) active dry
  yeast

½ cup warm water (105° to 115°F)

3 cups water, room temperature

3¾ cups (500 grams) durum flour

3¾ cups (500 grams) unbleached all-
  purpose flour

1 tablespoon sea salt

6 tablespoons olive oil

1 large ripe, full-flavored tomato,
  peeled and diced

¾ teaspoon coarse sea salt

Few sprigs fresh oregano, or ½ to ¾
  teaspoon dried oregano

You must make the *biga*, or starter, at least 12 to 24 hours before you prepare the dough. Because of the stickiness of the starter and the dough, this focaccia is easier to manage in a heavy-duty electric mixer. If you decide to brave the process by hand, be sure to have some extra flour nearby, but use it as sparingly as possible to avoid changing the nature of the dough.

Prepare the biga as described on page 213, and set it aside for at least 12 hours.

Stir the yeast into the warm water in a large mixer bowl; let it stand until creamy, about 5 to 10 minutes. Add the biga and the 3 cups water, and mix by hand or with the paddle attachment in a heavy-duty mixer until well blended. Add the flours and salt, and mix for 3 to 4 minutes; the dough will pull away from the sides of the bowl but not from the bottom.

Change to the dough hook, and knead at medium speed for about 5 minutes. (If you are kneading by hand, keep some extra flour nearby to dust on the work surface and your hands, but use it as sparingly as possible; knead for 6 to 8 minutes.) The dough should be elastic, sticky, and soft but not wet, with many bubbles visible under the skin.

First rise. Place the dough in a lightly oiled bowl, cover with plastic wrap, and let rise until doubled, about 1 hour.

Shaping and second rise. Prepare two 10½- × 15½- inch baking pans by pouring 3 tablespoons olive oil into each, then tilting to coat the bottoms and sides well. Turn the elastic, slightly sticky dough out onto a lightly floured work surface, cut it in half, and sprinkle very lightly with flour, just enough to counteract the stickiness. Place each half in an oiled baking pan, and flatten and stretch the dough to cover as much of the bottom as possible. Cover the pans with a towel and let the dough relax for 10 minutes. Then stretch the dough some more and leave to rise until well puffed, about 45 minutes to 1 hour.

Topping. Dimple the tops vigorously with your fingertips and brush them with oil, using some of the excess available by tilting the pan and siphoning it off from the bottom. Sprinkle with the pieces of tomato, crystals of coarse sea salt, and the oregano, and finish by drizzling with a little more oil.

Baking. Preheat the oven to 425°F. If you are going to use baking stones, preheat them in the oven for 30 minutes. Set the baking pans on the preheated stones, and reduce the heat to 400°F. Bake until golden, 20 to 25 minutes, spraying with water three times in the first 10 minutes. Remove the focacce immediately from their pans, and let them cool to room temperature on racks.

MAKES TWO 10½- × 15½-INCH FOCACCE

Focaccia Condita

DURUM PIZZA AND DURUM BREAD

People may visit the town of Altamura in Puglia to see the medieval cathedral and its wondrous carved doors, but they usually stay on to eat some of the city's famous breads and pizze. At one of the last bakeries in the city equipped with a wood-burning oven, I watched wheels of bread and round friselle being made from sensational durum flour dough all day long. Around seven in the evening, when the oven was roaring hot, the bakers took the bread dough, stretched it out like pizza on wooden peels, sprinkled oregano, slathered olive oil, and rubbed tiny juicy tomatoes right on its surface. They made a rim around the edge so the oil wouldn't escape, then sprinkled on some salt and slid it into the oven. In the next 2 hours dozens and dozens of pizze flew out the door into the arms and mouths of the people of Altamura.

Because this dough uses so little yeast, it fits wonderfully into busy American lives. You can make it in the morning, using mostly cool water, and let it rise all day long at a cool room temperature. When you return, it is ready to be made into pizza or bread.

Durum flour, the silky fine golden wheat used for making pasta, can be found in some specialty shops and health food stores and through a number of mail-order sources (see page 282). Don't substitute semolina (sometimes called pasta flour), or durum integrale (whole-wheat durum), which won't rise properly, or unbleached all-purpose flour, which makes an impossibly wet dough.

DOUGH

¼ teaspoon active dry yeast
½ cup warm water (105° to 115°F)
3 cups water, room temperature
¾ cup (150 grams) Durum Flour Biga (page 213), 1 to 5 days old
7½ cups (1,000 grams) durum flour
1 tablespoon sea salt

TOPPING FOR 3 PIZZE

3 to 3¾ teaspoons chopped fresh oregano
6 tablespoons olive oil
2 ripe juicy tomatoes, or about 24 ripe full-flavored cherry tomatoes, halved
3 green onions, white part only, trimmed and sliced (optional)
2 to 3 teaspoons capers (optional)
1½ teaspoons sea salt
Olive oil
Cornmeal (for bread)

If you want to make a single pizza or bread, you can freeze the extra dough for up to 4 months. Immediately after completing the kneading, remove the part you don't plan to cook, flatten it into a disc shape, and store it in a self-sealing freezer bag.

You can also precook pizza for later reheating. Omit any cheese the recipe calls for, and bake the pizza for half the time the recipe recommends, just until the crust has begun to take color. Remove the pizza from the oven and let it cool to room temperature. Finish baking at 400°F for 15 minutes, adding the cheese during the last few minutes.

If you have some leftover pizza, wrap it tightly in aluminum foil and set it in the freezer. Reheat at 400°F in the foil for 30 to 40 minutes, removing the foil during the final 10 minutes.

Stir the yeast into the warm water in a large mixing bowl; leave until creamy, about 10 minutes. Add the 3 cups water, and then squeeze the biga into the bowl through your fingers. To make the dough by hand, whisk in the flour and salt, ½ cup at a time, until the dough becomes too thick for the whisk. Using a heavy wooden spoon or your hands, continue mixing until a dough is formed. Set it on a floured work surface and knead for 13 to 15 minutes, until smooth, supple, and elastic although still sticky. Keep a small bowl of water nearby so you can dip your hands into it to keep them from sticking to the dough. Use a dough scraper to help you in the kneading.

If you are using a heavy-duty electric mixer, set the yeast mixture, water, and biga in the mixer bowl, and stir in the flour and salt with the paddle attachment; mix for 3 to 4 minutes. Change to the dough hook and knead energetically on medium speed for 5 minutes, until you have a dough that is moist, supple, soft, and velvety but not wet or sticky.

First rise. Set the dough in a large oiled bowl, cover tightly with plastic wrap, and leave to rise in a cool spot until tripled, about 8 hours.

Shaping. Turn the dough onto a lightly floured surface, and divide it into three pieces. Shape each one into a rough ball.

To make pizze. Oil three 14- or 15-inch pizza pans, or flour three pieces of parchment paper that have been set on baker's peels or on the back of heavy baking sheets. Place the balls of dough on the peels or pizza pans, and stretch each one out to form a 14- or 15-inch circle with a thick edge. (You may also roll the dough with a rolling pin on a lightly floured work surface to form a 12-inch circle, then spread it with your fingers to 14 inches. Alternatively, set the dough over your oiled fists and gradually pull them apart, turning and stretching the dough at the same time.) When the dough begins to resist, cover and let it rest for a few minutes; then resume rolling or stretching the dough. If it springs back, let it relax for a few minutes under a towel; then return to rolling or stretching it. Each pizza should be shaped like a plate with a 1-inch-high rim so that the oil doesn't escape during the baking. When you have finished the shaping, carefully place each round of dough on a prepared pizza pan or floured parchment paper. You can safely leave the dough for up to 1 hour before spreading the topping on it.

Sprinkle the oregano over the dough. Then drizzle on the oil, spreading it over the top. Finally squeeze the chunks of meaty tomato or the cherry tomatoes right on top of the dough and then scatter the rest over the top. If you want, add sliced green onions and capers. Finish by sprinkling the sea salt over the tops.

Preheat the oven to 450°F. If you are using baking stones, preheat them in the oven for 30 minutes before baking. Just before baking, sprinkle the stones with cornmeal. If the pizze are in pans or on parchment paper, set them in the oven directly on the preheated stones. Without stones, omit the cornmeal and bake on baking sheets. Bake until the edges of the crusts are golden, about 20 to 25 minutes. Immediately brush the edges with oil, and serve very hot.

To make bread. Shape the 3 balls of dough into rounds and place them, seam side up, on floured parchment paper set on baking sheets or on peels. Cover with towels and let rise until doubled, about 2 hours.

Preheat the oven and baking stones, if you are using them, to 450°F for 30 minutes before baking. Just before baking, sprinkle the baking stones with cornmeal. Gently invert the rounds onto the stones or leave them on the baking sheets, and bake for 30 to 35 minutes, until the loaves sound hollow when tapped on the bottom. Cool on racks.

MAKES 3 PIZZE OR 3 LOAVES OF BREAD

Focaccia Farcita

FILLED FOCACCIA

In Italy people now drop into a pizzeria to eat what used to be a typical homemade *merenda*. It starts by slicing open a focaccia already fragrant with olive oil and sea salt, filling it with creamy cheese and prosciutto or pancetta, then closing and warming it in the oven until the cheese melts and bubbles inside its lovely case. Serve small squares as an appetizer; cut it in wedges and make it part of an antipasto platter; or serve it for light lunch or Sunday supper. If you don't want to bake, buy a prepared focaccia and fill and warm it yourself.

1 recipe Pizza Dough, prepared
    through first rise (page 126)
About ¼ cup extra-virgin olive oil
Sea salt
8 ounces creamy cheese such as
    stracchino, taleggio, or
    mozzarella
20 to 24 very thin slices prosciutto
    or pancetta

Shaping and second rise. Divide the dough in half, and set each piece in an oiled 12-inch round metal baking pan. Flatten and stretch the dough to cover the bottom. If it doesn't quite reach, cover it with a towel and let it relax for 10 minutes, then stretch the dough some more. Leave it to rise, covered with a towel, until well puffed, 45 minutes to 1 hour.

Topping. Dimple the tops by poking them vigorously with your fingertips. Brush with the oil and sprinkle with sea salt.

Baking. Preheat the oven, and baking stones if you are using them, to 450°F for 30 minutes. Set the baking pans on the preheated stones and bake until golden, 20 to 25 minutes. Remove the focacce from their pans and let them cool to room temperature on racks. When they are cool, slice them in half horizontally, brush the insides lightly with olive oil, and fill with the cheese and prosciutto or pancetta. Bake them in a 375°F oven until the cheese is soft and melting, 10 to 15 minutes. Serve hot.

MAKES 2 FILLED FOCACCE

Focaccia All'Avena

HERB-FLAVORED OAT AND
WHEAT FOCACCIA

This focaccia may not be traditional—it was invented by Walter Redaelli, the very up-to-date chef at L'Amorosa in Tuscany—but it embodies the spirit of an ancient *merenda* in mixing rustic grains with wheat flour. The oat flour gives it a wonderful flavor and keeps it moist, so that it really stays fresh for a day or two. Please make the dough ahead of time and refrigerate it for 24 hours before baking it.

1 tablespoon active dry yeast

1¼ cups plus 3 tablespoons warm water (105° to 115°F)

1 tablespoon plus 1 teaspoon extra-virgin olive oil

1¾ cups plus 2 tablespoons (250 grams) unbleached all-purpose flour

Scant 2½ cups (250 grams) oat flour

2 tablespoons chopped fresh rosemary, sage, or mint leaves, separately or in combination

2 teaspoons sea salt

5 tablespoons olive oil

Salt

Whisk the yeast into the warm water and let stand until creamy, about 5 to 10 minutes. Stir in the olive oil, then the flours, herbs, and salt, and mix until the dough comes together. If you are making the bread by hand, knead the dough on a lightly floured surface for 8 to 10 minutes. In a heavy-duty electric mixer with a dough hook, knead for 2 minutes on low speed and 2 on medium, until the dough is firm and elastic. Transfer it to an oiled bowl, cover with plastic wrap, and refrigerate for 24 hours.

The next day, preheat the oven to 400°F. If you are using baking stones, preheat them in the oven for 30 minutes.

Oil a 10½- × 15½-inch rimmed baking sheet with 2 tablespoons of the olive oil, then spread the dough in a thin layer over the bottom of the pan. Since the dough is very stiff, it will take some time and strength to stretch it to the edges, but don't worry, you will succeed. Dimple the top with your knuckles—fingertips simply won't make much of an impression—and then drizzle the remaining 3 tablespoons oil over the top and sprinkle with salt. Let rise until puffy, about 1½ to 2 hours.

Bake the focaccia for about 25 minutes, until the top is a pale golden color. Remove it from the pan and let it cool on a rack.

MAKES ONE 10½- × 15½-INCH FOCACCIA

Pasta per Pizza

PIZZA DOUGH

I love this dough because it is so delicious, so versatile, and so malleable. If you would like it to rise more slowly to fit into your workday, cut the yeast by half or even three-quarters. If you want it to rise faster, use 1 package (2½ teaspoons) yeast. You can shape the dough into balls and set them in plastic bags in the refrigerator to use later, or you can make the dough one day and use it the next. It keeps in the refrigerator for 2 days. Use it for any pizza you make, but omit the oil for an authentic Neapolitan dough. I've given several traditional *merende* toppings in the recipes that follow, but your choice is close to endless. Wonder of wonders, this dough is also delicious when used for focaccia, all manner of savory treats, and even breads.

1 teaspoon active dry yeast
1½ cups warm water (105° to 115°F)
2 tablespoons olive oil (optional)
1½ teaspoons sea salt
4 cups (550 grams) unbleached all-purpose flour

*S*tir the yeast into the water in a large mixing bowl and leave until creamy, 5 to 10 minutes. Then stir in the olive oil, if you are using it.

If you are making the dough by hand, whisk in the salt and 2 cups of the flour, 1 cup at a time; add the remaining flour and stir with a wooden spoon until the dough comes together. Knead on a lightly floured surface until soft and velvety, about 10 minutes. Using a heavy-duty mixer, add the salt and flour at once and mix with the paddle for 1 to 2 minutes. Change to the dough hook and knead at medium speed until the dough is soft, velvety, and slightly sticky, 3 to 4 minutes.

(continued)

First rise. Place the dough in a lightly oiled bowl, cover tightly with plastic wrap, and let rise until doubled, 1¼ to 1½ hours.

Shaping and second rise. Punch the dough down, and divide it in half. Roll the halves into balls, and let them rest under a moist cloth for 20 to 30 minutes.

Note: This dough can be prepared in a food processor. See page 211 for instructions.

VARIATION

Whole-Wheat Pizza Dough Use 3¼ cups (450 grams) unbleached all-purpose flour and ¼ cup (100 grams) whole-wheat flour.

MAKES TWO 12- TO 14-INCH ROUND PIZZE, ONE 12- × 17-INCH PIZZA, 16 TO 20 SMALL PIZZETTE OR PANZEROTTI, 7 TO 8 CALZONE, OR 2 LOAVES PANE COI CICCIOLI E PEPE NERO (PAGE 222)

Pizza Bianca
SIMPLE CRISPY PIZZA

Born in the country homes of *contadini* and in the world of frugal Italians with little money but plentiful imagination, pizza bianca is the original *merenda*—fast food Italian-style, made with simple ingredients and extraordinary style.

When Neapolitan bakers started making pizza, tomatoes had not yet arrived in Italy, so they certainly weren't part of the equation. The simplest pizze were flavored with oil, garlic, and sometimes with tiny salty fish called *cecinielli* that have now been replaced by anchovies. Schoolchildren in Rome are more than familiar with pizza bianca, since they often pour en masse into bakeries and buy just that—pizza flavored with olive oil and sea salt, sometimes with the addition of a herb like rosemary—to eat as a midmorning snack.

Bakers take small pieces of bread dough, shape them into small flattened rounds, sprinkle them with sea salt and olive oil, and put them in the oven when the bread goes in. Since the pieces are smaller than the wheels of bread, the bakers pull them out and eat them first. Lore says they are the way a baker knows if the oven is hot enough, and that is why they are the baker's *merenda*. In some communities mothers do the same for their children, to reward them for their patience as they wait for the dough to rise.

1 recipe Pizza Dough (page 125)
2 to 3 tablespoons best-quality
   extra-virgin olive oil
1½ to 2 teaspoons coarse sea salt
2 or 3 cloves garlic, sliced into
   extremely thin slivers
Several sprigs fresh rosemary or
   oregano, chopped optional

On a lightly floured work surface, roll out each ball of dough with a rolling pin to form a 12-inch circle about ⅛ to ¼ inch thick, leaving a thick edge. Turn the dough over as you roll it so it won't shrink back later. Place each one on an oiled 12- or 14-inch pizza pan, baking sheet, or peel sprinkled with cornmeal. Dimple the dough with your fingertips or knuckles, brush the tops with the olive oil, and sprinkle with the sea salt, garlic slivers, and, if desired, rosemary or oregano.

Preheat the oven to 425°F. If you are using baking stones, preheat them in the oven for 30 minutes. Sprinkle the stones with cornmeal just before sliding the pizza bianca onto them. Bake until the crusts are crisp, 20 to 25 minutes.

MAKES TWO 12- TO 14-INCH PIZZE

Spianata

TOMATO-DAPPLED PIZZA BIANCA

Tomatoes arrived in Italy in the wake of Columbus's voyage to the New World, but it wasn't until the nineteenth century that Neapolitan bakers thought to add a wash of tomato on top of a simple pizza.

2 tablespoons olive oil
1 clove garlic, minced
1 pound juicy ripe tomatoes, peeled and chopped, or one 14-ounce can plum tomatoes, drained and chopped
1 recipe Pizza Dough (page 125)

Warm the olive oil over low heat in a medium-size heavy sauté pan. Add the garlic, and after a minute or two, the tomatoes. Cook over medium heat for 5 to 6 minutes, until the tomatoes have cooked down a bit. Allow to cool.

On a lightly floured work surface, roll out each ball of dough with a rolling pin to form a 12-inch circle about ⅛ to ¼ inch thick, leaving a thick edge. Turn the dough over as you roll it so it won't shrink back later. Place each one on an oiled 12- or 14-inch pizza pan, baking sheet, or peel sprinkled with cornmeal. Dimple the dough with your fingertips or knuckles, and brush the tops with the tomato sauce.

Preheat the oven to 425°F. If you are using baking stones, preheat them in the oven for 30 minutes. Sprinkle the stones with cornmeal just before sliding the pizze onto them. Bake until the crusts are crisp, 20 to 25 minutes.

MAKES TWO 12- TO 14-INCH PIZZE

Panzerotti Farciti

SMALL HALF-MOON FILLED PIZZE

Crispy little surprise packages full of the flavors of the Mediterranean, these portable bite-size treats are an ancient and much loved *merenda*. Etruscans and ancient Romans ate similar cheese-and-herb-filled pastries (there's history for you), and Italians continue the tradition with a myriad of fillings. You can bake the panzerotti or fry them, you can brush the tops with beaten egg yolk or leave them unglazed, and best of all, you can vary the fillings to your heart's content.

1 recipe Pizza Dough (page 125)
12 ounces fresh mozzarella, diced
1½ cups peeled, seeded, chopped
    fresh tomatoes, pressed lightly in a
    ricer to extract juice
3 tablespoons freshly grated
    Parmigiano-Reggiano cheese
¼ cup fresh basil leaves torn into
    small pieces or cut into thin ribbons
Salt and freshly ground pepper
Oil for deep-frying (optional)

Divide the dough in half. On a lightly floured work surface, use a rolling pin to roll each half out to form a sheet about ¼ inch thick. Cut out the panzerotti with a 4-inch cookie cutter.

Set a small mound of diced mozzarella in the center of each round, then a bit of chopped tomato. Sprinkle with the Parmesan and basil, and season with salt and pepper. Brush the edge of each circle well with water, and fold the top half over the mixture. Use your fingertips or the tines of a fork to press the edges together and seal them securely. Place them on oiled baking sheets.

Baking. Preheat the oven to 450°F. If you are using baking stones, preheat them in the oven for 30 minutes. Bake the panzerotti for 15 to 20 minutes, or until they are golden brown. Serve immediately.

Frying. Fill a deep heavy pot with about 3 inches of oil, and heat it to 375°F. Carefully slide a few of the panzerotti into the oil, being sure not to overcrowd the pan, and fry them until golden brown. Remove them with a slotted spoon and drain on paper towels. Serve immediately.

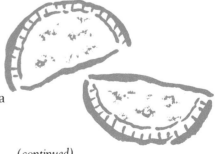

(continued)

Substitute 2 teaspoons dried oregano for the basil and add a pinch of red pepper flakes.

Use the Sausage and Pecorino Cheese mixture (page 67).

Use the Rustici filling (page 139)

MAKES ABOUT 20

Pizzette

INDIVIDUAL-SIZE PIZZE

These bite-size pizze can be as simple as Pizza Bianca or Spianata, or they can be covered with toppings that range from the obvious (Sugo di Pomodoro, page 193, and scamorza or fontina cheese with a scattering of torn basil leaves) to the exotic (fava beans and sautéed greens from 'Ncapriata, page 186). Other possibilities include baking the pizzette with a wash of olive oil and then covering them with the warm mussel topping (Le Cozze, page 57) and fresh black pepper, as well as combining any of the other Condimenti toppings.

1 recipe Pizza Dough (page 125)
Toppings of choice (see above)
Olive oil

Divide the pizza dough in half. Set one half aside under a tea towel. Roll the other half into a ball and then flatten it into a disc shape. Using a rolling pin, roll out the dough on a lightly floured work surface until it is ⅛ to ¼ inch thick. Cut out the pizzette with a 3-inch cookie cutter, keeping the circles as close as possible. Repeat with the other half of the dough.

Set the pizzette on baking sheets that have been oiled or lined with parchment paper. Place a spoonful of topping in the center of each circle of dough.

Preheat the oven to 425°F. If you are using a baking stone, preheat it in the oven for 30 minutes. Bake the pizzette for 12 to 15 minutes, or until the crusts are golden brown and crisp. Immediately brush the crusts with olive oil, and serve.

MAKES 16 TO 20

Calzone al Formaggio Fresco

CALZONE FILLED WITH MOZZARELLA

This folded stuffed pizza is delicious and filling, a neat portable dish that is especially well suited to informal occasions. Since the calzone crust is essentially a plate, you can eat your dish and skip the washing up. Perhaps that's why workers at olive mills in Puglia eat it between shifts as they work at an intense pace, pressing olives to create the pure green oil of the fruit.

1 recipe Pasta Dough (page 125)
1 pound fresh mozzarella, grated
7 or 8 flat anchovy fillets, rinsed
  and mashed
Salt and pepper
Olive oil

Divide the dough into 7 or 8 pieces. On a lightly floured work surface, use a rolling pin to roll each piece out to form a circle about ¼ inch thick.

Divide the mozzarella among the circles, mounding it in the center. Set a mashed anchovy on top of each portion, and season judiciously with salt and pepper. Fold the top half of the circle over the filling. Then fold the border over and press the edges together, crimping with your fingertips. Set the calzone on an oiled baking sheet or pizza peel sprinkled with cornmeal. Brush the tops with olive oil.

Preheat the oven to 450°F. If you are using a baking stone, preheat it in the oven for 30 minutes; sprinkle the stone with cornmeal just before you slide the calzone onto it. Bake for 20 to 25 minutes, until puffy and golden brown. Brush the tops with the oil, and serve hot.

VARIATION

Use the Rustici filling (page 139).

MAKES 7 OR 8

Pizza di Cipolle

ONION PIE

Every region has its savory tarts, and this one, I think, is particularly delicious. I discovered it in Puglia, at the antiques-filled Hotel Melograno outside of Monopoli. Once a great farmhouse, the beautifully restored hotel sits on a vast piece of land that is thick with orange and lemon trees and with mammoth twisted olive trees of a great age. The night I arrived the cooks were in high gear, turning out quantities of food for a big political reception. Platters and bowls filled with the tastes of the region covered a buffet table that stretched the length of a ballroom. The choices were staggering, but I couldn't get enough of this tart filled with the sweetness of sautéed onions and tomatoes, the savory bite of olives and capers, and the slight saltiness of mashed anchovies. The filling also makes an outstanding pasta sauce or antipasto salad.

DOUGH

1¼ teaspoons active dry yeast

¼ cup plus 1½ teaspoons warm water (105° to 115°F)

1 teaspoon sugar

⅓ cup white wine, room temperature

Scant 2 tablespoons olive oil

1½ cups plus 2 teaspoons (220 grams) unbleached all-purpose flour

2 tablespoons (30 grams) whole-wheat flour

1½ teaspoons sea salt

Whisk the yeast into the warm water in a large mixing bowl, sprinkle in the sugar, and let stand until foamy, about 10 minutes. Then mix in the wine and oil. Stir in the flours and salt, and mix using a wooden spoon or the paddle attachment of a mixer until the dough comes together, about 2 minutes. Knead by hand for 8 to 10 minutes on a lightly floured surface, or in a heavy-duty mixer at low speed for 3 minutes, until the dough is blistered, elastic, and firm. Transfer to a lightly oiled bowl, cover tightly with plastic wrap, and let rise just until puffy, about 45 minutes to 1 hour.

FILLING

3 tablespoons olive oil

⅔ pound onion, sliced very thin

2 cloves garlic, minced

⅔ pound fresh tomatoes, peeled, seeded, and chopped

7 ounces small black olives in brine, pitted and roughly chopped

3½ tablespoons small capers in salt, thoroughly rinsed

5 anchovy fillets in oil, rinsed

2 tablespoons grated ricotta salata cheese (see Note)

Salt and pepper

Olive oil

Heat the olive oil in a medium-size skillet over medium-low heat, and sauté the onions for 10 to 15 minutes. Add the garlic and continue cooking until the onions are soft and translucent, making certain that the garlic doesn't burn. Add the tomatoes and cook for another 15 minutes. Stir in the olives, capers, and anchovies, and continue cooking for another 10 minutes. At the very end sprinkle the ricotta into the mixture, stir it in well, and taste for salt and pepper. Cool before filling the tart shell.

Divide the dough into two pieces, one twice the size of the other. On a lightly floured work surface, roll out the larger piece to form an 11-inch circle. Slide it into an oiled 9-inch pie pan, with the dough completely covering the bottom of the pan and overlapping the sides slightly. Brush a light layer of olive oil over the dough, and spread the filling on top. Roll out the second piece of dough to form a circle the same diameter as the pan, about 9 inches, and lay it on top of the filling. Trim the edges of any excess dough, and with your fingers carefully press the two layers of dough together to seal in the filling and close the focaccia. Brush the top crust with olive oil, and prick it with a fork every inch or so. Bake in a preheated 400°F oven for 30 minutes until golden. Cool to room temperature. Slice into wedges to serve.

Note: It's much easier to grate ricotta salata cheese if you put it in the freezer for about 10 minutes. If you can't find ricotta salata, substitute feta.

Note: This dough can be prepared in a food processor. See page 211 for instructions.

SERVES 6 TO 8

Pizza di Scarola

ESCAROLE PIE

Escarole, a member of the endive family, goes by various names, including frisée; just be sure to choose the flat leafy variety with curly puckered leaves, not the long ribbed chicory type. Its slightly bitter flavor combines wonderfully with the sweetness of sautéed onions and the small mellow olives. French Niçoise, Taggia from Liguria, or some mellow Greek or Moroccan variety would be ideal. Avoid Kalamata olives—they are too strong and salty.

1 large head (about 1 pound)
   escarole
3 tablespoons olive oil
1 onion, finely sliced
2 cloves garlic, minced
7 ounces small black olives, pitted
Salt and freshly ground pepper
1 tablespoon grated pecorino
   cheese
1 recipe Pizza di Cipolle dough
   (page 132)
Olive oil

Wash the escarole well in cold water; rinse and dry it. Cut off part of the base of the heart, but do not eliminate it all, since its bitterness is important to the mingled flavors of the dish. Chop the leaves roughly.

Warm the olive oil in a large heavy sauté pan, and sauté the onion over medium-low heat until it is limp and translucent. Add the garlic and cook only until it begins to take on color; be careful not to let it burn. Add the escarole and olives, and continue cooking, stirring frequently, for 15 to 20 minutes, until the escarole has softened but is still somewhat crunchy. Add the salt, pepper, and cheese. Remove from the heat and allow to cool.

Divide the dough into two pieces, one twice the size of the other. On a lightly floured work surface, roll the larger piece out to form an 11-inch circle. Slide it into an oiled 9-inch pie pan, with the dough completely covering the bottom of the pan and overlapping the sides slightly. Brush a light layer of olive oil over the dough, and spread the filling on top. Roll out the second piece of dough to form a circle the same diameter as the pan, about 9 inches, and lay it on top of the filling. Trim the edges of any excess dough, and with your fingers carefully press the two layers of dough together to seal in the filling and close the pizza. Brush the top crust with olive oil, and prick it with a fork every inch or so. Bake in a preheated 400°F oven for 30 minutes, until golden. Slice into wedges, and serve warm or at room temperature.

SERVES 6 TO 8

Focaccia Ripiena
RUSTIC VEGETABLE PIE

The first thing to be said about this focaccia, which I discovered in Monopoli, is that it is absolutely delicious. The sweetness of the leeks and peppers plays beautifully against the slight bite of the capers and the saltiness of the olives. The second is that the focaccia is made like a vegetable pie, with the filling wrapped in bread dough. That means that to avoid a tough crust, you should be especially careful to moisten, then pinch together, the edges of the two pieces of dough, pressing them firmly with your fingers, instead of overlapping them the way you do a pie crust. The filling by itself makes a delicious antipasto or cool salad.

DOUGH
½ teaspoon active dry yeast
⅓ cup plus 2 tablespoons warm water (105° to 115°F)
1½ cups (200 grams) durum flour
2 tablespoons olive oil
½ teaspoon sea salt

Whisk the yeast into the warm water and leave until creamy, 5 to 10 minutes. Meanwhile, using a wooden spoon or the paddle attachment of a heavy-duty mixer, beat together ¼ cup of the flour and the olive oil. Add the dissolved yeast to the flour mixture, stir in the remaining ¼ cup flour and the salt, and mix until it becomes a dough. Knead by hand on a lightly floured work surface for 2 minutes, or in the mixer with the dough hook for just 1 minute.

Rise. Set the dough in an oiled bowl, cover it tightly with plastic wrap, and leave it to rise until puffy, if not doubled, about 2 hours.

(continued)

FILLING

¼ cup olive oil

2 pounds leeks, white part only, well cleaned and finely sliced

About 4 ounces dark olives in water or light brine, such as Niçoise, Taggia, or Gaeta, pitted

½ tablespoon capers, rinsed

8 ounces tomatoes, peeled, seeded, chopped, and drained

3 sweet red peppers, roasted, peeled, seeded, and chopped

Olive oil

While the dough is rising, warm the ¼ cup olive oil in a medium-size heavy sauté pan, and sauté the leeks over low heat until they are sweet and almost caramelized, about 25 minutes. Stir in the olives, capers, tomatoes, and peppers, and continue to cook for another 10 minutes. Allow to cool.

Preheat the oven to 400°F.

Divide the dough so that one piece is slightly larger than the other. On a lightly floured work surface, roll out the larger piece to form a disc about 11½ inches in diameter and ⅛ inch thick. Oil an 8-inch round baking pan and lay the dough in the bottom, letting the excess drape over the sides. Brush the dough lightly with olive oil, and cover it with the filling. Roll out the second piece of dough to form an 8-inch circle. Trim the edges, stretching them to keep them thin. Brush the edges of the bottom layer with water, lay the top crust over the filling, and carefully and firmly press the edges of the two layers together with your fingers to close the focaccia. Brush the top with olive oil and prick with a fork to allow steam to escape.

Bake for 25 to 30 minutes, until golden. Cool the focaccia in the pan, and do not unmold it until it is tepid. Serve at room temperature.

SERVES 6 TO 8

Pizza Rustica

HAM, SALAME, AND CHEESE—FILLED RUSTIC PIE

Rustic and elegant all at once: Abruzzo, Campania, and Puglia all have their own versions of *pizza rustica*, an envelope of dough enclosing a filling of ham, salame, and various cheeses. One of countless ancestors of Neapolitan pizza, this particular version is stuffed with ingredients available over much of Italy. Variations are limited only by the imagination of the cook. Peer into your refrigerator, look at the larder, visit your local delicatessen: you can use prosciutto, ricotta, mozzarella or provolone, tomatoes, even greens such as chard, and parsley or other herbs.

DOUGH

2 cups and 2 tablespoons (300 grams) unbleached all-purpose flour

½ teaspoon sea salt

7 tablespoons unsalted butter or lard, room temperature; cold if you are using a food processor

2 eggs, room temperature

2 tablespoons very cold water, if needed

Place the flour and salt in a medium-size bowl, and stir to mix. Cut the butter into small pieces, and cut or mix them into the flour with a pastry blender, two knives, or the paddle of a heavy-duty electric mixer until the mixture resembles coarse meal. Slowly stir in each egg, mixing thoroughly after each addition. Add the water if the dough is dry. Gather the dough and knead it roughly on a lightly floured work surface just until it comes together, about 2 minutes.

To prepare the dough in a food processor, set the flour and sea salt in the processor bowl outfitted with the steel blade. Pulse several times to sift. Scatter the pieces of cold butter over the top, and pulse until the mixture resembles coarse meal. With the motor running, pour the eggs down the feed tube and continue to process until a dough forms.

Wrap the dough in plastic wrap, and refrigerate for 1 hour.

(continued)

FILLING

6 ounces mozzarella, cubed

5 ounces cooked ham, cut thick and cubed

5 ounces salame, cut thick and cubed

5 ounces young sheep's-milk cheese, such as pecorino dolce, caciotta, pecorino sardo, or Greek sheep's-milk cheese, cubed

5 ounces ricotta cheese

3 eggs

3 tablespoons freshly grated Parmigiano-Reggiano cheese

Salt and pepper

GLAZE

1 egg white, beaten

*I*n a large bowl, mix together the mozzarella, ham, salame, and sheep's-milk cheese. In a separate bowl, press the ricotta through a sieve and then beat the eggs into it one at a time. Add this to the cheese and salame mixture, and then stir in the Parmesan cheese and the seasonings.

Preheat the oven to 400°F.

Divide the dough into two pieces, one twice as large as the other. Roll out the larger piece to form a 13-inch circle about ⅛ inch thick. Lay it inside a well-oiled 9-inch springform pan, making sure that some dough drapes over the edges. Spread the filling over the dough. Roll out the remaining piece of dough to form a 9½-inch circle. Cover the filling with the dough, and pinch the edges of the two layers together tightly to seal them. Prick the surface of the top crust with a fork, and brush the beaten egg white over it.

Bake until the top is golden, about 45 to 50 minutes. Cool on a rack; unmold the Pizza Rustica only when it is cool enough to handle. Serve at room temperature.

SERVES 8

Rustici

CHEESE- AND SALAME-FILLED PUFFS
FROM AVELLINO

How these elegant little bite-size turnovers came to be named *rustici* I can't imagine, unless the simple dough in which they are wrapped distinguishes them from true aristocratic splendors in Neapolitan cuisine. These are particularly wonderful eaten warm. You can use any leftover filling to stuff ravioli or tortellini, to fill calzone, or to spread on top of crostini.

DOUGH

Scant 3 cups (400 grams)
  unbleached all-purpose flour
¼ teaspoon sea salt
14 tablespoons (1¾ sticks)
  unsalted butter, room
  temperature; cold if you are
  using a food processor
3 eggs, room temperature

If you are preparing the dough by hand, place the flour and salt in a mixing bowl. Chop the butter into small pieces, and cut or mix it into the flour with a pastry blender or two knives until the mixture resembles coarse meal. Slowly stir the eggs, one at a time, mixing thoroughly after each addition. Gather the dough together and knead it briefly on a lightly floured surface, just until it comes together.

If you are using a food processor, set the flour and salt in the processor bowl outfitted with the steel blade. Pulse several times to sift. Cut the cold butter into small pieces and scatter them over the top; pulse until the mixture resembles coarse meal. With the motor running, pour the eggs down the feed tube and continue to process until a dough forms.

Divide the dough in half, form each piece into a ½-inch-thick disc. Wrap in plastic wrap, and refrigerate for 1 to 2 hours.

(continued)

FILLING

1/3 pound best-quality ricotta
    cheese
1 large egg, room temperature
2 tablespoons freshly grated
    Parmigiano-Reggiano cheese
1/4 teaspoon sea salt
1/3 pound salame and prosciutto,
    mixed, diced
4 1/2 ounces scamorza or fontina
    cheese, cut into 1/4-inch dice
2 tablespoons finely chopped flat-
    leaf parsley
Freshly ground pepper

GLAZE

1 egg white, beaten

Press the ricotta through a sieve or whirl it in a processor. Beat the egg, Parmesan, and salt together in a medium-size bowl, and add the ricotta. Mix in the salame and prosciutto, the scamorza or fontina cheese, and the parsley and pepper.

Preheat the oven to 375°F.

Divide the dough in half. On a lightly floured surface, roll out each half to form a sheet 1/8 inch thick. Use a 3-inch cookie cutter to cut circles out of one sheet of the dough. Keep the circles as close together as possible because you lose tenderness when you reroll the scraps. But reroll them you must and then cut out the remaining circles. Then use a 3 1/2- or 4-inch cookie cutter to cut out circles from the other sheet of dough.

Brush the circumference of the 3-inch circles with water, and place 1 tablespoon of the filling in the middle of each circle, leaving a border of at least 1/2 inch. Set a larger circle on top of each smaller one, and press gently around the filled center so that the outline of the filling shows clearly. Press the edges together firmly to seal in the filling. Place the puffs on a parchment-paper-lined or oiled baking sheet. Brush each puff with egg white.

Bake for 20 to 22 minutes, until golden. Serve hot or at room temperature.

Note: You can cut the dough recipe in half by dividing all the ingredients except the eggs in half; reduce the eggs to 1 egg and 1 egg yolk. For the filling, use 1 egg yolk and divide the remaining ingredients in half.

SERVES 8 TO 10

Uova Frittate e Tortine

Can there be any dish as versatile as the *frittata?* This flat Italian omelet can be eaten at almost any hour (except breakfast, when Italians never eat eggs). And cast your eye over the possible fillings: asparagus, artichoke hearts, spinach, chard, eggplant, cauliflower, beans, fried tomatoes, white onions, mushrooms, leeks, sweet peppers, potatoes, zucchini, zucchini flowers, wild greens, a handful of herbs. Frittate can be flavored with cubes of salame and ribbons of prosciutto, slices of cheese, even tangles of pasta.

In Italy many frittate are made to be eaten at room temperature. They may be served in the middle of the afternoon in the shade of a grape arbor or at the edge of a bocce court. They are even carried into the countryside for picnics, and are often tucked between two pieces of bread or cut in a wedge and eaten out of hand.

Here are a couple of secrets for making good frittate. Beat the eggs lightly with a fork or a whisk, just enough to blend the whites and yolks. Mix the vegetables and eggs together before putting them in the skillet. Use a nonstick pan. Set the mixture over the lowest possible heat so the frittata will cook very slowly (unlike a French omelet) and will remain rich, creamy, and substantial. If you find it difficult to invert the frittata onto a plate, place the skillet under a broiler briefly to cook the top part.

Other irresistible egg dishes for *merende* include the creamy artichoke tortino that is baked in the oven, and eggs scrambled with sweet peppers and served on a slice of country bread. Like the frittate, they can be served as appetizers, as part of an antipasto, or as a main dish for lunch or an informal supper. Toss a green salad, open a good bottle of wine, and it's time to eat. Anytime. Anyplace.

Frittata alle Erbe

FRITTATA WITH HERBS

"**B**etter an egg today than a chicken tomorrow" say the country people of Lombardy, who turn many of their eggs into frittate flavored with vegetables or herbs. This one is particularly beautiful, with its ribbons of green dappling the interior.

8 eggs
⅓ cup freshly grated Parmigiano-
    Reggiano cheese
⅛ teaspoon salt
Freshly ground pepper
⅓ cup finely sliced mixed fresh
    herbs: flat-leaf parsley, basil,
    sage, and/or mint
3 to 4 tablespoons unsalted butter
    or olive oil

Break the eggs into a bowl, and whisk them only until they are blended. Stir in the cheese, salt, pepper, and herbs.

Warm the butter or oil in a 10-inch skillet, preferably nonstick, and pour in the egg mixture. Cook over the lowest possible flame until the top is set, about 16 to 18 minutes.

Place a dinner plate over the skillet, and holding it firmly with one hand, very gently invert the frittata onto the plate. Slide the frittata, cooked side up, back into the skillet and continue cooking for just 2 to 3 minutes longer to set the bottom. Slide the frittata onto a serving dish and serve immediately, or let the frittata cool, slice it into wedges, and serve at room temperature.

SERVES 4 TO 6 AS AN APPETIZER, 2 TO 3 AS A MAIN DISH

Frittata alle Cipolle

ONION FRITTATA

Spring onions look like oversize scallions with fat red or white bulbs and long green tops. They appear at the same time as spring garlic and are mild enough to be eaten raw with bread as a midmorning *merenda* in Puglia, where they are known as *spunzale*, probably because they tend to grow close to each other in pairs, like *sposini*, or newlyweds. The onions give a wonderful flavor to this frittata (use leeks or a white onion if you can't find the real thing) and are also delicious roasted on a grill until they are charred on the exterior and still creamy inside.

2 to 3 tablespoons olive oil

6 spring onions, or 2 leeks and 1 white onion, finely sliced

6 eggs

¼ cup freshly grated Parmigiano-Reggiano cheese

Salt and freshly ground pepper

3 tablespoons unsalted butter or olive oil

Heat the oil over low heat in an 8- or 9-inch skillet (preferably nonstick), and sauté the onions until they are transparent and beginning to wilt, about 25 to 30 minutes. Remove them from the skillet with a slotted spoon, and allow to cool briefly.

Break the eggs into a bowl and beat them only until blended. Toss in the onions, Parmesan cheese, salt, and pepper and mix briefly. Add the butter to the skillet (you may want to wipe out the pan with paper towels first), and heat until it melts. Add the egg mixture, and cook over the lowest possible flame until the top is set, about 16 to 18 minutes.

Place a dinner plate over the skillet, and holding it firmly with one hand, very gently invert the frittata onto the plate. Slide the frittata, cooked side up, back into the pan, and continue cooking very briefly, just long enough to set the bottom. Slide the frittata onto a platter, and serve hot or at room temperature.

SERVES 4 TO 6 AS AN APPETIZER, 2 TO 3 AS A MAIN DISH

Tortino di Carciofi

CREAMY ARTICHOKE TORTINO

I'm not sure how to translate *tortino*: it's not quite an omelet, or a flan, or a vegetable tart. It is, however, a dish much loved by Ligurians, who now eat this traditional *merenda* at all hours of the day.

There are two varieties of artichokes in Italy: small conical ones with prickly leaves, and larger ones with round heads and no prickles at all (these are the Romanesco variety, which are known familiarly as *mammole* because of their shape). Ligurians make this creamy frittata with the smaller variety. The tortino is gold from the color of the egg yolks—Italian chickens feed on corn and produce yolks that are called *rossi*, or reds. This splendid dish is filling enough to serve for a light lunch or Sunday night supper.

6 medium-size or 4 large
   artichokes
1 lemon, sliced
½ onion, chopped
¼ cup olive oil
2 tablespoons extra-virgin olive oil
1 clove garlic, lightly crushed
2 tablespoons minced flat-leaf
   parsley
6 eggs, beaten
Salt and freshly ground pepper

Clean, trim, and cut the artichokes as in Torta di Carciofi (page 194). Set the cleaned artichoke slices in a saucepan of water and add the lemon slices, onion, and ¼ cup olive oil. Bring to a boil. Then reduce to a simmer, cover, and cook for about 10 minutes, until the artichokes are almost tender. Remove from the heat, drain, and allow to cool briefly.

Preheat the oven to 350°F.

Heat the oil in an 8-inch ovenproof sauté pan. Add the garlic clove and artichoke pieces, and sauté over medium heat until the garlic begins to turn golden. Remove the garlic. Spread the artichoke pieces evenly over the bottom of the pan, and sprinkle the parsley over them. Pour the eggs over the top, add salt and pepper, and immediately set in the oven. Cook until golden brown and set, about 15 to 18 minutes. Serve hot.

VARIATION

Clean 6 medium-size artichokes, halve them, remove the chokes, and proceed with the recipe.

SERVES 4

Frittata di Pasta e Uova

FRITTATA OF LEFTOVER
PASTA AND EGGS

I used to worry about what to do with leftover pasta—until I learned the trick of turning it into a succulent frittata. Now I purposely make too much. Use any kind of pasta with any kind of sauce for this dish; if you want to toss in sautéed sausage or pancetta or some leftover vegetables, that's fine too.

4 cups cooked pasta

8 eggs

Salt and freshly ground pepper

½ cup grated Parmigiano-
   Reggiano cheese

¼ cup olive oil

8 ounces soft fresh cheese, such
   as taleggio, sliced

*I*f your pasta has become dense and firm as it sat in the refrigerator, chop it into small pieces. Beat the eggs well with the salt, pepper, and Parmesan cheese. Incorporate the pasta into the mixture.

Heat the olive oil over medium heat in a heavy 10-inch sauté pan. Pour half the egg and pasta mixture into the pan, spread the soft cheese over the top, and cover with the remaining egg and pasta mixture. Sauté over medium-high heat, occasionally stirring the mixture with a wooden spoon, until the bottom is golden. Now you have a choice: you may either crisp the top of the frittata under the broiler until it is golden, or you may invert it onto a plate and slide it back into the pan to brown the other side. Serve immediately or at warm room temperature.

SERVES 4 TO 6

Peperoni e Uova

EGGS SCRAMBLED WITH
SWEET PEPPERS

This delicious combination of creamily scrambled eggs with sweet peppers is the *merenda* of hunters in Abruzzo, who turn it into a sandwich between two long thin slices of country bread. Nicoletta Peduzzi, an extraordinary cook who took me into her kitchen for days, likes to simply sauté the peppers, but I've found that the dish is every bit as delicious when they're roasted first for easier peeling. Take your choice. This is a fine light lunch or Sunday night supper dish.

2 sweet red peppers
2 tablespoons extra-virgin olive oil
2 cloves garlic, finely minced
4 large eggs
Salt
2 tablespoons finely minced flat-leaf parsley
4 to 6 slices country-style bread (for sandwiches)

Peel the peppers with a vegetable peeler, remove the seeds, and cut them into thin strips. Or roast them under the broiler, charring the skins; set them in a tightly closed paper bag for 15 minutes, then peel them, remove the seeds, and cut into thin strips. Heat the oil in a heavy sauté pan, and sauté the peppers and garlic over medium-low heat until soft but not mushy. In a separate bowl, beat the eggs and salt very slightly. Pour the eggs into the pan, and scramble them with the peppers over a low flame, adding the parsley, until they are creamy and set.

If you are making sandwiches, grill or broil as many long thin pieces of country-style Italian bread as you need. Arrange the egg mixture between the slices, allowing the delicious flavors to permeate the bread as it absorbs the oil.

SERVES 2 TO 3

Pancotto

BREAD CRUMB AND EGG SOUP

Call it a *minestra* (a soup) or a nourishing bowlful to fill a hungry stomach, *pancotto* is yet one more inventive Tuscan dish made with eggs and crumbs of leftover bread. Every region has its variation on this simple theme, and every household has the ingredients on hand to make the filling main attraction of an informal meal. This is a particularly appealing version because the cheese, bread crumbs, and bright green herbs dapple the broth, while the eggs float like golden ribbons in the bowl.

3 to 4 tablespoons olive oil

3 cloves garlic

4½ cups chicken broth, preferably homemade

Breadcrumbs from 6 to 8 slices stale country-style bread, crusts trimmed

¼ cup shredded or torn fresh basil

¼ cup chopped flat-leaf parsley

¼ cup freshly grated Parmigiano-Reggiano cheese

3 to 4 eggs, lightly beaten

Salt and freshly ground pepper

Heat the olive oil over medium-low heat in a 2-quart saucepan. Sauté the garlic until it is soft, but be careful that it doesn't burn. Pour in the broth, bring it to a boil, turn down the heat, and simmer for about 5 minutes.

Combine the bread crumbs, basil, parsley, and grated cheese. Whisk the mixture into the broth and cook, whisking constantly, until the soup is hot but not boiling. At the last minute whisk the eggs into the hot broth; simmer for about 1 minute, until the eggs are cooked and have shredded. Do not let the broth boil. Season with salt and pepper, and serve immediately.

VARIATION

Panata For an elegant lemony version of the countrified Pancotto, grate the zest of 1 lemon directly into the crumb mixture before you add the eggs.

SERVES 4 TO 6

Polenta

Traditionally cooked in a gleaming round-bottomed copper pot called a *paiolo* until it is as golden as the sun, polenta is more than just a mixture of cornmeal and water that thickens as it cooks to become a soft pudding. One of the oldest dishes in Italy and the mainstay of the Roman diet, *puls* or *pulmentum* was first made with a wheat called *farro*. In medieval and Renaissance times the same dish was made with spelt, chestnut flour, or millet and was much more important than bread or pasta. Corn didn't even arrive in Italy until the sixteenth century, but in the space of two hundred years, cornmeal polenta made deep inroads into the Italian diet. It became the chosen food of people living in the mountainous areas of northern Italy, a perfect and substantial one-dish meal when accompanied by fresh local ingredients. It may have begun as a poor person's dish, but these days it is a rustic food that has become chic in both America and Italy.

Polenta is so versatile that it can be eaten as an antipasto, a first course, or an entrée. It may be prepared and immediately served in a soft hot mound topped with butter and Parmesan cheese, with mascarpone, or with other sauces. Or it may be turned out onto a wooden board or a baking dish and left to cool until it is firm enough to slice and then grill (*polenta ai ferri*) or fry (*polenta fritta*). Slices of fried polenta were once sold as a snack for people shopping near the central market in Florence. They were fried until crisp outside and still creamy inside, drained, sprinkled with sea salt, and then served on pieces of brown paper. Even today, if you happen to be near the Cathedral of San Nicola in Bari, you can find women frying big ovals of polenta, then sprinkling them with sea salt and serving them as splendid walk-around food.

Tuscans make polenta out of chestnut flour, for the dense woods around Lucca and Mount Amiata produce an extraordinary quantity of chestnuts. The flour is made into a polenta called *pattona*, a rosemary-and-raisin-dappled flan called *castàgnaccio*, and crepes called *necci* that are filled with fresh ricotta cheese. For their *merende*, Tuscan children once ate ditalini, little mounds of chestnut flour packed tightly into a thimble, cooked quickly in the embers of the fire, and tapped sharply to release them: a perfect child-size snack.

In the mountainous Valtellina of Lombardy, polenta is made with buckwheat and called *polenta taragna*; both in that form and in its more common cornmeal version in Lombardy it is often spread with *pistada*, a delicious topping of lardo or pancetta, garlic, and salt; sometimes it is even topped with goose liver. In Tuscany walnuts and rosemary may be folded right into the polenta, or a mound of it may be covered with a layer of grilled radicchio. Elsewhere in Italy it is sliced and served cold with cooked greens and chips of Parmesan cheese, or enriched with mascarpone cheese beaten right into the warm mound.

Making Polenta Ahead. You can make polenta for crostini a day ahead. Spread the cooked polenta out on a shallow oiled baking sheet, pat it to an even ½- to ¾-inch thickness, cover it with plastic wrap, and refrigerate. It will be firm and ready for use anytime within 24 hours. Polenta makes delicious crostini, fried or brushed with olive oil and grilled to a lightly crunchy exterior while remaining creamy inside. The crostini can be topped with any number of spreads and sauces, as you will see in the recipes that follow.

Polenta

BASIC POLENTA

When you are making polenta, be sure that you sprinkle the cornmeal into the pot in a fine, thin stream. I always use a whisk at the beginning and then stir constantly with a wooden spoon to prevent it from getting lumps or sticking to the sides. Some Italian experts insist you should always stir in the same direction to be sure to keep lumps from forming! Polenta for crostini and its accompanying sauce can be made ahead to be assembled and cooked at the last minute.

6 cups water
2½ teaspoons coarse salt
2 cups finely ground cornmeal, or
  1 cup finely ground and 1 cup
  coarsely ground cornmeal

Bring the salted water to a vigorous boil in a very large pot. Reduce the heat to medium-low, and slowly sprinkle in the cornmeal in a thin stream, first whisking it in and then stirring constantly with a wooden spoon, being very careful to eliminate any lumps by crushing them against the sides of the pot. Keep the water at a steady simmer and stir frequently. The polenta will thicken, bubble, and hiss as it cooks. When it comes away from the sides of the pot, after 25 to 35 minutes, the polenta is ready. Be sure to taste for salt.

Serve it immediately, or allow it to cool for use as crostini. To do so, pour the polenta out onto a marble slab, wooden board, or 10½- × 15½-inch oiled baking sheet. Wet your hands or a spatula, and pat the polenta into a smooth flat rectangle about ½ to ¾ inch high. Let it cool for about 10 minutes or until firm. Use it immediately and proceed to grill, bake, or fry it (see page 161), or cover and keep it for use later in the day, or refrigerate it for 24 hours.

SERVES 4 TO 6 AS A MAIN COURSE

Polenta Facile allo Stile di Carlo Middione

CARLO MIDDIONE'S TROUBLE-FREE POLENTA

Now that I have described the traditional way of preparing polenta, let me tell you about the ingenious invention of my friend Carlo Middione, who makes his in a double boiler. It is a splendid procedure that frees the cook from the burden of constant stirring. The recipe is adapted, with his permission, from his book *The Food of Southern Italy*.

8 cups water

2 cups finely ground cornmeal, or
   1 cup finely ground and 1 cup
   coarsely ground cornmeal

1 tablespoon coarse salt

Bring the 8 cups water to a vigorous boil in the top half of a double boiler, directly over the flame. At the same time, add as much water to the bottom half of the double boiler as is needed to just reach the top half when it is set in. Bring it to a vigorous simmer.

Put the cornmeal in a container with a spout from which you can pour it easily. Add the salt to the boiling water. Using a whisk or a wooden spoon, begin stirring the water in one direction, creating an obvious whirlpool. Now you can begin drizzling in the cornmeal in a thin steady stream, stirring constantly as you pour. When all the cornmeal is incorporated, continue to stir, reaching into the corners of the pot Lower the heat so that the polenta bubbles, hisses, and spits.

Continue to stir the polenta for about 5 minutes. When it begins to thicken, put a lid on the pot and set it into the bottom half (with the simmering water reaching just underneath the top piece). Cook for about 1½ hours, stirring every half hour or so. Taste for doneness. The polenta should be smooth, shiny, and sweet-tasting. If it is still slightly bitter, cook it a bit longer.

Use the polenta immediately, or keep it warm in a slowly simmering double boiler for up to 4 hours. If you are making crostini, pour it onto an oiled 10½- × 15½-inch baking sheet. With wet hands smooth the polenta into a flat rectangle. Let it cool until firm, about 10 minutes.

SERVES 4 TO 6 AS A MAIN COURSE

Polenta Lampo

LIGHTNING-QUICK POLENTA

I know that this may sound like heresy, but even Italians are now using instant polenta from a box. While it might not be my first choice for creamy polenta served in a mound, it is a fine solution for polenta that will be cooked a second time—either fried, grilled, or broiled and served with other tasty ingredients. It is a speedy and trouble-free way to produce polenta in a flash.

6 cups water
2 teaspoons coarse salt
1 13-ounce package, 2 cups, instant polenta

*B*ring the water to a vigorous boil, add the salt, and when the water returns to a boil, let the polenta fall into the pot in a steady stream, stirring with a wooden spoon. Cook, stirring continuously for 5 minutes or until the mixture is solid but still soft. Pour onto an oiled 10½ × 15½-inch baking sheet, and with your wet hands or a wet spatula, pat the polenta into a smooth flat rectangle. Let it cool for about 10 minutes or until firm.

SERVES 8 TO 10 AS CROSTINI

Crostini di Polenta alla Pizzaiola

POLENTA CROSTINI WITH TOMATO SAUCE

3 to 4 tablespoons olive oil

2 cloves garlic, finely minced

6 ripe tomatoes, seeded, finely chopped, and drained

Salt and pepper

1½ tablespoons chopped parsley, or a handful of torn basil leaves

1 recipe Basic Polenta (page 155), Carlo Middione's Trouble-Free Polenta (page 156), or Lightning-Quick Polenta (page 157), spread out into a flat rectangle and cooled

Olive oil

Warm the olive oil in a medium-size skillet over medium heat, and sauté the garlic gently, just until it begins to take on color. Add the tomatoes, salt, and pepper, and cook uncovered for 8 to 10 minutes, or until the tomatoes lose their juices. Stir in the parsley or basil.

Preheat the broiler. Cut the polenta into 2-inch squares, and brush them with a light wash of olive oil. Broil until they are firm and lightly crisp, with a bit of crust on the first side. Turn the squares over, spread the sauce over them, and broil for 5 to 7 minutes. Serve immediately.

SERVES 8 TO 10

VARIATION

Crostini di Polenta alla Pizzaiola con Mozzarella Brush a little olive oil over each polenta square, and place a slice of best-quality mozzarella cheese, cut to the same size, on each square. Drop a spoonful of the tomato topping right in the center of the cheese, drizzle with a little more olive oil, and broil about 4 inches from the heat (or bake in a 425°F oven) until the mozzarella is golden and melting, about 5 minutes.

Polenta Crostini and . . .

Many sauces and toppings are delicious over Polenta Crostini, as appetizers or additions to an antipasto platter. Here are some suggestions to stir your imagination.

Sweet Pepper Topping. Spread Acquasale (page 60), a chunky topping of red peppers sautéed with onions and tomatoes, over squares of crispy polenta.

Red Pepper Sauce. For an appetizer as tantalizing to contemplate as it is delicious to eat, spread Peperoni Arrostiti (page 86) or the sauce from Focaccia Rustica (page 139) over Polenta Crostini.

Mussel Topping. A marriage of mountain and seaside: crunchy squares of polenta crowned with Le Cozze (page 57).

Garlic-Walnut Topping. Spread Agliata (page 66) over squares of warm polenta for an aromatic antipasto with the crunch of walnuts, the tantalizing taste of deep green parsley, and the glorious bite of garlic.

Salami and Prosciutto. Top each warm Polenta Crostini with a thin square of warmed soppressata sausage and a paper-thin slice of prosciutto. Or try pancetta as an alternative to prosciutto, cotechino in place of the soppressata.

Pistada or Pesto Sauce. Spread Polenta Crostini with the garlicky Pistada of Emilia (page 63) or with Liguria's Pesto (page 54), blended with just a little unsalted butter.

Crostini di Polenta
ai Funghi

POLENTA CROSTINI WITH MUSHROOMS

In this sauce the dark musky fragrance of porcini mingles with nutty brown cremini mushrooms to re-create the taste of wild mushrooms freshly pulled from the earth. Spoon the sauce onto slices of golden polenta, the ultimate comfort food, and you have a combination as irresistible as it is versatile. Serve it as an appetizer, as part of an autumnal antipasto plate, as a main course, or as a side dish with roast meat or poultry.

1 ounce dried porcini mushrooms
3 to 4 tablespoons extra-virgin olive
   oil
1 large red onion, finely minced
2 small cloves garlic, finely minced
1 pound fresh brown mushrooms, such
   as cremini or portobello, well
   cleaned and sliced
3 or 4 small ripe plum tomatoes,
   chopped
1 tablespoon chopped flat-leaf parsley
Salt and freshly ground pepper
1 recipe Basic Polenta (page 155)
   Carlo Middione's Trouble-Free
   Polenta (page 156), or Lightning-
   Quick Polenta (page 157), spread
   out into a flat rectangle and cooled
Olive oil

Soak the dried porcini mushrooms in warm water to cover for at least 45 minutes or until softened. Remove them from the liquid carefully, and rinse them well under cold running water to remove any sand still clinging to them. Chop the mushrooms roughly and dry them thoroughly. Strain the soaking liquid at least twice through a sieve lined with cheesecloth or paper towels, and reserve for use in another dish.

Heat the olive oil in a heavy sauté pan, and sauté the onion until it is translucent and soft, 15 to 20 minutes. Add the garlic and all the mushrooms, turn the heat to low, and cook, stirring intermittently, for 20 to 25 minutes, until tender. Then add the tomatoes, parsley, salt, and pepper, and continue cooking for another 5 minutes.

Cut the polenta into slices that are 2 inches wide and 3 to 4 inches long, and brush them lightly with olive oil. Broil until they are firm and lightly crisp on both sides. Place a spoonful of the hot mushroom sauce on top of each crostino and serve.

VARIATION

To make a main-course Polenta with Mushrooms, cook the polenta and serve it immediately as a steaming mound on a large platter; pour the hot mushroom sauce over the top. Pass some freshly grated Parmigiano-Reggiano cheese.

SERVES 8 TO 10 AS AN ANTIPASTO, 4 TO 6 AS A MAIN COURSE OR SIDE DISH

Crostini di Polenta

POLENTA CROSTINI

Polenta is every bit as versatile as bread when it comes to creating *crostini*, those handy croutons that are a perfect platform for any number of toppings. Begin by making polenta, spreading it into a flat rectangle about ½ inch thick, cooling it until it is firm, and then cutting it into squares. Grill, bake, or fry them and you'll have the beginning of dozens of possible antipasti.

1 recipe Basic Polenta (page 155), Carlo Middione's Trouble-Free Polenta (page 156), or Lightning-Quick Polenta (page 157), spread out into a flat rectangle and cooled
Olive oil

Cut the sheet of firm cooled polenta into 2-inch squares. Then cook the crostini by one of these methods: Brush them lightly with olive oil and grill them until they are lightly crispy and marked with the characteristic brown stripes from the grill, about 4 minutes a side; or broil them 4 to 6 inches from the heat for 4 to 5 minutes a side; or deep-fry them in ⅜ inch vegetable oil over medium-high heat, turning once to brown them evenly on both sides, about 5 minutes a side; or bake them at 400°F for about 6 to 8 minutes.

MAKES 25

Polenta Toscana

TUSCAN POLENTA

Here's Tuscan ingenuity: Take polenta, stir in a little fresh rosemary and a handful of toasted walnuts, and *ecco*: a delicious twist on a country classic.

1 recipe Basic Polenta (page 155), partially cooked
3 tablespoons olive oil
2 teaspoons chopped fresh rosemary
⅔ cup walnuts, toasted and chopped
Salt and freshly ground pepper

While the polenta is cooking, warm the olive oil over medium-low heat in a small heavy sauté pan. Add the rosemary and walnuts, and sauté for about 5 minutes, being careful not to let either one brown. Sprinkle the walnut mixture with salt and pepper, and stir it into the polenta about 10 minutes before it is completely cooked. Continue stirring and cooking until the polenta is ready. Serve immediately, or cool and make crostini.

SERVES 8 TO 10 AS AN ANTIPASTO, 4 TO 6 AS A MAIN COURSE

Crostini di Polenta Toscana

TUSCAN POLENTA CROSTINI

---

1 recipe Tuscan Polenta
Olive oil

Turn out the cooked polenta onto an oiled 10½- × 15½-inch baking sheet. Pat it out into a smooth flat rectangle with wet hands or a wet spatula. Allow to cool to room temperature until firm.

Cut the firm polenta into 2-inch squares, brush them lightly with olive oil, and bake at 400°F for 6 to 8 minutes or until golden and crusty, or grill or broil 4 to 6 inches from the heat for 5 minutes each side, or deep-fry in vegetable oil over medium-high heat, turning once to brown evenly on both sides.

SERVES 8 TO 10 AS AN ANTIPASTO, 4 TO 6 AS A MAIN COURSE

Polenta al Radicchio ai Ferri

POLENTA WITH GRILLED RADICCHIO

Radicchio, the slightly bitter, purplish-crimson-long-leaf chicory from Treviso in the Veneto region, is delicious when grilled and served as a vegetable with a little oil and vinegar. Imagine how glorious it is when paired with polenta! Use the more familiar round red variety if you can't find the elongated one.

1 recipe Basic Polenta (page 155), spread out into a flat rectangle and cooled
Olive oil
1 medium head radicchio (about 1 pound), preferably the long-leaf variety
¼ cup extra-virgin olive oil
Salt and freshly ground pepper
Few drops of vinegar (optional)

Fire up a grill or preheat a broiler. Cut the polenta into 1½- × 3-inch rectangles, and brush them lightly with olive oil. To grill, cook the polenta until it is lightly crispy and marked with the characteristic brown stripes on both sides, about 8 minutes. To broil, set the polenta on a broiler pan about 4 inches from the heat, and broil, turning once, until the slices are lightly golden and slightly crisp at the edges, about 4 minutes a side. Remove and set on a platter.

While the polenta is broiling, discard any bruised outside leaves of the radicchio, cut it in half lengthwise, and then cut into quarters. Wash and dry each piece carefully. Drizzle half the olive oil over the radicchio, and season with salt and pepper. Set them on an oiled broiler pan or on the barbecue. Cook over charcoal or under a hot broiler, about 4 to 6 inches from the heat. As the radicchio begins to soften and darken in color, turn it to broil it evenly all over.

Using your fingers or a knife, tear or cut the grilled radicchio into small pieces. Arrange the radicchio over the polenta crostini, and drizzle with the remaining olive oil and the optional vinegar. Taste for salt. Add some freshly ground pepper, and serve immediately or at room temperature.

SERVES 8 TO 10 AS AN APPETIZER

Polenta con Baccalà
Mantecato

POLENTA WITH CREAMY SALT COD

*B*accalà (dried cod), once a dish of the poor, has gone upscale, especially in this Venetian version, which is both elegant and refined, the Italian equivalent of *brandade de morue*. The Venetians still use the old system of drying the salt cod on a wickerwork shelf in the cold air, but in America you can find small boxes filled with pieces of boned baccalà, all of uniform size, at your fish store.

This recipe is amazingly easy: You do need to plan ahead so you can soak the dried fish for 3 days in advance, but after that, you can prepare it in no time with the aid of a heavy-duty mixer, using the paddle attachment and beating in the olive oil as if you were making mayonnaise.

You can serve this fabulous mixture at room temperature on top of slices of grilled or broiled polenta, as they do in the *osterie* of Venice, or you can briefly warm it under the broiler and serve it as a first or main course. I even scramble it into a *frittata*.

*T*hree days before you plan to serve this dish, set the baccalà in a pan of cold water to cover. Soak the fish (this removes excess salt), turning the

1 pound baccalà, preferably boned fillets of equal size
3 black peppercorns
3 cloves garlic, crushed
1 onion, quartered
1 cup olive oil
2 tablespoons chopped flat-leaf parsley
1 teaspoon minced garlic
½ teaspoon sea salt, or to taste
Freshly ground pepper
1 recipe Polenta Crostini (page 161)

pieces several times and changing the water twice a day, for 3 days. The baccalà will be white and no longer firm in the center when it is ready. Taste to see if it still seems salty. Discard any bones or hard skin.

At the end of that time drain the baccalà, place it in a saucepan with fresh water to cover, and add the peppercorns, garlic cloves, and quartered onion. Bring to a boil, and after 3 to 4 minutes turn off the heat. Cover, and let the baccalà sit for 20 minutes.

Drain the baccalà, and using your fingers, remove any bones. Put the fish in the bowl of a heavy-duty mixer, and beat it well with the paddle attachment for 5 to 7 minutes at medium speed, until it has the consistency of flaked crabmeat. With the mixer running, slowly add the olive oil in a thin stream, as if you were making mayonnaise. Continue beating until you have a soft, creamy, mousse-like purée, another 5 to 7 minutes. Then beat in the parsley, minced garlic, and lots of pepper, and taste for salt. Spoon over the crostini, and serve.

SERVES 6 TO 8

Crostini di Polenta con Seppie in Umido

POLENTA CROSTINI WITH STEWED SQUID

Venetians have been fishing squid from the waters of the Adriatic for centuries, for they know how tasty these mollusks can be. They fry them, cook them in their own ink, and toss them with strands of spaghetti, but when it comes to an afternoon *merenda*, they stew the squid with tomatoes and wine until it is velvety, then pile it on crostini of golden polenta.

Stewed squid can be prepared ahead of time and kept in the refrigerator for up to 2 days. To serve, warm them slowly over low heat.

2 pounds small squid
1 small onion, finely chopped
3 to 4 tablespoons olive oil
1 clove garlic, finely chopped
2 tablespoons finely chopped flat-leaf parsley
½ cup dry white wine
8 ounces fresh tomatoes, chopped, or ¾ cup canned Italian tomatoes, coarsely chopped, with their juices
Salt and freshly ground pepper
1 recipe Basic Polenta (page 155), Carlo Middione's Trouble-Free Polenta (page 156), or Lightning-Quick Polenta (page 157), cooked, spread on a baking sheet, and cooled
Olive oil

Buy cleaned squid if your fish seller has them. To clean them yourself, hold the sac in one hand and gently remove the tentacles. Cut the head off just above the eyes, saving the tentacles and discarding the other parts. Clean the sac by washing the interior under cold running water and removing the clear thin cartilage (it resembles a bone of plastic), the ink bag, and any other material that remains. Wash and peel away any purplish skin from the sac and tentacles, rinse both thoroughly, and dry well. Cut the squid into ¼-inch rings and the tentacles into 1-inch pieces.

Set the onion in a large heavy skillet with the olive oil, and sauté over medium heat until it is pale golden and limp. Add the garlic and sauté only until it begins to color; do not let it brown or burn. Stir in the parsley, then add the squid and sauté it for about 2 minutes. Stir in the white wine and tomatoes, season with salt and pepper, cover, and cook until the squid is easily pierced and is velvety in texture, about 40 to 45 minutes. Taste for salt and pepper.

Cut the polenta into slices 2 inches wide and 3 to 4 inches long, and brush them lightly with olive oil. Broil until they are firm and lightly crisp on both sides. Spoon the stewed squid over the Polenta Crostini, and serve.

V A R I A T I O N

For a main course, serve the squid over a steaming mound of hot polenta.

SERVES 10 TO 12 AS AN APPETIZER, 4 TO 6 AS A MAIN COURSE

P O L E N T A

Polenta Taragna

BUCKWHEAT POLENTA

*F*or an earthy dappled beige polenta, use buckwheat polenta, a mixture of cornmeal and dark buckwheat flour. See the Source Guide (page 282) if you can't find buckwheat polenta.

6 cups water
2½ teaspoons coarse salt
2 cups buckwheat polenta

*F*ollow the instructions for Basic Polenta (page 155).

SERVES 8 TO 10 AS CROSTINI

Le Verdure

Man may not live by bread alone, but toss in some olive oil and the panoply of Italian vegetables, and the idea seems eminently appealing. Italians treat vegetables with a care that borders on reverence, whether they are to be eaten raw or turned into dishes for every course. Vegetables grow in profusion in Italy's kitchen gardens and fields, and turn up in markets as a mass of brilliant colors in bountiful and seductive displays.

The vegetables in this section can be divided into four categories. Some are eaten raw. Italians have traditionally gathered wild plants and served them at home. Arugula, today's trendy pungent green, dandelion greens, and wild chicory are all edible weeds that turn up in *merende*. Many *merende* salads, in fact, are based on a mixture of wild greens like arugula, radishes, watercress picked from streams, and fennel plucked from the fields. The greens have a real bite and marry well with hard-boiled eggs and with soft salami like soppressata. Workers commonly carry little bottles of olive oil so that making salads (or bruschetta) in the great out-of-doors presents no problem.

Other vegetables are cooked in such simple ways that they barely need a recipe. Onions, for example, are rubbed with olive oil and baked or roasted, then peeled and eaten with olive oil, garlic, and a sprinkling of hot red peppers, or with just salt, pepper, and a splash of vinegar. Artichokes, mushrooms, even asparagus, can be cooked on a grill and eaten in the fingers, dipped into a simple dressing of lemon juice and oil. Fresh fava beans can be eaten raw when they are young and newly picked; once their tender skins begin to thicken, they are boiled and shelled before they are eaten. Dried favas are easily cooked to a nutty purée that can be spread on toasted bread and topped with a swirl of cooked greens.

Some vegetables are preserved under oil or made into spreads that, when filmed with oil, keep in the refrigerator for a week or longer. They offer amazingly diverse possibilities for foods that may turn up in almost every course. Slide out a few slices of eggplant under oil and spread them on crostini or toss them with strands of pasta. Serve preserved mushrooms with a plate of your favorite salame and prosciutto. Toss pencil-thin asparagus with a lemon-scented dressing to make a delicate salad. Set a whole panoply of vegetables in a bowl with leftover bread to make a quick, dazzling cold plate.

Vegetables take on a more complicated existence in soups, *pizze*, and *torte rustiche*, savory vegetable-filled pies. These may be as elegant as Liguria's Easter tart, which is made with thirty-three layers of fine pasta, one for each year of Jesus' life. Such complex dishes do not appear for *spuntini* or *merende*, but you can be certain that as soon as the countryside turns green in springtime and gardens begin to offer chard and spinach, there isn't a house in Emilia-Romagna that doesn't serve the spinach tart called *erbazzone* as part of an afternoon *merenda*.

Vegetable-based tortes and focacce have been made in Italy for centuries and are still found from Liguria and Tuscany in the north all the way south to Campania and Puglia. They may fold in prosciutto, pancetta, or sausage, or they may get their zest from anchovies, capers, and olives. The first recipe for such a savory green tart was published in 1567, when Cristoforo di Messisbugo created a *Torta d'Erbe alla Ferrarese o Romagnola*, which is surprisingly similar to the *erbazzone* of Modena. In Italy such savory tarts are eaten for a midmorning *spuntino* or late-afternoon *merenda*, although we would serve them as part of an antipasto, as the center of a light lunch, brunch, or informal dinner, or as one of a number of dishes on a buffet.

ROASTING AND PEELING SWEET RED AND YELLOW PEPPERS

Choose peppers with smooth unblemished skins and firm flesh. To roast them, set the peppers on a broiler pan and broil them about 3 inches from the heat, or bake them at 425°F for about 45 minutes, or roast them over a high gas flame or an electric burner. The idea is to char the skins so that they blister and are easy to pull away from the flesh. Be sure to turn the peppers so they are evenly blistered. Set the charred peppers in a bowl or a plastic bag, cover or close it tightly, and allow them to rest for 15 to 30 minutes. Then cut the peppers in half, remove the stems, internal ribs, and seeds, and peel off the skins—you will find that they come off easily. Carefully reserve the juices. You can keep roasted peppers with their juices in a sealed container in the refrigerator for a week.

PEELING TOMATOES

Bring water to a boil in a medium-size saucepan, and plunge the tomatoes into it for no more than 2 minutes, just long enough to loosen the skins. Drain the tomatoes, run cold water over them, and you will be able to peel the skins off easily.

CLEANING ARTICHOKES

Snap off and discard all the tough outer dark green leaves of the artichoke. Trim the stubby bits that remain with a sharp knife. Cut off and remove the top half of the remaining leaves until you reach the core, where the pale leaves have only a slight tinge of purple-green at the top. Turn the artichoke on its side, and with a large sharp knife cut off the remaining tops of the leaves. Slice a lemon in half, and as you cut, rub it over all the parts that are exposed to the air, then squeeze the remaining lemon juice into a large bowl of water. Set the artichokes in the acidulated water until you are ready to use them.

FAVA BEANS

Also known as broad beans, favas can be eaten fresh and young in their pods when their skins are still tender. They can also be shelled and cooked, or shelled and dried for use later. When cooking the dried beans, drain and discard the soaking water, then put them in fresh water and bring it to a boil before adding the salt.

Pappa al Pomodoro

THICK TOMATO AND BREAD SOUP

*H*ere's every Tuscan's idea of comfort food: Plunge a few pieces of stale bread into good homemade broth, add some tomatoes, and film the top with fine ribbons of fruity Tuscan olive oil. It's the soup Tuscan grandmothers have been making for centuries. The secret is in the ingredients: good dense country bread, preferably whole wheat, and the best tomatoes you can find.

6 cups chicken broth, preferably
   homemade
Salt and pepper
1 pound stale Italian country bread,
   preferably one with some whole
   wheat, thinly sliced or in chunks
¾ cup extra-virgin olive oil
2 large cloves garlic, minced
2 pounds fresh ripe tomatoes, peeled,
   seeded, and chopped
10 to 12 basil leaves
Extra-virgin olive oil

*S*eason the broth with salt and pepper, and bring it to a boil in a large saucepan. Stir in the bread, and cook over medium heat for 2 to 3 minutes.

Heat the olive oil in a large heavy sauté pan over low heat, add the garlic, and sauté for 3 to 4 minutes, being careful not to allow it to burn. Stir in the tomatoes and the basil and simmer for 5 minutes. Add the tomatoes to the broth and cook, uncovered, for 3 to 4 minutes. Remove from the heat and let stand 1 hour so the flavors can mingle.

You may serve the pappa hot or cold, but in either case drizzle a fine thread of extra-virgin olive oil over the top.

SERVES 6

Zuppa Matta

BREAD SALAD WITH TOMATOES, CUCUMBERS, FENNEL, AND CELERY

Zuppa matta? Crazy soup? This is more salad than soup, made with everything from the kitchen garden but leafy greens. It is a perfect cold dish to serve in hot weather, another tasty Tuscan invention using leftover bread. Olives and cornichons give it a bite. There is nothing exact about the recipe, so don't worry if you don't have all the ingredients. Use what you have, and if you like, toss in marinated artichokes, sweet peppers, and any other vegetables preserved under oil that you have in your pantry. Start by soaking the onion in cold water for an hour or two before you plan to make the soup.

4 1-inch-thick slices stale Italian country-style bread
1 red onion, finely sliced, soaked in cold water for 1 to 2 hours
2 ripe tomatoes, finely sliced
1 cucumber, peeled and finely sliced
2 ribs celery, finely sliced
1 bulb fennel, quartered and finely sliced
1 sweet red pepper, ribs and seeds removed, finely sliced
1 handful radishes, finely sliced
2 handfuls small black olives in brine
6 to 8 cornichons, chopped
About 12 fresh basil leaves, roughly torn
2 tablespoons red wine vinegar
6 tablespoons extra-virgin olive oil
Lots of salt and freshly ground pepper

Soak the slices of bread in cold water to cover until moist, 10 to 15 minutes. Squeeze each slice between your hands to get rid of any excess moisture and then tear it into small chunks.

Place the bread in a large bowl, and add the onion, tomatoes, cucumber, celery, fennel, pepper, radishes, olives, cornichons, and basil leaves. Mix the vinegar and oil, adding salt and pepper, and pour over the salad. Serve at room temperature.

SERVES 4

Fave alle Sette Insalate

BROAD BEANS SURROUNDED BY
SEVEN SALADS

*F*avas, sometimes called broad beans, are an ancient legume that were so important in Rome that a powerful ruling family took its name, Fabi, from them. People in Puglia still eat the beans with such passion and reverence that they have a saying: "Of all the vegetables there are, broad beans are the queen, sovereign of all, cooked in the evening, reheated in the morning." They certainly command the place of honor in this appealing informal dish.

Fava Bean Salad (page 179)

Black Italian olives, such as Gaeta, rinsed

Slices of sweet onions, such as Vidalia or red torpedo, soaked in water for 1 hour, drained, and soaked again for 1 hour

Arugula leaves or other slightly bitter greens

Sweet peppers in brine, or Ribbons of Sweet Peppers (page 86)

Lightly Pickled Eggplant (page 192)

Boiled and sautéed wild greens ('Ncapriata, page 186)

Braised leeks

*T*o enjoy this specialty from Bari, arrange the fava beans in the center of the plate, and surround them with the colorful collection of vegetables. Then start eating: Begin with a bite of favas, then try one of the salads, drink a little wine, return to the favas, go to the next salad, drink some more wine, and so on around the plate until nothing is left. This dish is always eaten in that rhythm and is always accompanied by a glass of wine.

Insalata Verde e Rossa

RED AND GREEN SALAD OF FRISÉE, RADISHES, AND WATERCRESS

Many small rivers flow from the Alps into Lombardy. They are ice cold, crystal clear, and extremely clean, any impurities filtered by the rocks that line them. The wild greens, watercress, and other plants that flourish in these crystalline waters are obvious picking for *merende*.

In this particular Lombard salad the bite of watercress, the spiciness of radishes, and the crunchy texture and slightly bitter taste of the dandelion greens or frisée, a crisp escarole with a white heart, make a fresh-tasting combination that is especially good with grilled or roasted meats and game. If you can't find frisée, use young chicory or arugula.

¾ to 1 pound dandelion greens,
   frisée, or young chicory
1 large bunch watercress
10 to 12 large red radishes
Salt
6 tablespoons extra-virgin olive oil
2 tablespoons red wine vinegar
Salt and freshly ground pepper

Thoroughly rinse the dandelion leaves or frisée and the watercress. Remove tough stems. Shred dandelion leaves. Slice away some of the base of the heart of the frisée, where the bitterness is concentrated.

Wash the radishes and remove the stems, leaves, and roots. Cut them in quarters, or eighths if they are very big.

Put the dandelion greens and radishes in a bowl (if you are using frisée, reserve it until later), cover with cold water, add salt, and leave for 1 hour. Shortly before serving, drain and dry them and put them in a serving bowl. Add the watercress and the frisée if you are using it.

Beat the oil and vinegar together, adding salt and pepper to taste, until well blended. Pour over the salad, toss well, and serve.

VARIATIONS

People who live in the countryside around Milan often eat a *merenda* of slices of salame served with a salad of radishes, watercress, and sliced young spring onions.

A salad gathered in the fields of Lombardy in springtime combines greens such as frisée, escarole, and dandelion greens with slices of hard-boiled eggs and salame.

SERVES 6

Insalata della Campagna

COUNTRY SALAD

In Italy, this satisfying salad relies on greens picked in the countryside and on soppressata, a large pork sausage that is almost soft enough to spread. If you can't find arugula, use watercress or the tender inner leaves of escarole.

2 cups arugula or other greens
2 hard-boiled eggs, sliced
2 ounces soppressata, cubed
2½ tablespoons extra-virgin olive oil
1½ teaspoons red wine vinegar
Salt and freshly ground pepper

Clean, trim, and wash the greens. Then dry them and tear them roughly. Set the greens in a bowl with the sliced eggs and soppressata. Beat the oil and vinegar together, add salt and pepper to taste, and pour over the salad.

SERVES 4

Insalata di Fave

FAVA BEAN SALAD

The rich, slightly nutty flavor of the fava bean purées that once nourished Roman gladiators still sustains workers in the fields of southern Italy. This particular salad is the *merenda* eaten by shepherds as they take their flocks across the mountainous Gargano promontory, which thrusts out from the northern part of Puglia into the wild uneven coastline of the Adriatic—the spur of the Italian boot. This is excellent as part of an antipasto plate or as a southern Italian equivalent of our potato salad.

8 ounces dried fava beans
1 onion, quartered
1¼ teaspoons sea salt
2 teaspoons lemon juice
2 to 2½ tablespoons extra-virgin
    olive oil
1½ tablespoons finely chopped
    flat-leaf parsley
½ teaspoon sea salt
Freshly ground pepper
1 clove garlic, minutely minced
    (optional)

Soak the beans overnight in cold water to cover.

The next day, drain and slip them out of their skins. If the skins cling too tightly, cook the beans in boiling water for 5 to 10 minutes, drain, and peel.

Set the skinned beans in a saucepan with the onion and just enough water to cover. Turn the heat to medium, bring to a boil, add the salt, and immediately turn down to a simmer. Cover, and cook until the water has almost evaporated and the beans are tender but not pulpy, about 20 to 25 minutes.

Drain the beans. Mix together the lemon juice, olive oil, parsley, salt, pepper, and the optional garlic, and toss with the beans.

SERVES 4

Minestrone Genovese

VEGETABLE SOUP WITH PESTO

The spoonfuls of green pesto that are stirred into the depths of this thick minestrone give away its beginnings, for the basil and garlic mixture comes only from Genoa, home of sailors who embrace its fresh taste after months away at sea. So dense that you can eat it with a fork or stand a spoon in it upright, this minestrone is an informal meal by itself. Drizzle threads of a light extra-virgin olive oil over the top, pass freshly grated Parmesan cheese, and serve it with slices of country bread.

If you don't want to wait for the dried beans to soak overnight, put them in a large pot of cold water with a pinch of bicarbonate of soda, and bring to a boil. Cook for 5 minutes, then drain and rinse the beans, discarding the cooking water. Proceed as directed.

All the vegetables are tossed into the pot without being sautéed and then simmer until they form a thick, nourishing mass. Don't worry if you don't have all the ingredients; just use whatever you find in your garden or refrigerator. Stir in peas, fresh green beans, strips of red cabbage or spinach, even cubes of eggplant that have been salted and drained first. All the vegetables meet in the big pot on the stove and are given a new depth by the short tubular pasta that cooks in their midst.

I love the rituals that surround this minestrone: The pesto must be added precisely when the heat is turned off under the pot, and the cooked rind of Parmigiano-Reggiano cheese is traditionally eaten with the last spoonfuls of the soup.

1⅓ cups dried white kidney or cranberry beans

8 cups water

2 large or 3 medium-size potatoes, peeled and diced

½ pound butternut squash, peeled and diced

3 large zucchini, finely chopped

1 tomato, peeled, seeded, and chopped

⅓ pound mushrooms, sliced

1 carrot, peeled and finely chopped

2 ribs celery, finely chopped

1 large clove garlic, finely minced

1 yellow onion, finely sliced

⅓ cup olive oil

1½ teaspoons coarse sea salt or kosher salt

Piece of rind from Parmigiano-Reggiano cheese (optional)

⅓ to ½ pound short tubular pasta, such as penne or ditalini

1 to 2 tablespoons Pesto (page 54)

Light extra-virgin olive oil

Freshly grated Parmigiano-Reggiano cheese

This soup only gets better the next day and keeps in the refrigerator for up to three days. Eat it at warm room temperature and feel suffused with good feelings.

Soak the dried beans overnight in cold water to cover.

The next day, drain the beans and combine them with the 8 cups water (no salt) in a large deep heavy pot or Dutch oven. Bring to a boil and cook at high heat for about 10 minutes; then reduce the heat and simmer, covered, for 5 to 10 minutes longer.

Add the potatoes, squash, zucchini, tomato, and mushrooms to the pot, and cook over medium heat, stirring from time to time to keep the vegetables from sticking to the bottom. After about 15 minutes, add the carrot, celery, garlic, and onion. Continue cooking for another 15 to 20 minutes. Now add the olive oil, salt, and the optional Parmesan cheese rind. Continue simmering, pressing the potatoes and beans against the sides of the pot to make the soup dense. When the vegetables are cooked, after another 15 or 20 minutes, add the pasta and simmer until it is cooked *al dente*, about 8 to 9 minutes. Just as the heat is turned off under the pot, stir in the pesto with a wooden spoon. Let this thick soup cool to tepid, and serve it with drizzles of light extra-virgin olive oil on top. Pass the freshly grated Parmigiano-Reggiano cheese to sprinkle over the soup.

SERVES 6 TO 8

Cipolle Arrostite

ROAST ONIONS

Onions roasting on an open fire may not seem as romantic as chestnuts, but they are a delicious *merenda* in many parts of Italy. Northern Italians eat large purple onions rubbed with olive oil and roasted in their skins until they are soft (they are sometimes cooked in the baker's oven once the breads have come out), while southern Italians grill *spunsale*, long leek-like wild onions, over grapevine cuttings until they are charred on the outside but tender and creamy inside. Serve these as an antipasto, as a side dish with any roasted or grilled meat or poultry, or as a salad—sliced and tossed with olive oil, salt, pepper, and fresh herbs such as thyme or oregano.

4 small yellow onions
2 tablespoons olive oil
Salt and pepper

Preheat the oven to 400°F.

Do not peel the onions. Rub the outer skins well with the olive oil. Set them in an oiled baking pan, sprinkle with salt and pepper, and bake for about 1 hour, until soft and golden. Serve warm or at room temperature.

VARIATION

Cut the onions in half vertically, through the blossom and root ends, rub with the olive oil, and proceed as described.

SERVES 2 TO 4

Zucchine a Fiammifero

MATCHSTICK ZUCCHINI SALAD

Choose firm, glossy zucchini for this light vegetable salad and steam them very briefly, so that they remain slightly crisp. Overcooking makes them watery, something to avoid at all costs. Toss them gently with the herbs, and serve forth a delicate and delicious dish.

8 small fresh zucchini
1 tablespoon extra-virgin olive oil
1 large clove garlic, minced
1½ tablespoons finely minced
  fresh rosemary
1½ tablespoons finely minced
  fresh sage leaves
1 tablespoon lemon juice or red
  wine vinegar
¼ cup extra-virgin olive oil
1 teaspoon sea salt
Freshly ground pepper

Bring a deep pot of water to a boil. Set the zucchini in a steamer basket, place it over the pot, cover, and steam for a very few minutes, so that the zucchini are cooked but still slightly crisp and *al dente*. Remove, and allow to cool.

Warm the 1 tablespoon olive oil in a small sauté pan over very low heat, and add the garlic; let it sweat so that the flavor of garlic infuses the oil. Add the minced rosemary and sage and let them wilt in the oil for a minute or two.

Cut the cooled zucchini into strips the size of kitchen matches, and place them in a salad bowl. Whisk together the lemon juice or vinegar, ¼ cup olive oil, salt, pepper, and the garlic-infused oil with the herbs. Toss carefully with the zucchini because it is very fragile. Serve at warm room temperature.

SERVES 4 TO 6

Asparagi di Campo

COLD MARINATED PENCIL-THIN ASPARAGUS

For a few weeks every springtime, Italian hillsides bloom with wild asparagus that are as fine as the tip of a pencil. Wise Italians race out to pick them and turn them into pasta sauces, frittate, or wonderfully simple vegetable salads like this one.

¾ small onion, very finely minced

3 flat anchovy fillets, mashed, drained and rinsed

1½ teaspoons capers, rinsed and chopped

1 teaspoon lemon juice

Salt and pepper

1 mint leaf

1 pound pencil-thin asparagus

Choose a bowl large enough to hold the asparagus, and put the onion and anchovies in it. Mix well and let steep for 30 minutes. Then add the capers, lemon juice, and mint leaf, and marinate for a minimum of 1 hour. Mix thoroughly from time to time.

Meanwhile bring an asparagus cooker or a pot half filled with water to the boil, add the asparagus, and cook very briefly, just so they are tender but still crisp and slightly firm, 3 to 5 minutes. Drain.

Add the still-warm asparagus to the marinade, taste for salt and pepper, toss gently, and serve.

VARIATION

To turn this salad into a warm vegetable dish, warm 3 tablespoons extra-virgin olive oil in a sauté pan over medium-low heat. Add the onion and sauté, stirring from time to time, until it wilts; do not let it brown. Add the mashed anchovies and cook a bit longer. Remove from the heat, and mix in the capers, lemon juice, and mint leaf. Leave to mellow for 30 minutes to 1 hour. Toss gently with the still-warm asparagus, and serve.

SERVES 4 TO 6

Peperoni alle Acciughe

SWEET PEPPERS WITH ANCHOVY SAUCE

Sweet peppers from the vine, anchovies from the sea, and oil pressed from olives carefully picked from ancient trees: a triumphant mix of the best of Italy. Spoon this surprisingly light anchovy sauce over meaty roasted sweet peppers for a wonderful antipasto or a light meal. Try it on grilled eggplant slices as well.

4 meaty sweet red peppers,
   roasted and peeled (page 173)
6 flat anchovy fillets
3 cloves garlic
2 tablespoons finely chopped flat-
   leaf parsley
2 to 3 tablespoons extra-virgin
   olive oil

Cut the peppers in half, and discard the seeds and ribs.

If you are using salted anchovies, remove the central bone and rinse them well. If you are using anchovies in oil, merely drain them. Chop the anchovy fillets finely with the garlic and parsley. Set the anchovy mixture in a small heavy saucepan, add the olive oil, and slowly heat the mixture over medium-low heat. Keep mashing the anchovies and cooking slowly for about 5 to 7 minutes, being careful not to let the garlic burn. Remove from the heat.

Set the peppers cut side up on a platter, spoon the anchovy sauce over the top, cover, and leave them to marinate at room temperature for 3 to 4 hours. Drain any excess oil before serving.

VARIATION

Substitute 1 eggplant for the sweet peppers, and grill it as instructed on page 92.

SERVES 4

'Ncapriata di Fave

CREAMY FAVA BEAN PURÉE WITH
WILD GREENS

*L*uigi Sada, the author of an astonishing number of books about the food of Puglia, calls this traditional fava dish "a lyric symphonic poem to an ancient rhythm." The smooth nutty flavor of the favas is a wonderful counterpoint to the bitterness of the wild greens. If you can't find wild bitter greens, substitute cultivated chicory, frisée, or escarole. You could spread the purée (also called Fave e Foglie) on grilled lightly oiled bread, as olive mill workers do during the pressing, and then set a swirl of boiled or sautéed wild greens on top to make crostini, or you could serve 'Ncapriata as a very thick soup or as part of the Seven Salads (page 176). Serve it too with sautéed sweet peppers with tomatoes and onions or scallions—but always with slices of porous rustic country bread and a glass of white wine. I love it with leg of lamb, grilled fish, or chicken.

8 ounces dried fava beans
2 ribs celery, chopped
1 medium onion, chopped
2 teaspoons sea salt
2 tablespoons fruity olive oil
12 ounces broccoli rabe, chicory,
    other wild greens, or cultivated
    chicory, washed and well
    trimmed
⅓ to ½ cup water
1 tablespoon sea salt
3 tablespoons fruity olive oil
2 cloves garlic, finely minced

Soak the beans overnight in cold water to cover.

The next day, drain and slip them out of their skins. If the skins cling too tightly, cook the beans in boiling water for 5 to 10 minutes; then drain and peel.

Put the peeled beans in a saucepan with the celery and onion, add just enough water to cover, and bring to a simmer over medium heat. Add the 2 teaspoons salt, cover, and cook for 25 to 30 minutes, or until the beans are very soft. Check to be sure there is enough liquid; if the water has evaporated, add more. Drain the beans, and purée them in a food processor with the 2 tablespoons olive oil.

If you are using broccoli rabe, clean it by peeling off any thick skin covering the larger stems, and cut it into 2-inch pieces. Rinse the greens well. Bring the water to a boil, add the greens and the 1 tablespoon salt, cover, and cook until the greens are soft but not mushy, about 5 to 10 minutes. Drain.

Warm the 3 tablespoons oil in a sauté pan and slowly sauté the garlic just until it is soft and barely golden; do not let it brown. Add the greens and swirl them well in the flavored oil. Serve on a platter, spooning the garlic-infused greens over or into creamy favas.

SERVES 4 TO 6

Rape Affogate

BROCCOLI RABE IN WHITE WINE

I casually put my fork into the tangle of dark leaves on my plate, little expecting anything out of the ordinary. I don't know if that first taste literally stunned me into speechlessness, but I certainly will never forget the haunting combination of flavors. I was delighted to be able to re-create this broccoli rabe dish, for I had visions that only by traveling back to the far reaches of Puglia could I taste it again. The recipe was given to me by the extraordinarily talented and very generous chef Dora Ricci, at the Al Fornello da Ricci restaurant in the little town of Ceglie Messapico in Puglia.

1 pound 2 ounces broccoli rabe
3 tablespoons olive oil
4 ounces pancetta, diced
2 small tomatoes, peeled, seeded, and chopped
1 leek, white part only, well washed and finely sliced
1 onion, finely sliced
½ cup dry white wine
1 bay leaf
⅛ teaspoon red pepper flakes
Salt

*R*emove the tough upper leaves and large stems of the broccoli rabe. If the main stem is tough, peel it with a vegetable peeler. Wash the greens well in several changes of water, drain, and dry them well. Chop them roughly.

Warm the olive oil in a deep heavy pot, and cook the pancetta, tomatoes, leek, and onion over low heat until the onion and pancetta are soft and transparent, about 20 minutes. Add the broccoli rabe and the white wine and simmer, covered, over very low heat for 20 minutes. At the end of that time add the bay leaf, the red pepper flakes, and salt. Stir the mixture well and continue cooking over low heat for 10 more minutes. Serve at room temperature.

SERVES 4 TO 6

Tocchetti

CRISPY EGGPLANT ROUNDS

These may look like little meatballs but they are really eggplant, broiled until they are lightly crunchy outside and still creamy inside. You can sauté the eggplant cubes up to 2 days in advance and refrigerate them; then just pull them out, stir in the other ingredients, and broil them in a flash. Another recipe from Dora Ricci, these are a sensational antipasto as well as a vegetable to serve with grilled or broiled meats or poultry.

1 small eggplant (about ¾ pound)
Salt
¼ cup olive oil
⅓ cup fine-textured bread crumbs, preferably freshly made
½ cup freshly grated pecorino or Parmigiano-Reggiano cheese
2 tablespoons finely chopped flat-leaf parsley
¼ teaspoon sea salt

Peel the eggplant and cut it into ½-inch cubes. Place them in a colander, sprinkle with salt, and let them stand for at least 30 minutes to drain off the bitter juices. Then pat them dry with paper towels.

Heat the olive oil in a large heavy sauté pan, and when it is hot, add the eggplant cubes without crowding the pan. Sauté until they are golden in color and creamy and soft in texture, about 6 to 8 minutes, stirring frequently. Remove them with a slotted spoon and set them in a bowl. Add the bread crumbs, cheese, parsley, and salt to the eggplant. Mix together very well to form a paste, and shape into rounds the size of small walnuts.

Preheat a broiler. Set the eggplant rounds on a broiler pan about 3 to 4 inches from the heat. Broil for about 3 minutes, until they are a crunchy chestnut brown on the outside but still creamy inside. Serve at warm room temperature.

MAKES 24

Sedano Ripieno

STUFFED CELERY

Wedged between mountains and the sea, most of Liguria is rugged and steep, but that has not prevented people from terracing and cultivating the land, prodding vegetables and herbs to grow in astonishing abundance. Sonia Lorenzini, the talented cook who gave me this recipe, says that Ligurians, faced with adversity and relatively limited products, have had to be inventive in combining ingredients. As the chef at a century-old trattoria that once specialized in making *merende* for workers, she exemplifies that Ligurian innovation, for her distinctive and imaginative dishes rely on a modest number of ingredients to accentuate the amazing flavors of local vegetables.

10 large thick ribs celery, cut into
  4-inch lengths
¾ cup milk
2 slices country-style bread, torn in
  chunks and crusts removed
4 ounces finest-quality mortadella or
  prosciutto di Parma
4 ounces ground lean veal
2 ounces prosciutto di Parma
2 eggs
¼ cup finely chopped flat-leaf parsley
1 teaspoon minced garlic
Substantial gratings of nutmeg
Salt and freshly ground pepper
½ cup freshly grated Parmigiano-
  Reggiano cheese
1 recipe Sugo di Pomodoro (page 193)

This unusual stuffed celery, a *merenda* Sonia learned from her grandmother, is so local that it may not even be known 10 kilometers away. Although it looks complicated, you can make the tomato sauce up to a week ahead and refrigerate it. If you don't have celery, try zucchini. Serve it as part of an elegant antipasto, as a first course, or as the centerpiece of a light meal.

Bring a medium-size pot full of water to a boil, and set the celery in it. Cook only until barely tender when pierced with a knife, about 7 to 10 minutes. Drain and dry well.

Meanwhile, warm the milk in a small saucepan, add the slices of bread, and cook at a very low simmer for 10 to 15 minutes, stirring occasionally, until the mixture is creamy and oatmeal-like. Set aside to cool.

Grind the mortadella, veal, and prosciutto in a meat grinder or in a food processor outfitted with the steel blade.

In a medium-size mixing bowl, beat together the eggs, parsley, garlic, nutmeg, salt and pepper, and ¼ cup of the cheese. Stir in the ground meats and the milk mixture to make a creamy filling.

Preheat the oven to 400°F.

Lightly oil a 9- or 10-inch baking dish. Spoon a thin layer of the tomato sauce over the bottom, and cover with a layer of celery. Spread the filling over the celery, then the rest of the tomato sauce, and finish by sprinkling with the remaining grated Parmigiano-Reggiano. (If you have enough for a second layer, repeat the steps but set the celery stalks at a 90-degree angle to the first layer, so they form a woven pattern. Cover with filling and sauce and finish with grated cheese.)

Bake for 30 to 40 minutes, until the top is dappled golden brown and is brown at the edges.

Serve hot or at room temperature.

SERVES 6 TO 8

Melanzane Sott'Olio

LIGHTLY PICKLED EGGPLANT

This eggplant from Puglia is cooked in water and vinegar, then layered with mint, garlic, and hot pepper flakes, and marinated in olive oil. The recipe comes from Maria Pignatelli Ferrante, a passionate and knowledgeable source of information about the region's food, and I have made it two ways. In this one I have increased the amount of water and cooked the eggplant until it is creamy, a perfect foil for the crunch of grilled bread. It is an excellent antipasto, wonderful as one of the Seven Salads (page 176), and a fine vegetable to serve with boiled or cured meats.

2 pounds eggplant, preferably the
   long thin Italian or Japanese
   variety
4 cups red wine vinegar
4 cups water
1 tablespoon coarse sea salt
About 30 fresh mint leaves
5 large cloves garlic, thinly sliced
½ teaspoon red pepper flakes
2 cups olive oil, or as needed

Peel the eggplants and cut them into ¼-inch-thick slices. Bring the vinegar, water, and salt to a boil in a heavy 4- or 5-quart saucepan. In the boiling liquid, immerse as many of the eggplant slices as possible in one layer. Lower the heat to a simmer, and set a weighted plate on top of the eggplant to keep it submerged. Cook for about 10 minutes, until the eggplant is soft and easily pierced by a knife. Remove with a slotted spoon. Repeat until all the eggplant is cooked. If the liquid becomes too concentrated, add 1 cup more of both water and vinegar.

Arrange a layer of eggplant slices in a glass bowl or a 1-quart glass jar with a wide neck. Sprinkle with some of the mint, garlic, and red pepper flakes. Repeat the layers until the eggplant is used up, and cover with the olive oil. Cover, and allow the eggplant to marinate at room temperature for 2 days before serving. (It may also be refrigerated, but not for much longer than 2 days unless packed in sterilized jars immediately after cooking.) Bring back to room temperature, and serve.

Melanzane Sott'Olio II This is the stronger pickled eggplant recipe as given to me by Maria Ferrante.

Cut the peeled eggplant into 1½-inch-thick slices. Bring 4 cups red wine vinegar, 2 cups water, and 1 tablespoon coarse sea salt to a boil. Cook the eggplant, submerged, for about 5 minutes, just until it can be pierced by a knife but is in no way soft. As the eggplant cooks, skim off any foam. Drain well in a colander, pressing out any remaining liquid, and proceed as described.

MAKES 1 QUART

Sugo di Pomodoro
TOMATO SAUCE

This very simple tomato sauce has many possible lives: it is delicious on pasta (add a few basil leaves), it is splendid on pizza, and it can be painted as a wash on focaccia. It keeps in the refrigerator for a week and can be frozen for up to 4 months.

3½ tablespoons extra-virgin olive oil
2 red onions, minced
1 35-ounce can Italian plum tomatoes, preferably San Marzano, roughly chopped, with their juice
1 clove garlic, lightly crushed
Salt and freshly ground pepper

Heat the olive oil in a large heavy non-aluminum sauté pan, and sauté the onions over low heat until soft and transparent, about 15 to 20 minutes. Pour in the tomatoes and juice, crushing them with a fork or the back of a wooden spoon. Add the garlic and bring to a boil over medium heat; then lower the heat and simmer uncovered for about 30 minutes. Taste for salt and pepper.

SERVES 6 TO 8 AS A PASTA SAUCE

Torta di Carciofi

ARTICHOKE TART

*E*very nuance of green can be found in the palette of herbs and vegetables that grow in Liguria, thriving on adversity on the rugged vertical hillsides. This delicious artichoke tart enfolds many of them: the silvery green of the olive trees that produce the region's acclaimed delicate oil; the dusty green of marjoram, the major herb of Liguria; and the gray green of the artichokes that are the center of this fine tart. The dough is so easy to make that it shouldn't frighten even a novice baker.

DOUGH
1½ cups (200 grams) unbleached
   all-purpose flour
¼ to ½ teaspoon sea salt
½ cup water
5 tablespoons olive oil

*T*his dough takes about 30 seconds to make. Set the flour and salt in a food processor outfitted with the steel blade, and pulse briefly to sift. Then with the motor running, pour the water and olive oil down the feed tube, mixing only until it masses as a ball. Transfer the dough to a bowl and cover it, or wrap it in a self-sealing plastic bag, and chill in the refrigerator for 30 minutes.

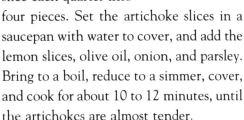

FILLING

8 medium-size artichokes
1 lemon, sliced
¼ cup olive oil
½ onion, finely chopped
3½ tablespoons finely minced flat-
   leaf parsley
5½ tablespoons grated
   Parmigiano-Reggiano cheese
Salt and freshly ground pepper
5 ounces ricotta cheese, sieved
3 eggs, room temperature, beaten
¾ teaspoon minced fresh
   marjoram
Olive oil

Clean the artichokes as instructed on page 173. Cut them in quarters, remove the chokes, and slice each quarter into four pieces. Set the artichoke slices in a saucepan with water to cover, and add the lemon slices, olive oil, onion, and parsley. Bring to a boil, reduce to a simmer, cover, and cook for about 10 to 12 minutes, until the artichokes are almost tender.

Remove the artichokes from the heat, drain them, set them in a large bowl, and allow to cool briefly. Then stir in the Parmesan, salt and pepper, ricotta, eggs, and marjoram.

Preheat the oven to 375°F.

Divide the dough into two pieces, one about 60 percent of the total, the other 40 percent. Roll the larger one out to form a 13-inch circle. Oil the bottom of a 9-inch springform pan or quiche pan with removable bottom, and ease the dough into it so it covers the bottom and overlaps the sides slightly. Brush the dough with oil, and spoon the filling over it. Roll out the top sheet of dough to form a 10-inch circle, and set it on top of the filling. Trim the overhanging dough, and use your fingers to press the two edges together, crimping them decoratively and closing the tart well. Lightly brush the top crust with oil. Pierce the crust with a fork in a few places to allow steam to escape.

Bake for 35 to 40 minutes, until the top is lightly golden. Cool on a rack, and serve warm or at room temperature.

SERVES 6 TO 8

Scarpaccia Viareggina

SAVORY ZUCCHINI TART

Once a common midafternoon *merenda* in the Tuscan coastal towns of Viareggio and Camaiore, today this light and creamy zucchini tart is rarely found outside of people's homes. If you can find zucchini flowers, be sure to include them; several of my sources swore they were the crucial ingredient. While I wouldn't go quite that far, they do add depth and richness to the flavor and make the tart look especially beautiful. Milk and/or egg make a creamier scarpaccia, although some Tuscans use only water in their batter. Easy to make and versatile in its uses, scarpaccia is a perfect little bite to serve with a glass of wine. You can also cut it in wedges and serve it as an antipasto or as a perfect centerpiece for a light lunch or supper.

The secret to making a successful scarpaccia lies in pouring the batter no more than ¼ inch deep in the baking pan. Just oil two round 10- or 11-inch metal pie pans, divide the batter between them, and you'll have the real thing.

Salt
8 ounces young zucchini, finely sliced
1 medium-size white onion, finely diced
1 cup (140 grams) unbleached all-purpose flour
½ teaspoon sea salt
1⅓ cups milk or water
½ cup olive oil
1 egg (optional)
8 ounces zucchini blossoms (if you can find them), roughly sliced
Abundant freshly ground pepper

Salt the zucchini and onions, and leave them to drain in a colander for 30 minutes.

Preheat the oven to 450°F.

Sift the flour and sea salt together. Whisk in the milk or water, then ¼ cup of the olive oil, to make a batter that is quite liquid. Whisk in the egg, if you are using it. Stir in the zucchini, the zucchini flowers if you are using them, and the onions.

Use two 10- or 11-inch metal pie pans. Pour 2 tablespoons of the remaining olive oil into each pan, rubbing a little on the

sides to prevent the scarpaccia from sticking. Divide the batter between the two pans, pouring it into a depth no greater than ¼ inch. Smooth the top to prevent the zucchini slices from protruding from the batter. Grind a substantial amount of pepper over each one.

Bake for 20 minutes, then reduce the temperature to 425°F and continue baking for 8 to 15 minutes, until deep golden. Grate more pepper over the top, cut in wedges, and serve warm or at room temperature.

SERVES 10 TO 12

Torta dell'Erbe

VEGETABLE TART

All morning long, people line up at the metal counter in the tiny Osteria Bacciottini in Pontremoli for a glass of wine or grappa and something to eat. Most of them come to work from the forested Lunigiana mountains that are squeezed in between the Apennines and the Apuan Alps, and they need reinforcement by the middle of the morning. The glass case is full of various vegetables *sott'olio* along with sweet pecorino cheese and salami, but as good as they are, they cannot challenge the sublime vegetable tarts on display.

This pastry dough is extremely light and flaky and simple to make. Be sure to cut the chard, potatoes, and onions very, very fine. There's no Cuisinart in the kitchen in this tiny trattoria—there isn't even a dishwasher, and the mixing bowls are small and unmatched—but the grandmotherly cook sends out superb traditional plates.

DOUGH

2 cups plus 1 tablespoon and
   1 teaspoon (300 grams)
   unbleached all-purpose flour
½ tablespoon sea salt
¼ cup olive oil
10 to 11 tablespoons cold water

To make the dough by hand, combine the flour and salt in a bowl. Make a well in the center and add the oil. Blend until the mixture resembles coarse meal. Sprinkle with 8 tablespoons of the water, and mix with a fork until the dough comes together. If it is dry, add more water. If you are using a heavy-duty electric mixer, combine the flour, salt, oil, and water in the bowl and mix with the paddle attachment until they come together as a dough.

Knead the dough briefly by hand on a lightly floured work surface. Cover with plastic wrap, and leave at room temperature for 30 minutes.

FILLING

2 pounds 2 ounces Swiss chard, washed well, dried, white ribs removed

1 large boiling potato

½ yellow or white onion

¼ cup grated Parmigiano-Reggiano cheese

6½ tablespoons freshest possible ricotta cheese, sieved

2 eggs, lightly beaten

Salt and pepper

Substantial gratings of nutmeg

Scant ½ cup extra-virgin olive oil

Put about 1 quart of water in a pot large enough to hold the chard later and bring it to a boil. Add salt and when the water boils rapidly, add the chard. Cook until tender, 10 to 15 minutes. Drain well, squeezing the moisture out of the chard, and set aside to cool. At the same time, bring another quart of water to boil in a medium size pot, add salt, and when the water boils rapidly, add the potato and onion and cook until each is tender. Set aside to cool.

Set the vegetables in a food processor and pulse until they are finely chopped. Transfer them to a large bowl, and mix in the Parmesan, ricotta, eggs, salt, nutmeg, and olive oil.

Preheat the oven to 375°F.

Divide the dough into two pieces, one slightly larger than the other. Roll the larger piece out to form a 15-inch round; it should be almost as fine and transparent as the dough for the thinnest pasta. Lift the dough on a rolling pin, and lay it inside an oiled 8½- or 9-inch springform pan so that it completely covers the bottom and the sides. Fill with the vegetable mixture. Roll the second piece of dough out to form a 9- or 9½-inch circle as thin as the first, and lay it over the filling. Trim the edges, and crimp them together well to seal the tart. Pierce the crust with a fork in a few places to allow the steam to escape.

Bake for 50 to 60 minutes, until the top is a pale golden brown. Unmold, and serve warm or at room temperature.

SERVES 6 TO 8

Erbazzone

SPINACH PIE

The top crust of this spinach pie has a satiny finish from the wash of oil and the pancetta, and its pale golden color contrasts splendidly with the dark green of the spinach. Cut it into wedges or squares and serve it hot, warm, or at room temperature with a glass of red wine.

Every family in Emilia-Romagna serves *erbazzone*, the quintessential *merenda* that appears as soon as spinach returns in the springtime, but the recipes are carefully kept secrets. My friend Renato Bergonzini introduced me to his friend the winemaker, whose aunt cooked this one for me at home. The three of us sat around a table, talking and drinking a wonderful pale rosé wine, until to our amazement we noticed that we'd eaten almost the entire erbazzone.

DOUGH

2 cups plus 1 to 2 tablespoons (300 grams) unbleached all-purpose flour

1½ teaspoons sea salt

4 tablespoons unsalted butter or best-quality lard, room temperature

8 to 10 tablespoons ice-cold water, preferably sparkling mineral water

Mix the flour and salt together in a large bowl. Cut the butter or lard into small pieces, and then cut it into the flour with a pastry blender, two knives, or in a heavy-duty electric mixer until it resembles coarse meal. Slowly stir in the cold water and mix until smooth. Gather the dough into a ball, cover it with plastic wrap, and refrigerate it for at least 30 minutes.

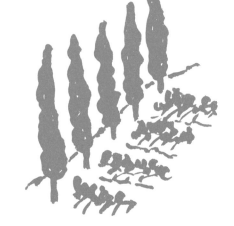

FILLING

2¼ pounds fresh spinach

2 tablespoons unsalted butter

2 tablespoons extra-virgin olive oil

4 ounces pancetta, diced

2 large onions, diced

2 large cloves garlic, minced

2 tablespoons finely chopped flat-
   leaf parsley

2 eggs, room temperature, beaten

¾ cup freshly grated Parmigiano-
   Reggiano cheese

Substantial gratings of nutmeg

Salt and pepper

GLAZE

2 tablespoons olive oil

¼ cup finely minced pancetta

1 small garlic clove, flattened

Wash the spinach very well to remove all traces of dirt from the leaves. Set the spinach in a large pot with only the water still clinging to the leaves, cover, and cook until barely tender, 4 to 5 minutes. Drain, chop very fine, and set in a bowl.

Heat the butter and olive oil in a medium-size sauté pan, and sauté the pancetta, onions, garlic, and parsley until the onion is pale and limp, being very careful not to burn the garlic. Remove from the heat, and using a slotted spoon, transfer the contents to the bowl containing the spinach. Stir the eggs, Parmesan, nutmeg, and salt and pepper into the spinach mixture. Set aside the sauté pan for use later.

Preheat the oven to 350°F.

Divide the dough in half, and roll one part out on a very lightly floured work surface to form a circle about 12 inches in diameter, large enough to line the bottom and drape over the sides of a well-oiled 9- or 10-inch round or square baking pan with a removable bottom. Cover with the vegetable mixture. Roll the remaining dough out to form a circle about 9 to 10 inches in diameter and set it over the filling. Press the edges of the two pieces of dough together. Trim the edges of the larger piece with a sharp knife, fold over the overhanging dough, and crimp the two together to seal the edges.

Combine the olive oil, pancetta, and garlic in the sauté pan you used earlier, and cook over medium-low heat until the fat of the pancetta has melted, about 5 to 6 minutes. Discard the garlic, but scrape up any bits remaining on the bottom of the pan. Brush the top crust with half of this glaze. Pierce the crust with a fork in a few places to allow steam to escape.

Bake the pie for 20 minutes, then brush on the rest of the glaze and continue cooking for another 25 minutes, until the crust is satiny and lightly golden. Serve hot or slightly warm, cut in wedges or in squares the size of large brownies.

SERVES 6 TO 8

Torta dell'Erbe Nicolese

GARDEN GREENS VEGETABLE MOLD

Just because the little dishes served for *merende* are the original Italian version of fast food doesn't always mean that they are as fast to make as they are to eat. One solution is to make *torte* as vegetable dishes and eliminate the dough entirely. This spinach-and-chard-filled "pie" is the oldest of all *merende* in the area around the tiny walled town of Nicola in southern Liguria, but the women there sometimes also bake it as a *sformato,* a vegetable dish that is a cross between a pudding and a soufflé. It is always served cold or at room temperature and is never reheated.

This particular recipe uses borage, a cucumber like herb with lovely blue blossoms; if you have trouble finding it, simply substitute finely minced cucumber. Cut the pie in slices or wedges for a first course or appetizer, serve it as a main dish for lunch, brunch, or supper, or use it as a delicious vegetable side dish.

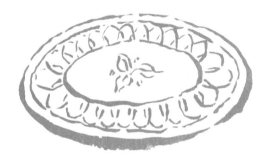

3 tablespoons light extra-virgin olive oil, either Ligurian or French

4 leeks, washed very well, green and white parts finely chopped

3 small white boiling onions, minced

14 ounces fresh Swiss chard leaves, washed, ribs removed

14 ounces fresh spinach, washed very well, stems removed

14 ounces borage, minced, or cucumber, peeled, seeded, and finely chopped

1½ teaspoons coarse sea salt or kosher salt

1 bay leaf

6 eggs

1½ cups freshly grated Parmigiano-Reggiano cheese

10 ounces best-quality ricotta cheese

Salt and freshly ground pepper

Heat the oil in a large sauté pan over medium heat, and sauté the leeks and the white onions until they are limp and pale. Transfer them to a 5-quart pot, and add the chard, spinach, borage or cucumber, salt, and bay leaf. You will probably not need any liquid other than the water still clinging to the spinach and chard leaves, but add a little if the chard needs more moisture. Cover and cook, stirring, over very low heat for about 10 minutes, until the vegetables are barely tender. Remove the bay leaf. Drain well, chop roughly, transfer to a large bowl, and set aside to cool.

Meanwhile, beat the eggs and Parmesan cheese together with the salt and pepper in a mixing bowl. Press the ricotta through a sieve into the bowl or pulse it briefly in a food processor, then whisk it into the bowl, and mix well. Stir the egg and cheese mixture into the vegetables, and mix well again.

Preheat the oven to 400°F.

Oil a 9-inch deep ring mold or a 9- × 5- × 3-inch loaf pan, and pour in the vegetable mixture, smoothing the top. Fill a baking pan with about 1½ inches of hot water, set the mold or loaf pan in it, and bake for 45 to 50 minutes, until a tester comes out clean and the top is lightly golden. Cool and unmold to serve.

VARIATION

For an authentic torte, make the dough for the Spinach Pie (page 200), following the instructions for rolling it out. Line an oiled 12-inch low-sided baking dish with the dough, fill with the vegetable mixture, seal the top crust. Pierce with a fork in a few places to allow steam to escape, and bake for 50 minutes to 1 hour.

SERVES 10 TO 12 AS AN APPETIZER, 6 AS A MAIN COURSE

Funghi Sott'Olio

MUSHROOMS PRESERVED IN OIL

Another delicious preserved vegetable from Maria Pignatelli Ferrante in Puglia, these mushrooms can be served as part of an antipasto platter with a variety of salame, prosciutto, and olives.

1 pound fresh brown mushrooms,
　　such as cremini
2 cups water
1 cup white wine vinegar
1½ teaspoons coarse sea salt
15 fresh mint leaves
3 large cloves garlic, thinly sliced
¼ teaspoon red pepper flakes
Olive oil

Clean the mushrooms well by wiping them with a moist cloth. Bring the water, vinegar, and sea salt to a boil in a heavy saucepan. Immerse the mushrooms, and simmer for only 2 to 3 minutes. Remove the mushrooms with a slotted spoon, drain well, and dry on tea towels.

Layer the mushrooms in pint glass jars, sprinkling the mint, garlic, and red pepper flakes between the layers. Cover with olive oil. Allow the mushrooms to marinate for at least 3 days before using—they will keep for months in the refrigerator. Bring back to room temperature before serving.

MAKES 3 CUPS

Merende di Pane

Many of the simplest and most evocative *merende* are based on bread, the elemental food that has nourished the people of Italy for millennia. The bread may be fresh or it may be stale and need to be moistened with sprinklings of water, with drizzlings of olive oil, or with the juices of vegetables or fruits. *Merende* often begin (and sometimes end) with bread and something to eat with it, for even the poorest people have a chunk of bread, a small bottle of olive oil, and herbs and wild greens from the fields. Workers have always brought along bread to cut with a large penknife, dip into water and squeeze dry, then spread with tomato, garlic, oregano, and salt and pepper. Simple, basic, nourishing: what the earth renders is set upon a slice of bread.

Take a quick look at *merende* in any part of Italy and one thing stands out: any number of them start with bread dough. It may be baked, it may be fried, it may be grilled, it may be cooked on an old-fashioned griddle or under the embers, but it often turns out to be round in shape—the *piadina* from Romagna, the *crescentina* from Emilia, the hard-baked *gallette* and *friselle* of soldiers and shepherds, the famous huge loaves of Puglia, even the famous pizza of Naples, are all as round as the sun.

Bread is the Ur-food of Italy. It takes the grains of the earth and the yeasts of the air and in a miraculous alchemy turns them into the simple food that nourishes the people of the country. It is, says Carlo Levi, "as though all the juices and values of the earth it came from, the labor of its people, the solitude and the sun, the antiquity of the place, its human thoughts and the simplicity of the daily round had been gathered into a substance that was delicious, life-giving and maternal."

Every day bakers' ovens in every region pour forth wheels of bread, cylinders of bread, long thin grissini and rolls of various forms, for a meal without bread is unthinkable. And that is why, of course, it is so easy for Italians to make many of these little tastes. Anyone can buy bread or bread dough from the neighborhood baker and turn it into one of hundreds of breads and *spuntini* and *merende* that feed the soul as well as the body. We can do the same.

The breads in this chapter include a simple dough that can be transformed into many local specialties, a fantastic whole-wheat bread from a very young baker I discovered outside of Rome, and several flavored breads that are delicious by themselves but also make extraordinary bases for a whole range of *spuntini e merende*.

Many of the basic forms of such *merende* turn up in different regions with different names. No matter where I went, I kept discovering that every region has a different word for the test piece of bread dough thrust into the oven to see if the temperature is hot enough. In some places this treat is known as the baker's *merenda*—who better to get the first taste of the fruits of his labors?—and elsewhere it is considered a reward for children when bread is being baked at home. In the region of Le Marche it is known as *cacciannanze* and is essentially pizza bianca. The baker adds oil to risen bread dough, spreads it out like a pizza or focaccia, pleats the edges to make a low border, dimples it, sprinkles salt on top, drizzles a thread of oil over it, and slides it into the oven before any breads go in. With little pieces of tomato on top, it becomes *spianata*. In Puglia this basic snack is called *cice*, but the bread dough is rolled like grissini or flattened like schiacciata, and it is cooked to a crunchy finish. That same long thin breadstick is fried and called *sgabei* in Liguria and *panzanelle* in Tuscany, where it is sprinkled with salt and slit open to make room for a bit of salame or stracchino cheese that melts in the heat of the steamy interior.

These tasty treats are sometimes sprinkled with sugar instead of salt and given an entirely different incarnation—with new names, of course. I was once at Regaleali, the great wine-producing estate in the interior of Sicily, watching the two women who have been making bread there for decades. When all the loaves had been shaped, some dough was left over, so they fried it in small rounds in very little oil, sprinkled it with sugar, and ate it hot out of the pan, without draining it even briefly on a paper towel. Ambrosial! The rest of the dough went up the hill to the celebrated chef at the great house. He rolled it out into a very thin layer, put a piece the size of a dinner plate in hot oil, and we watched it puff up into a giant pillow that sent out legs like a huge stingray. He turned it over, time and again, and finished this thin crunchy treat with a spritzing of sea salt. These two *merende* began with the same bread dough and were both fried, but the similarity ends there: they were treated differently and tasted different, although they were both called *cuddurone*.

ABOUT PREPARING DOUGHS

All the recipes in this book are written for active dry yeast. If you prefer to use fresh cake yeast, use slightly cooler water (95° to 105°F) and calculate that 1 package of dry yeast (2½ teaspoons, 7 grams) is equal to 1 small cake of fresh yeast (18 grams).

Since everyone measures flour differently—some people scoop while others spoon it delicately into measuring cups, some start with densely packed flour still in the bag, others pour it into a big bowl and scoop it from there—I strongly recommend measuring by weight so nothing is left to chance. Variations of as much as ½ cup of flour can occur, and they will produce radically different breads.

The same instructions apply to the *biga*, or starter, since it grows as it sits at room temperature. If you are using cup measures, please measure the biga as soon as you take it out of the refrigerator; otherwise weigh it at room temperature.

Some of these doughs are not for beginners—they are very wet. They really work, although your eyes and fingers may say otherwise the first time you try them. Just remember to have a bowl of water nearby for your hands (sticky doughs don't stick to wet hands), flour on your work surface, and courage. If you make them by hand, whisk in the first cup of flour to prevent lumps from forming. If you make them in a heavy-duty mixer, always use the paddle attachment to mix the dough and the dough hook to knead it. Please do not punch the dough down after the first rise unless specifically instructed. Parchment paper is a baker's best friend. You can let dough rise directly on floured parchment paper set on baking sheets or pizza peels and then place the dough, still on the paper, in the oven. Just be certain not to let any paper overhang the baking stones or it will burn, and instead of the lovely smell of baking bread, your house will be permeated by an acrid scent. If you wish, you can remove the parchment paper after about 15 or 20 minutes, when the wet doughs have set.

BAKING TERMS

Some of the terms used in this chapter may be unfamiliar to you.

A *sponge* is simply a small bit of bread dough that is prepared a short time before the true dough to give the entire dough a little boost. Yeast is dissolved in a small amount of water, and flour is beaten in to make a soft batter. In some cases eggs, milk, and/or sugar may be added. The bowl is covered with plastic wrap and the sponge is allowed to ferment and froth for anywhere from a matter of minutes to an hour or two. The sponge gives a head start to the true dough, which is made with more water, flour, and perhaps even a bit more yeast.

A *biga* is a starter dough prepared anywhere from 6 to 24 hours before you plan to bake. It is made simply of flour, water, and a small amount of yeast, and permits an initial fermentation that flavors the consequent bread dough. In Italy it gives strength to their weak flours, but it also produces the secondary fermentation that imparts rich, complex flavors and irresistible fragrances to the myriad wheels and loaves of country breads.

Italian bakers use a bit of dough saved from the previous day's bake for their biga, but home bakers can't rely on such a steady source of supply to start a new dough. Instead, you can make your own biga by dissolving a minuscule amount of yeast in water, then beating in flour to make a soft batter; covered and left to rise, it will start bubbling madly and tripling in bulk as the yeasts expand and feed happily on the sugars in the flour. Once the sugars are absorbed, the biga will collapse a bit, but that is normal. The biga is ready to be used in bread recipes anywhere from 6 to 24 hours after you've made it, but it may be kept in the refrigerator for about 5 days after that, becoming sourer and tangier as it ages. If you like sourdough bread, use a biga that has aged for 2 or 3 days. You can freeze the biga; it will come back to life in a mere 3 hours at room temperature, bubbling actively and ready for use. Because breads made with a biga use so little yeast, they stay fresh longer than loaves with large amounts of commercial yeast. The relatively long rises of doughs made with a biga accentuate the taste of the grain, resulting in breads with wonderful rich flavors and more complicated structures and textures.

USING A FOOD PROCESSOR

Not all the doughs in this book can be made by food processor; some are just too wet for the machine. I have indicated on the individual recipes where you can use a processor. Here, for those breads, is the procedure: Stir the yeast into the warm water as in all recipes. Set the flour and salt in a food processor outfitted with the steel blade. Pulse several times to aerate the mixture. In a container with a spout, mix together the yeast, the water (which must be *cold* for the processor), the cold biga, and any other liquid, such as olive oil or eggs. With the motor running, pour the mixture down the feed tube as quickly as the flour can absorb it, until the dough gathers into a ball. Then you may either process the dough for 45 seconds longer and finally knead it briefly on a lightly floured work surface, or you may take the dough out of the bowl immediately and do all the kneading on the floured work surface.

Biga Pugliese

BREAD STARTER FROM PUGLIA

This is a biga that I discovered in Puglia. It makes a fabulous dough. Just mix it and leave it to rise in the same bowl.

½ teaspoon active dry yeast
¼ cup warm water (105° to 115°F)
1½ cups water, room temperature
3¾ cups (500 grams) unbleached
all-purpose flour

Stir the yeast into the warm water in a medium-size or large mixer bowl and let stand until creamy, about 10 minutes. Stir in the remaining water and then the flour, 1 cup at a time, and mix by hand with a wooden spoon for 3 to 4 minutes or with the paddle of a heavy-duty mixer for 2 minutes. Leave the biga in the mixing bowl; or if you need that bowl, wet your hands and transfer it to an oiled bowl. Cover it with plastic wrap and let it rise at cool room temperature for anywhere between 6 and 24 hours. The starter will triple in volume and then collapse a bit. The biga will still be wet and sticky when it is ready. Cover and refrigerate until ready to use.

To use the biga, scoop out the needed amount. It is best to weigh the starter, but if you don't have a scale, measure it into cups and teaspoons while it is still cold and hasn't begun to grow and expand at room temperature.

MAKES ABOUT 3½ CUPS (ABOUT 750 GRAMS)

Biga di Grano Duro

DURUM FLOUR BIGA

Be sure that you use golden durum flour, not durum integrale, which contains the whole husk of the wheat berry and is not right for this recipe.

½ teaspoon active dry yeast
¼ cup warm water (105° to 115°F)
1 cup plus 2 tablespoons water, room temperature
2¼ cups plus 2 tablespoons (335 grams) durum flour

Stir the yeast into the warm water in a medium-size or large mixer bowl and leave until creamy, about 10 minutes. Add the rest of the water and the durum flour, 1 cup at a time, and mix vigorously by hand with a wooden spoon for 6 minutes or in a heavy-duty mixer with the paddle attachment for 3 minutes. The mixture will clear the sides of the bowl but will remain soft and sticky. Cover with plastic wrap and leave to rise at room temperature for 24 hours. The starter will triple in volume and then collapse a bit. It will still be wet and sticky when it is ready. Cover and refrigerate until ready to use.

To use the biga, scoop out the needed amount. It is best to weigh the starter, but if you don't have a scale, measure it into cups and teaspoons while it is still cold and hasn't begun to grow and expand at room temperature.

MAKES 2½ CUPS

Casareccio

RUSTIC WHOLE-WHEAT BREAD

Valentino, a young man of twenty, his mother, and his two aunts produce wheels of a wonderfully aromatic whole-wheat country bread with a crunchy crust and porous interior. They bake five times a day, seven days a week, in the countryside outside Rome, thrusting all their loaves into a wood-burning oven stoked by armloads of chestnut wood. This is my interpretation of their casareccio dough, which can be flavored with toasted walnuts, pistachios, olives, sweet peppers, or sautéed onions. It is a wonderful bread without any additional ingredients, and it also makes an excellent pizza bianca drizzled with extra-virgin olive oil and sprinkled with crystals of sea salt.

You will need to use a heavy-duty mixer to make this wet dough. Be sure to keep a bowl of water nearby and to dip your hands in it before kneading or shaping the dough; wet dough does not stick to wet hands.

1 teaspoon active dry yeast

¼ cup warm water (105° to 115°F)

3½ cups water, room temperature

⅘ cup (200 grams) Biga Pugliese (page 212), made with 2 tablespoons less water

3¾ cups (500 grams) whole-wheat flour

3¾ cups (500 grams) unbleached all-purpose flour

1 tablespoon plus 1 teaspoon sea salt

⅓ pound walnuts, toasted and roughly chopped; or ½ cup shelled pistachio nuts; or ⅓ cup pitted Italian black olives (all optional)

Stir the yeast into the warm water in the large bowl of a heavy-duty mixer; let it stand until creamy, about 10 minutes.

Add the remaining water and the biga, then the flours and the salt, and mix with the paddle for 5 minutes. The dough will not pull away from the sides of the bowl. Change to the dough hook, and knead at medium speed for 7 minutes. The dough will be soft and elastic, but it still will not pull away from the sides of the bowl. You can pour the sticky dough directly into an oiled bowl for the first rise, but although it is very moist, it will come together nicely when kneaded on a lightly floured work surface. Sprinkle a little flour over it and knead the dough briefly, using a dough scraper and wet or well-floured hands at the beginning.

First rise. Place the dough in a large lightly oiled bowl, cover it tightly with plastic wrap, and let rise until almost tripled, about 3 to 5 hours. This dough rises very well overnight or for as long as 24 hours in the refrigerator. Let it come back to room temperature before shaping.

Filling, shaping, and second rise. Flour your work surface well, flour a dough scraper, and keep a mound of flour or a small bowl of water nearby for your hands. Pour the bubbly dough out of the bowl, but do not punch it down, lightly flour the top, and divide it into two or three equal pieces. Work in the nuts or olives, if you are using them, by flattening the dough and sprinkling equal amounts of filling over each piece. Then turn in the sides of the dough and roll each into a ball, being gentle but at the same time pulling the skin taut. Turn the dough 90 degrees, pat it flat, and roll it up again. If you are not using a filling, simply roll the dough as directed into a ball.

Place the loaves on floured parchment paper set on baking sheets or peels, cover with a heavy towel or cloth, and let rise until doubled, about 1 hour.

Baking. Thirty minutes before baking, preheat the oven to 450°F with baking stones in it. Just before baking, sprinkle the stones with cornmeal. You can turn the doughs over directly onto the stones, leaving the parchment paper in place (on top of the loaves) for about 15 minutes, when the doughs will have set and the paper will be easy to remove. Or you can slide the loaves, on the paper, onto the baking stones or leave them on baking sheets without turning them over. Bake until golden and crusty, about 30 to 35 minutes.

MAKES 2 LARGE OR 3 SMALLER ROUND LOAVES

Friselle

RING-SHAPED CRISPS

Friselle are ring-shaped rolls that are cut in half midway through the cooking and returned to the oven to become really crunchy. When I offered some to a boy in my neighborhood, he took a handful and said, "Great! Bagel chips!"—a perfect description of what they look like.

Even though it sounds strange, their delicious taste and lovely texture are the result of boiling the dough briefly before baking. I learned the secret from Antonio Marella, who collects and, with his wife, makes some of the best products of Puglia. Friselle are made with either whole-wheat or durum flour and come in sizes that range from little rings to rolls as large as a dinner plate. The sticky dough is best left to a heavy-duty mixer, although it is not impossible to make by hand.

Use friselle for bruschetta: Soften them with water, rub with a mashed garlic clove, brush with extra-virgin olive oil, rub with really juicy ripe tomatoes, and sprinkle with salt, pepper, and finely chopped fresh oregano. This dough also makes a great pizza, which you can top with those very same ingredients.

1¼ teaspoons active dry yeast

1¾ cups warm water (105° to 115°F)

⅔ cup plus 2 teaspoons (175 grams) Biga Pugliese (page 212) or Durum Flour Biga (page 213) measured cold

3¾ cups (500 grams) durum flour or whole-wheat flour

2½ teaspoons sea salt

Stir the yeast into ½ cup of the warm water in a large mixer bowl, and let it stand until creamy, 5 to 10 minutes. Stir in the biga and the remainder of the water and with the paddle attachment of a heavy-duty mixer, mix until the starter is broken up. Add the flour and salt and mix for 3 to 4 minutes, until the dough comes together well. You may need to add more water to ensure that the dough is soft and does not come away from the bottom of the bowl. Switch to the dough hook and knead at medium speed, 3 to 4 minutes for whole-wheat flour, 5 minutes for durum. The durum dough will be wet and the whole-wheat will be sticky, but when you knead them on a very lightly floured board, both doughs will come together without sticking.

First rise. Set the dough in an oiled bowl, cover tightly with plastic wrap, and let rise until doubled, 1¼ to 1½ hours.

Shaping and second rise. Divide the dough into ten pieces. Shape each one into a cylinder 8 inches long and as fat as a thumb by rolling it on a lightly floured work surface with the palms of your hands. The dough will be very springy and elastic. As you roll each out, cover the others to allow them some time to relax and recover. Set the rolls on an oiled or parchment-lined baking sheet and connect the ends, forming rings about 4 inches in diameter. Pat the tops so they are level, cover with a towel, and leave to rise until very puffy and doubled, about 1 hour.

Cooking and baking. Preheat the oven to 400°F. Bring a large pot of water to a boil.

Leave the friselle on the parchment paper—simply cut the paper into little individual squares, one friselle to a square—and put them right into the boiling water, 2 to 3 at a time. Turn them over to submerge both sides, but leave them for only 1 to 2 minutes in all. The parchment paper will come off easily. Remove the friselle carefully with a large slotted spoon—they stretch easily—and drain on paper towels.

Set the friselle on oiled or parchment-lined baking sheets and bake for 20 minutes, until golden and toasty. Remove from the oven, let cool slightly, and then cut them in half horizontally, using a serrated knife. Set them cut side up on the baking sheets.

Turn the heat down to 350°F and return the friselle to the oven for 15 minutes, until crisp and crunchy.

MAKES 20

Puccia

OLIVE-STUDDED ROLLS

These popular olive-studded rolls were once made of coarse whole wheat, but these days bakers are more likely to use golden durum flour. Just be prepared for a sticky dough that can be made only in a heavy-duty electric mixer. Despite any initial misgivings you may have about this dough, the recipe really works, although it is not for beginners. Just take these precautions: Sprinkle your work surface with flour, and keep a bowl of water nearby so you can moisten your hands to prevent them from sticking to the dough. Persevere. The rolls are worth it.

Puccia come in a variety of sizes ranging from small 2-ounce rolls to giants that weigh in at a bit less than a pound. Some people make little sandwiches of them filling them with marinated fish.

1¼ teaspoons active dry yeast
⅓ cup warm water (105° to 115°F)
3 cups water, room temperature
1 cup plus 3 tablespoons (300 grams) Biga Pugliese (page 212)
About 5½ to 5¾ cups (760 grams) unbleached all-purpose flour
1 cup (140 grams) whole-wheat flour
1 heaping tablespoon sea salt
4⅓ ounces small meaty black olives in water or brine, pitted
Cornmeal

Stir the yeast into the warm water in the large bowl of a heavy-duty mixer. Let it stand until creamy, about 10 minutes. Add the remaining water and the biga and mix with the paddle until well blended. Add the flours and salt and mix until the dough comes together, 1 to 2 minutes, although it will not come away from the sides of the bowl. Change to the dough hook and knead at medium speed for 3 to 4 minutes. The dough will be very silky, soft, and elastic, and it will definitely stick to your hands. Kneading it on a lightly floured board until it comes together will eliminate the stickiness. You may knead the olives in the mixer during the last 2 minutes of the kneading, but it is preferable to knead them in by hand so they stay whole.

First rise. Set the dough in a lightly oiled bowl, cover it tightly with plastic wrap, and leave to rise until tripled, 3 to 4 hours.

Shaping and second rise. Pour the wet and oozy dough out of the bowl onto a floured work surface. Do not punch it down. Flour the top and divide it into 12 or 16 pieces. Have a bowl of water nearby for your hands. Flatten each piece and roll it up lengthwise, using your fingers as a guide for the tightness of the rolls. Turn the pieces 90 degrees, pat them flat, and roll them up again. Shape each piece into a ball. Set the rolls on floured parchment paper on baking sheets or on floured baking peels. Toss a light hailstorm of flour over the tops, cover with a heavy cloth, and leave until doubled, about 1 to 1½ hours.

Baking. Thirty minutes before baking, heat the oven with the baking stones in it to 425°F. If you bake the rolls directly on the stones, sprinkle the stones with cornmeal just before setting them in the oven. Bake the rolls until the crusts are golden, about 25 to 30 minutes.

VARIATIONS

Puccia di Grano Duro Substitute 7½ cups (1 kilogram) durum flour for the whole-wheat and all-purpose flours, and knead the dough an extra 2 minutes.

Puccia di Uva Passa Sometimes raisins are substituted for the olives. Soften them in warm water for 30 minutes before adding them to the dough.

Pizzi You can use this dough to make rolls called *pizzi* by adding ¼ to ⅜ teaspoon hot pepper flakes to the vegetables of Cucuzzara (page 220) and folding them into the dough in place of the olives.

MAKES 12 LARGE OR 16 SMALL ROLLS

Cucuzzara

SQUASH BREAD LACED WITH TOMATOES, ONIONS, AND SWEET PEPPERS

This golden-colored squash bread is made in Lecce and in the small villages of the Salentine peninsula of Puglia, the southeastern end of Italy and the true heel of the boot. It is laced with tomatoes, onions, and sweet peppers, as if someone had gone into the garden in the autumn, picked the best of its crops, and simply thrust them into the bread dough. I've seen cucuzzara shaped in round loaves, long thin breads, or made as many little rolls. Use it for crostini or the bruschetta of Puglia; try it topped with cheese and grilled; serve it warm with soup, salad, or with cold roast meats. In some places bakers sprinkle in a large pinch of hot pepper flakes to give the bread a real bite.

This bread keeps well for several days. To freeze a loaf, simply wrap it tightly in aluminum foil, place it in a tightly closed self-sealing plastic bag, and set it in the freezer. Don't let it thaw; just set it in a preheated 350°F oven for about 30 minutes, and it will be ready to serve.

¾ cup olive oil

1 medium-size onion about ½ pound, cut in the thinnest possible slices

⅔ pound butternut squash or pumpkin, about 2 cups, peeled, seeded, and cut in large dice

1 sweet red pepper, roasted, ribs and seeds removed, cut into 1-inch strips

4 ounces full-flavored tomatoes, peeled, seeded, and diced

1½ teaspoons active dry yeast

1½ cups plus 3 tablespoons warm water (105° to 115°F)

⅘ cup (200 grams) Durum Flour Biga (page 213)

7 to 7¼ cups (1 kilogram) durum flour

1 tablespoon plus 2 teaspoons sea salt

Red pepper flakes (optional)

About 1 hour before you are ready to make the bread, warm ¼ cup of the olive oil in a skillet and sauté the onions over medium-low heat until they are soft but still slightly crunchy, about 15 minutes. Add the squash and pepper, cover, and cook for 20 minutes longer. Add the tomatoes and cook another 3 to 5 minutes. Cool.

Stir the yeast into ½ cup of the warm water in the bowl of a heavy-duty mixer. Leave until creamy, about 10 minutes. Add the biga and the remaining warm water and squeeze it through with your fingers or mix well with the paddle of the mixer. Add the remaining ½ cup olive oil and mix well. Stir in the cooked vegetables. Add the flour and salt slowly, mixing until the dough comes together, although it will not clear the sides of the bowl. Change to the dough hook and knead at medium speed until the dough is firm, velvety, and elastic, about 3 to 4 minutes. If it climbs up the collar of the dough hook, just stop the machine and push it down into the bowl.

First rise. Place the dough in an oiled bowl, cover with plastic wrap, and let rise for about 3 hours, or until doubled.

Shaping and second rise. The dough will be velvety and elastic. Divide it into four equal pieces, and shape them into long cylinders, rounds, or 16 small rolls. Place them on peels sprinkled with flour or on baking sheets lined with parchment, cover well, and leave to rise until well doubled, 1 hour.

Baking. Thirty minutes before baking, preheat the oven to 400°F with the baking stones in it. If you like, sprinkle the tops of the loaves with a light veiling of flour. Sprinkle the stones with cornmeal just before sliding the cucuzzara into the oven. Bake the breads for 35 to 45 minutes, the rolls for 18 to 20 minutes, until golden.

MAKES 4 LOAVES OR 16 ROLLS

Pane coi Ciccioli e Pepe Nero

BREAD WITH CRACKLINGS AND BLACK PEPPER

While the dough is rising, cook the cracklings or pancetta. If you are using cracklings, slice the pork fatback into small pieces. Set in a small saucepan, cover with cold water, and cook slowly over medium-low heat until the fat is completely rendered. Remove the crisply golden cracklings with a slotted spoon and drain on paper towels. Turn up the heat under the saucepan and boil until the water has evaporated. Save 3 tablespoons of the fat. Allow the cracklings to cool.

If you are using pancetta, heat the olive oil in a small heavy skillet. Sauté the pancetta over medium-high heat until it is crunchy and crisp, about 10 minutes. Cool. Reserve the pan drippings.

1 recipe Pizza Dough (page 125) made
    with 2 tablespoons olive oil,
    prepared through the first rise
2 pounds pork fatback, or 1 tablespoon
    olive oil and ½ cup, about 3 ounces,
    diced pancetta
1¼ teaspoons coarsely ground pepper
1 tablespoon olive oil
Cornmeal

Shaping and second rise. Set the soft, velvety dough on a lightly floured work surface and flatten it out. Scatter the cracklings and the reserved fat, or the pancetta and its drippings, over the surface, leaving a 1-inch margin around the edges. Grind the pepper over the dough and pat all the flavorings into it. Tuck in all the edges and roll the dough up to form an 18-inch-long log. Set the dough on a lightly oiled baking sheet, connect the ends to form a ring, and pinch them together well to seal. Cover with a towel and let rise until doubled, about 1 to 1¼ hours.

Baking. Preheat the oven to 425°F. If you are using a baking stone, preheat it for 30 minutes. Just before you slide the loaf into the oven, sprinkle the stone with cornmeal. Brush the top of the dough with olive oil and set it directly on the stone if you are using one. Bake for 15 minutes, reduce the heat to 375°F, and continue baking until the top is golden and a tap on the bottom of the ring produces the characteristic hollow sound confirming that the loaf is cooked, about 20 to 25 minutes.

Note: This dough can be prepared in a food processor. See page 211 for instructions.

MAKES 1 LOAF

Pizza di San Lorenzo in Campo

CHEESE BREAD FROM LE MARCHE

This bread, so rich with the flavor of cheese, is the *merenda* that sustains workers in the fields of the Marches as they busily thresh grain under the hot summer sun. It is similar to many glorious celebratory Easter breads that rise high above the rims of their baking forms, but with one very significant difference: those brioche-like breads are made with butter, while this one uses only olive oil.

4¾ teaspoons active dry yeast

6 tablespoons warm water (105° to 115°F)

4 eggs, warm room temperature, beaten

3 egg yolks, warm room temperature, beaten

¾ cup plus 2 tablespoons olive oil

3¾ cups (500 grams) unbleached all-purpose flour

2 teaspoons sea salt

5 ounces freshly grated Parmigiano-Reggiano cheese

1¾ ounces freshly grated pecorino romano cheese

GLAZE

1 egg, beaten

Stir the yeast into the water in a large mixing bowl; let stand until creamy, about 10 minutes. Stir in the eggs, egg yolks, and the oil by hand or with the paddle attachment of a heavy-duty mixer. Add the flour and salt, and mix until the dough comes together, about 2 minutes. If you are making the dough by hand, turn it out onto a lightly floured work surface and knead in the cheeses for 8 minutes, adding them in ½-cup portions and letting the dough rest briefly at the halfway point.

If you are using a heavy-duty mixer, change to the dough hook and knead at medium speed for 3 to 4 minutes, until the dough is velvety, golden, and rich. Sprinkle in about ½ cup of the grated cheese, 1 tablespoon at a time, while the mixer is running. Then set the dough on a lightly floured work surface and gradually knead in most of the remaining cheese. Let the dough rest, covered by a towel, for about 10 minutes, then knead in the final sprinkles of cheese. The dough should be soft but elastic.

First rise. Place the dough in a lightly oiled bowl, cover with plastic wrap, and let rise until doubled, about 2½ hours.

Shaping and second rise. Turn the dough out onto a lightly floured surface and cut it in half. Shape each half into a tight ball and let rest under a towel for 10 minutes. Then place the two rounds, seam side down, in well-oiled 1-quart charlotte molds, soufflé dishes, or even coffee cans lined with parchment paper circles on the bottom. The taller and narrower the form, the more dramatic the bread will be as it domes up in the baking. The dough should fill the container about halfway. Cover with plastic wrap held by a rubber band and let rise to the top of the containers, anywhere from 2½ to 4 hours.

Baking. Preheat the oven to 425°F. If you are using baking stones, preheat them in the oven for 30 minutes. Brush the tops of the dough with the beaten egg, and bake until the loaves are a deep chestnut color, about 40 to 45 minutes. Let the breads cool for 15 minutes, then unmold and cool on racks.

MAKES 2 LOAVES

Roschette

CRISPY SAVORY RINGS

These crisp little rings come from the Sephardic Jewish community in Livorno, the last place in Italy where they are still made. They are reminiscent of taralli (page 228) in taste and shape, but their texture is different.

1½ teaspoons active dry yeast
¾ cup water (105° to 115°F)
½ cup plus 2 tablespoons olive oil
3¾ cups (500 grams) unbleached
    all-purpose flour
1½ teaspoons sea salt
1 egg beaten with 2 tablespoons
    water

Stir the yeast into the warm water and leave until creamy, about 10 minutes. Stir in the olive oil.

Set the flour and salt in a mixing bowl, and work in the yeast mixture until the dough comes together and feels firm and rough. If you are preparing the dough by hand, knead it vigorously for 10 minutes on a lightly floured surface, until it is velvety and smooth. If you are using a heavy-duty mixer, knead with the dough hook for 3 minutes at low speed, until the dough is velvety and slightly rough; then knead it by hand for 1 minute on a lightly floured board, and it will become smooth.

First rise. Set the dough in a lightly oiled bowl, cover tightly with plastic wrap, and leave to rise until doubled, about 2 to 2¼ hours.

Shaping and second rise. Take walnut-size pieces of dough, flatten them, and fold them in thirds like a business letter, pressing down firmly. Roll each out into a log 6 inches long. Bring the ends together, and press them firmly to seal well. They will look like little wreaths. Don't worry if you have to press them very hard; the dough recovers nicely. Set the rings on oiled or parchment-lined baking sheets, cover with a towel, and leave to rise until well puffed, about 45 minutes.

Baking. Preheat the oven to 350°F. If you are using baking stones, preheat them for 30 minutes. Just before baking, brush the roschetti with the egg glaze. Bake them for 20 to 25 minutes.

Note: This dough can be prepared in a food processor. See page 211 for instructions.

MAKES ABOUT 22

Taralli Scaldati col Finocchio

TARALLI WITH FENNEL SEEDS

*E*verywhere you go in Puglia and Campania, you will find people eating little ring-shaped *taralli*, a delicious snack food similar to pretzels. No outer sprinkles of salt dapple the taralli, however, for the flavor of fennel seeds or peppercorns is incorporated right in the dough. The secret of their crumbly texture is a brief plunge into boiling water, just long enough for the dough to sink to the bottom and rise to the top again, before baking. If you decide simply to bake the taralli without boiling (they are delicious that way, too), leave them in the oven for 30 to 35 minutes, then lower the temperature to 225°F and bake for 1 hour until golden crisp. The long cooking time dries them out until they are really crisp. That's why they last for a long time in a well-sealed tin, perfect for snacks or little bites to enjoy with a glass of wine or beer. The peppery Pugliese variety, called *asciuga-bocca* (parch the mouth), are always accompanied by a glass of wine.

2½ teaspoons (1 package) active dry yeast

1 cup dry white wine, warmed to 105° to 115°F

½ cup olive oil

3¾ cups (500 grams) unbleached all-purpose flour

1 teaspoon sea salt

1½ teaspoons fennel seeds, or 2 teaspoons cracked black pepper

*S*tir the yeast into the warmed wine in a large bowl, and let it stand until creamy, about 10 minutes. Stir in the olive oil and then add the flour, salt, and fennel or pepper, and mix until the dough comes together. If you are working by hand, knead the dough on an unfloured surface (the amount of oil prevents it from sticking) for 5 to 7 minutes, until it is smooth and responsive. If you are using a heavy-duty mixer, knead with the dough hook for 3 minutes on low speed; finish by kneading briefly by hand, until the dough is smooth and responsive.

First rise. Set the dough in a lightly oiled bowl, cover it tightly with plastic wrap, and leave until puffy but not doubled, about 1 to 1¼ hours.

Shaping and second rise. Break off a piece of dough the size of a lime, and roll it between your palms and fingers to form a rope 18 inches long and as thin as a breadstick. Let the first ropes rest while you roll out the remainder (about 12 in all). Cut each piece into 6-inch lengths, and connect their ends to form rings about 2 inches in diameter. Press the ends together very firmly; don't worry if you need to pinch tightly where the ends join, because the dough has great recuperative powers. Set the rings on oiled or parchment paper–lined baking sheets, cover with a tea towel, and let rise again for 1 hour.

Boiling and baking. While the rings are rising, preheat the oven to 350°F and bring a big pot of water to a boil. When they are fully risen, plunge the taralli into the boiling water, a few at a time, immersing them only until they bob to the surface, a matter of several seconds. Remove them with a slotted spoon, and drain on absorbent paper towels. Let them cool slightly. Bake on oiled or parchment paper–lined baking sheets for about 20 to 24 minutes, until crunchy.

MAKES 30 TO 36

Brioche Rustica

NEAPOLITAN CHEESE AND SALAME BREAD

A *merenda* is often merely a slice of cheese or salame eaten with a slice of bread, but wily Neapolitans bake all the ingredients right into a single dough.

SPONGE

2½ teaspoons (1 package) active
    dry yeast
1 teaspoon sugar
½ cup milk, warmed to 105° to
    115°F
½ cup (70 grams) unbleached all-
    purpose flour

DOUGH

Approximately 3 medium-size
    boiling potatoes, slightly more
    than 8 ounces, peeled
4 large eggs, room temperature
1½ teaspoons sea salt
3 cups and 2 teaspoons (430
    grams) unbleached all-purpose
    flour
4 tablespoons unsalted butter,
    room temperature
½ cup freshly grated Parmigiano-
    Reggiano cheese
2 ounces salame, finely chopped
2 ounces piquant provolone
    cheese, diced
Freshly grated pepper

GLAZE

1 egg, beaten

Bring a pot of water to a boil and boil the potatoes until tender, about 10 minutes. Drain, and set them aside to use while still warm but not hot.

While the potatoes are boiling, prepare the sponge: Stir the yeast and sugar into the warm milk in a large bowl and leave until foamy, about 10 minutes. Whisk in the flour to make a soft dough. Cover and leave until doubled in volume, about 15 minutes.

As soon as the potatoes are no longer hot, mash them until no lumps remain.

First rise. Beat the eggs and salt together and add to the sponge. With a wooden spoon or the paddle attachment of a heavy-duty mixer, mix in the flour and potatoes. Add the butter, then the Parmesan, salame, provolone, and pepper. Knead the dough by hand on a floured work surface for 7 to 9 minutes or with the dough hook in a heavy-duty electric mixer for 2 minutes on low and then 3 minutes on medium speed, until it is firm, responsive, and slightly sticky. Set in an oiled bowl, cover tightly with plastic wrap, and leave to rise until well doubled, about 1 to 1¼ hours.

Shaping and second rise. Divide the dough in half and shape each piece into a long roll. Join the ends to make two rings, leaving as large a hole as possible in the center. Set the rings on greased or parchment-lined baking sheets, cover with towels, and let rise until puffy, 1 to 1¼ hours.

Baking. Preheat the oven to 400°F. If you are using baking stones, preheat them for 30 minutes and place the baking sheets directly on the stones. Just before baking, brush the tops of the rings well with the beaten egg. Bake the brioche for 25 minutes, until glossy and golden.

MAKES TWO 10-INCH RINGS

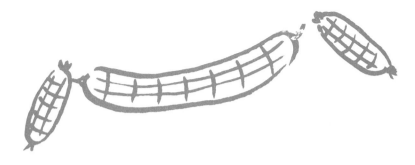

Gnocco Fritto

PUFFY CRISP PILLOWS

W hat do people on the plains of Emilia eat for antipasti, for *merende*, and for irresistible snacks? A crunchy fried diamond of dough that is cut open and served with slices of local prosciutto or coppa. In Parma it is known as *torta fritta*, in Modena *gnocco fritto*, and in Bologna *crescentina fritta*, and everywhere it is delicious.

1¾ teaspoons active dry yeast
¼ cup warm water (105° to 115°F)
3½ tablespoons water, room
   temperature
7½ tablespoons milk, room
   temperature
2 tablespoons unsalted butter, room
   temperature, or best-quality lard
2 cups plus 2 tablespoons (300 grams)
   unbleached all-purpose flour
1 teaspoon sea salt
Vegetable or olive oil for deep-frying

FILLING
⅓ pound thinly sliced prosciutto or
   coppa; ⅓ pound stracchino or
   taleggio cheese; 1 recipe Pistada II
   (page 64); or 1 recipe Emilian Pesto
   (page 63)—untraditional but
   definitely delicious

S tir the yeast into the warm water in a large bowl and leave until creamy, about 10 minutes. Stir in the remaining water, milk, and butter or lard. Add the flour and salt, mixing until the dough comes together. If you are working by hand, knead the dough on a lightly floured work surface until it is smooth and tender, about 8 to 10 minutes. In a heavy-duty electric mixer, knead with the dough hook for 3 minutes.

First rise. Set the dough in a lightly oiled container, cover it well with plastic wrap, and let it rise until doubled, about 1¼ to 1½ hours.

Shaping and second rise. Turn the dough onto a lightly floured work surface, punch it down, and knead it briefly. Roll it out to form a square that is ⅛ inch thick. Use a ravioli cutter to cut out diamond shapes 3½ inches long. Set them on parchment-lined cookie sheets, cover with a towel, and leave for 15 minutes to allow the dough to relax.

Frying. Pour the oil to a depth of 3 inches in a deep heavy pot, and bring to 375°F. Slide in a few pieces of dough at a time, and cook until they are golden, puffy, and crisp at the edges, turning them over once or twice. Drain on a double layer of paper towels.

Just before serving, make a cut in the center of each pillow and fill it with one of the fillings.

Note: This dough can be prepared in a food processor. See page 211 for instructions.

MAKES ABOUT 40

Ficatolle Dolce
SWEET DOUGH DIAMONDS

These sweet treats were childhood favorites for many people, including Gabriele d'Annunzio, who discovered them during his student days in Prato. One crunchy bite and you'll understand why.

1 recipe Pizza Dough made without oil (page 125), prepared through the first rise
6 cups peanut, canola, or olive oil
Sugar or vanilla sugar

On a lightly floured surface, divide the dough into two balls and flatten each into an 8-inch square. Cut the squares into 4-inch diamonds.

Pour the oil into a deep heavy saucepan or Dutch oven and heat it to 350°F. Slide the ficatolle into the oil, two or three at a time, being sure not to overcrowd them. As they puff up and turn golden, 4 to 6 minutes, turn them over. Once they are golden on both sides, remove them with a slotted spoon and set them on a platter lined with paper towels to drain. Roll them in the sugar, and eat while they are still warm.

MAKES 24

Paste Fritte

FRIED AND FLAVORED LEFTOVER BREAD DOUGH

Variations on the theme of leftover bread dough are too numerous to count in a country where bread is revered as part of the cultural patrimony, the birthright of every citizen. When bread dough is left over at home, various flavorings are often kneaded right in. Tiny bits of rosemary or finely chopped sage leaves are particularly nice, as are small cubes of pancetta or ribbons of prosciutto with grindings of pepper sprinkled right into the dough. The dough is rolled into strips and fried into tasty treats.

1 recipe Pizza Dough made
    without oil (page 125), prepared
    through the first rise
3 to 4 tablespoons finely minced
    rosemary or sage or 3 to 4
    tablespoons cubed pancetta or
    prosciutto
6 cups peanut, canola, or olive oil
Sea salt

On a lightly floured surface, flatten the dough, sprinkle the herbs, pancetta, or prosciutto over the top, turn in all the edges, and roll up the dough. Pat it flat and divide into two balls; flatten each with your hand, roll it out to a ¼-inch thickness, then cut it into strips the size of a finger or into 2-inch diamonds. Fry them in hot oil, as for Sgabei (page 235), drain, and sprinkle with sea salt. Eat immediately or at room temperature.
Serve with a glass of wine.

Sgabei

CHEESE-FILLED FRIED DOUGH WANDS

As long as Italians have made bread dough, they have shaped and fried it in a wonderful variety of forms. The sgabei of Liguria and the panzanelle of Tuscany are wand-shaped; elsewhere dough is formed into fat sausages as thick as a finger or rolled into little squares with bite-size anchovies hidden inside.

1 recipe Pizza Dough made without oil (page 125), prepared through the first rise

FILLING
8 ounces stracchino or taleggio cheese; you may have a little left over

FOR FRYING
6 cups (48 fluid ounces) peanut, canola, or olive oil
Sea salt

On a lightly floured surface, divide the dough into two balls and flatten each into a 7-inch-long rectangle. Cut each rectangle into 12 equal pieces and using your palms, roll them into 6-inch-long breadsticks.

Pour the oil into a deep heavy saucepan or Dutch oven, and heat it to 375°F. Slide the sgabei into the oil, two or three at a time, being sure not to overcrowd them. As they puff up and become golden, turn them over. Once they are golden on both sides, remove them with a slotted spoon to a platter lined with paper towels to absorb the excess oil. Sprinkle with sea salt. Using a sharp knife, open a slit down the center and stuff it with about 2 teaspoons of the cheese. Eat while they are still hot and the cheese is melting inside.

VARIATION

Sgabelletti Cut the dough into ½-inch dice and fry as described. Serve in a basket with similar-size chunks of cheese and/or salame.

MAKES ABOUT 24

Streghe

CRUNCHY CRACKERS

In Bologna these crunchy focaccia-like crackers used to be made from bread dough to which a bit of lard had been added. Later they were fried in sheets and set out so people could break off pieces in their fingers. In this version from Margherita Simili, a supreme baker in Bologna, the dough is rolled very thin, cut into diamonds, brushed with oil, and sprinkled with salt. But why are they called *streghe* or witches? Probably because on the day bread was baked, a small piece of the dough was traditionally tossed into the oven before the baking began to exorcise the evil spirits in the fire and to ensure an abundance of delicious loaves. Serve them alone or with prosciutto and a delicate cheese like taleggio.

DOUGH
1 tablespoon active dry yeast
1 cup plus 1 teaspoon warm water
   (105° to 115°F)
1 tablespoon plus 1 teaspoon olive
   oil or best-quality lard
About 3¼ cups (450 grams)
   unbleached all-purpose flour
1 teaspoon sea salt

TOPPING
3 tablespoons olive oil
1½ teaspoons coarse sea salt

Whisk the yeast into the warm water in a large bowl, and leave until creamy, about 10 minutes. Stir in the oil or lard. If you are working by hand, add the flour and salt in two additions, mixing only until the dough comes together, and then knead on a lightly floured surface for about 4 to 6 minutes until firm. The entire process should take no more than 8 to 10 minutes. If you are using a heavy-duty mixer, stir in the flour and salt with the paddle attachment, then change to the dough hook and knead only 1½ to 2 minutes on slow speed. The dough will be firm, velvety, and slightly blistered.

Rise. Set the dough in a lightly oiled bowl, cover with plastic wrap, and let rise until doubled, about 50 minutes to 1 hour.

Shaping. Divide the dough in half, and use a rolling pin to roll each half out on a lightly floured surface to form a 10½- × 15½-inch rectangle. If the dough tears or is stiff, do not worry. It can be rerolled and patched like a quilt, setting the pieces next to each other on the baking sheet. Each half of the dough should fit an oiled 10½- × 15½-inch baking pan; it is essential that the pieces be of uniform thickness so they brown evenly. Brush with the olive oil and sprinkle with the coarse sea salt. Using a serrated ravioli cutter, cut on the diagonal into 1- to 1¼-inch diamonds.

Baking. Preheat the oven to 425°F. If you are using baking stones, preheat them for 30 minutes. Place the baking sheets directly on the stones and bake for 12 to 15 minutes, until the bubbles that surface in the dough are a deep golden and the streghe themselves are lightly golden.

Note: This dough can be prepared in a food processor. See page 211 for instructions.

MAKES ABOUT 48

P i a d i n a

CRISPY FLATBREAD

Piadina is a rustic tortilla-like bread made of a circle of dough that becomes dappled and lightly crunchy as it cooks on a griddle on top of the stove. Piadine were originally made on a *testo*, a thick unglazed terra-cotta stone, in the hot embers of the fireplace, but today even the vendors who cook them at stands throughout rural Romagna use metal griddles to make stacks of the versatile flatbread. The ancestor of focaccia and schiacciata, piadina is the emblematic *merenda* of Romagna, a tender textured unleavened bread that was once so important that Pascoli, the famous nineteenth-century poet, called it *il cibo nazionale dei romagnoli,* the national dish of the people of Romagna.

Legend says that it takes an expert hand to make a piadina, but I find that the dough comes together with ease if you follow the instructions. I learned this variant from Margarita Simili, a *bravissima* baker in Bologna, who uses milk along with the water and substitutes olive oil for lard. The trick is to roll out the circles of dough to less than ⅛ inch, then cook the piadine quickly over a high flame.

The closest way to replicate authentic Romagnoli piadine made on a testo is by using a baking stone that has been soaked overnight in water and allowed to dry. Set a flame deflector over a burner, then place the baking stone on top and turn the heat to a very low flame to prevent the stone from cracking. Gradually increase the temperature until it is at a medium setting in 15 minutes, and cook the piadine on the stone.

Piadine make fabulous sandwiches or antipasti. Fold the piadina in half and fill it with finely sliced prosciutto or coppa, with chard or spinach that has been wilted with garlic in olive oil, or with a delicate buttery cheese like stracchino combined with ribbons of arugula and a thread of extra-virgin olive oil drizzled over the top. You can fold the piadina over the stuffing to make a half-moon-shaped sandwich, or you can put filling between two piadine and serve it cut in wedges. You can also eat it all by itself.

3¾ cups (500 grams) unbleached
     all-purpose flour
1½ teaspoons sea salt
½ teaspoon baking soda
⅓ cup olive oil or best-quality
     lard, melted, warm room
     temperature
½ cup warm milk (105° to 115°F)
½ cup warm water (105° to 115°F)
Olive oil

Mix the flour, salt, and baking soda together in a large bowl. Make a well in the center, and slowly pour in the olive oil or lard, then the warm milk and water. Blend until the dough is a rough shaggy mass, then knead on a lightly floured surface for 4 to 5 minutes until it becomes smooth and velvety. You can either roll out the dough immediately or cover and let it rest for up to 30 minutes.

Divide the dough into 10 to 12 balls the size of limes and roll each out to form a 7- to 8-inch circle.

Heat a cast-iron frying pan or an aluminum griddle over medium-high heat until a drop of water dances and then disappears in seconds. Brush a little olive oil on the pan or griddle and cook the piadine, one at a time, for about 45 to 60 seconds. Check the underside to be sure that it becomes speckled with medium- to dark-brown spots. Pierce the bubbles on top with a fork and turn the piadina over to cook the other side briefly, no more than 1 minute, until the bottom is speckled with slightly paler brown spots.

If you plan to serve the piadine immediately, wrap them in aluminum foil as they are cooked and keep them warm in the oven. Or you can set them aside, tightly wrapped, for several hours and reheat them in a 325°F oven for 10 to 15 minutes.

Note: This dough can be prepared in a food processor. See page 211 for instructions.

MAKES 10 TO 12

Panzanelle Versiliese

FRIED BREAD TWISTS WITH SOPPRESSATA

Panzanelle, from the northern coast of Tuscany just across the Ligurian border, are made with the same dough as sgabei, but they have an entirely different shape and filling. *Soppressata* is a large, round, rather soft salame made of pork; it is almost soft enough to spread. Tuscan babies are frequently fed these panzanelle, and the marble workers of Carrara eat them for a *merenda*, always accompanied with white wine.

1 recipe Pizza Dough made without oil (page 125), prepared through the first rise
6 cups peanut, canola, or olive oil
4 ounces soppressata or soft salame
Salt

Set the dough on a lightly floured surface, and crumble the salame over the top. Divide the dough in half, roll into two balls and pat each ball into a 4-inch square. Cut each square into 12 equal pieces. Using your palms, roll them into 6-inch breadsticks. Twist the breadsticks the opposite way from both ends. It is hard to keep the twists from coming out, but don't worry. Let the dough rest, covered with a towel, for 15 to 20 minutes.

Pour the oil into a deep heavy saucepan or Dutch oven, and heat it to 375°F. Slide the panzanelle into the oil, two or three at a time, being sure not to overcrowd them. As they puff up and turn golden, turn them over. Once they are golden on both sides, remove them with a slotted spoon and set them on a platter lined with paper towels to drain.

MAKES 24

Dolci e Pani Dolci

The Italian sweet tooth exercises itself many times a day, more often between, rather than at, meals. Italians love cookies—they even eat them for breakfast, and they certainly eat them with their midmorning or afternoon cappuccino or espresso, when they can dip them in the warm liquid. I've seen people in cities as far removed as Palermo and Bologna tuck scoops of ice cream inside brioche rolls in midmorning, and I've seen Tuscan villagers pick up *brigidini*, wafer-thin cookies made in a kind of waffle iron and filled with sweetened ricotta, to nibble as they pass through the piazza during the day.

Lucky children come home from school to *dolci al cucchiaio*, creamy desserts eaten with a spoon, or to simple fruit-based desserts. They may eat lightly sweetened breads topped with marmalades made from fruits that have ripened on nearby trees or *ciambelle*, wreath-shaped coffee cakes that have been part of the country tradition for hundreds of years. This is comfort food, Italian style.

Sweet breads are often special to the city where they are made. Certainly the people in Lucca love their *buccellato*, with its raisin and citrus-flavored filling, with an almost mystical passion. They consume quantities of it in thin slices, toasted as if it were a biscotto, or as a cakelike layer heaped high with fruit. Sweet breads may be as refined as the delicate Neapolitan bun served by aristocratic families at midafternoon or as simple as the lightly sweetened bread dough treated like focaccia and strewn

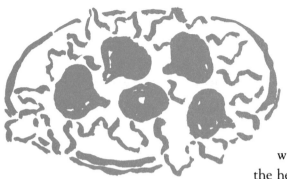

with ripe, juicy figs during the height of their season.

I have included a number of biscotti in this selection. Healthy, portable, and long keeping, they are quintessential *merende*. Since there are several recipes here, I've written one for the food processor, another for the electric mixer, and another for making by hand. Just choose your method and apply it to any of the biscotti recipes.

Biscotti di Nocciole e Mandorle

HAZELNUT AND ALMOND BISCOTTI

Anise, hazelnut, and almonds: a triumvirate of flavors for a crunchy biscotto.

2 cups (280 grams) unbleached
    all-purpose flour
1 cup sugar
Pinch salt
1 teaspoon baking soda
2½ teaspoons anise seeds
3 large eggs, room temperature
½ cup shelled hazelnuts, toasted
½ cup unblanched almonds,
    toasted

Set the dry ingredients in the bowl of a heavy-duty mixer. Add the eggs, and mix with the paddle until the dough comes together. Sprinkle in the nuts in two additions. The dough will be soft and sticky. Knead it briefly on a lightly floured work surface, cover with a tea towel, and leave to rest for 5 minutes.

Preheat the oven to 350°F.

Butter and flour or line with parchment paper two baking sheets that are at least 15 inches long. Divide the dough into three pieces. Roll each piece out on a lightly floured surface to form a 14-inch-long, 2-inch-wide log. Place them at least 3 inches apart on the prepared baking sheets.

Bake the logs for 30 minutes, until light golden. Remove from the oven and let cool until they are comfortable to handle, about 10 minutes. Cut the logs diagonally into ½-inch-thick slices, and lay them, cut side up, on the baking sheets. Return them to the oven and bake for another 7 minutes on each side until golden. Cool on racks.

MAKES ABOUT 48

Biscotti di Greve in Chianti

CLASSIC TUSCAN ORANGE-FLAVORED ALMOND BISCOTTI

Medieval towers, churches, and fortified castles may claim the conical hilltops of Tuscany, but the rolling green hills of Chianti belong to olive groves, cypresses, and to the grapevines that are planted in serried rows across a landscape that still looks like the background in a Renaissance fresco. In springtime the fields are splashed with red poppies and thick rivers of yellow sunflowers course through the flatlands.

Wandering through the little towns of Chianti while nibbling on special farmhouse cheeses and bakery sweets is one of the nicest ways to become acquainted with Tuscany. I have especially wonderful memories of buying these orange-scented almond biscotti at the bakery in Greve in Chianti and eating them on my terrace at the vineyard/hotel called Vignamaggio, not being able to get enough of them or of the view of the undulating green hills. These are a local variation of the classic *biscotti di Prato*.

2 cups (280 grams) unbleached
   all-purpose flour
1 cup sugar
1 teaspoon baking soda
Pinch salt
2 eggs, room temperature
1 egg yolk, room temperature
1 teaspoon vanilla extract
2 teaspoons grated orange zest
1½ cups unblanched almonds,
   toasted

GLAZE
1 egg, beaten with 1 teaspoon
   water

Preheat the oven to 325°F.

Set the flour, sugar, baking soda, and salt in the bowl of a processor outfitted with the steel blade. Pulse several times to mix. In a container with a pouring spout, mix together the eggs, egg yolk, vanilla, and orange zest. With the motor running, pour the mixture down the feed tube. Continue processing only until the dough is a shaggy mass, not yet collected into a ball. Pour half the nuts down the feed tube and pulse several times; repeat with the remaining half.

Transfer the dough to a lightly floured surface, and shape it into two or three logs, each 2 inches wide. Set them at least 3 inches apart on buttered and floured or parchment paper–lined baking sheets. Brush them with the egg wash.

Bake the logs for 25 to 30 minutes, until pale gold. Remove them from the oven and leave until they are cool enough to handle comfortably. Then, using a serrated knife, cut the logs diagonally into ¾-inch-wide pieces. Return the cookies to lightly buttered baking sheets, cut side down, and bake 12 minutes longer on each side until golden. Cool on racks.

MAKES ABOUT 24

Biscotti di Falconara Marittima

BISCOTTI FROM FALCONARA MARITTIMA

*I*t was pure chance that brought these delicate raisin-studded biscotti into my life. I was at a remarkable restaurant in Le Marche, the lovely unspoiled area between Umbria and the Adriatic. Both sophisticated and dedicated to the tastes of the region, such places were rare until recently, when several young men opened hotels with their mothers in charge of the kitchens. One of them, Lamberto Ridolfi, put Villa Amalia on the culinary map (on the geographical map, it's in Falconara Marittima, on the coast near Ancona). Ridolfi named the restaurant for his mother, Amalia Ceccarelli, a natural cook whose own mother cooked for the great families of Urbino. Now she's the chef and Ridolfi's wife, Angela, is the pastry chef. Both women make these exceptional biscotti, which I found sitting unobtrusively on a tiny plate to taste along with the restaurant's special vin santo. I did just that and immediately leapt up to learn the secret of their wonderful flavor and texture.

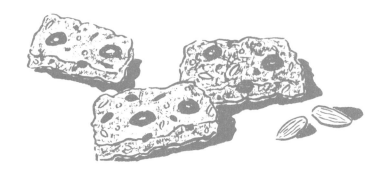

¾ cup raisins

6 tablespoons Cointreau or
    Curaçao

5 eggs

2¼ cups sugar

1 teaspoon vanilla extract

Scant 1½ cups unblanched
    almonds, toasted and roughly
    chopped

About 3¾ cups (500 grams)
    unbleached all-purpose flour

1½ teaspoons baking soda

Pinch salt

Preheat the oven to 350°F.

Soak the raisins in the liqueur for 20 minutes and then drain, reserving the liqueur.

Separate the eggs. Beat the yolks with 2 cups of the sugar until thick and pale; beat in the reserved liqueur and the vanilla. In another bowl, beat the egg whites until they just hold stiff peaks; slowly add the remaining ¼ cup sugar, beating until they hold stiff peaks. Whisk one quarter of the egg whites into the yolk mixture to lighten it, then fold in the remaining whites delicately but thoroughly, and finally fold in the drained raisins and the nuts.

Mix together the flour, baking soda, and salt. Using a rubber spatula fold the flour mixture into the egg mixture in four separate batches. Butter a jelly-roll or half-sheet pan (18 × 13 inches or 17 × 14 inches). Gently spread the dough to cover the prepared pan as evenly as possible.

Bake for 20 to 22 minutes, until pale golden; remove from the oven and let cool until comfortable to handle, about 10 minutes. Ease out of the pan onto a cutting board, and use a serrated knife to cut into 1½-inch strips. Cut the strips into ¾-inch-thick slices. Arrange them on the baking sheets, cut side down, and return them to the oven to bake for another 7 to 8 minutes on each side, until pale golden. Cool on racks.

MAKES 60 to 72

Biscotti di Lagaccio

ANISE-SCENTED BISCOTTI FROM LAGACCIO

Did Columbus and his sailors sail to the New World with these traditional Ligurian biscotti among their provisions? It's entirely possible, although theirs would have been cooked much longer to drive off all the moisture, allowing them to keep for an entire ocean crossing. These biscotti start with enriched bread dough instead of traditional cookie dough and have a somewhat softer texture, although they keep well when stored in an airtight container.

SPONGE

2½ teaspoons (1 package) active
    dry yeast
½ cup warm water (105° to 115°F)
¾ cup (100 grams) unbleached all-
    purpose flour

DOUGH

½ cup sugar
½ cup plus 2 tablespoons water
4 tablespoons unsalted butter,
    room temperature
2 cups plus 1 tablespoon
    (295 grams) unbleached
    all-purpose flour
½ teaspoon sea salt
1 tablespoon anise seeds

Make a sponge, following instructions for combining ingredients on page 280. Stir the sugar, water, and butter into the sponge. Add the flour, 1 cup at a time, salt, and anise seeds, and mix until a dough forms. Knead for about 8 to 10 minutes by hand on a lightly floured work surface or for 3 minutes with the dough hook of an electric mixer, until the dough is soft and smooth but still sticky. Transfer the dough to a lightly oiled bowl, cover it tightly with plastic wrap, and let it rise until doubled, about 1½ hours.

Prepare a baking sheet by lining it with parchment paper or by buttering and flouring it. Divide the dough in half. On a very lightly floured surface, shape each piece into a log about 2 inches wide and 15 inches long. Transfer to the baking sheet, cover with a towel, and let rise until doubled but still a bit sticky, about 2 hours.

Preheat the oven to 350°F.

Bake the logs for about 30 minutes, until golden brown. Cool for about 10 minutes. Cut each log diagonally into 1-inch-thick pieces and return them to the oven, cut side down. Bake for 10 to 15 minutes. Turn the biscotti over and finish cooking for another 10 to 15 minutes or until they are pale golden. Cool on racks.

MAKES ABOUT 24

Marzapane Pugliese

CINNAMON-FLAVORED ALMOND COOKIES

Marzipan, a sweet eaten all over Europe for centuries, was first mentioned in Puglia in 1398. Now, almost six hundred years later, baker Vincenzo Tamburini of Gioia del Colle has worked a delicious twist on the traditional almond paste sweet by flavoring it with lemon and cinnamon. Use a soft almond paste, such as Odense or Blue Diamond brand, to make these cookies. They keep for a long time when sealed tightly in a cookie tin.

1 cup plus 2 tablespoons blanched
　almonds
½ cup sugar
7 ounces soft almond paste
1 large egg white, room
　temperature
½ teaspoon cinnamon
Grated zest of 1 lemon
¾ teaspoon vanilla extract

GLAZE
1 egg white, very lightly beaten

Preheat the oven to 350°F, and toast the almonds for 10 to 15 minutes. Cool to room temperature. Reduce the oven temperature to 300°F.

Using a food processor outfitted with the steel blade, pulse the almonds with ¼ cup of the sugar just until the almonds are in small chunks. Transfer to a heavy-duty mixer bowl and mix in the almond paste with the paddle attachment. Add the remaining ¼ cup sugar and the egg white and mix at the lowest speed until well blended. Add the cinnamon, lemon zest, and vanilla extract and blend well. The mixture will be firm but sticky.

If the dough feels very sticky, flour your work surface lightly and moisten your hands. Set the dough on the work surface and pat it into a rectangle 6 inches wide and about 10 inches long. Cut it crossways into five 2-inch-wide strips. Then cut the strips into bars that are about 1½ inches wide. Neaten the edges. Set the cookies on a greased or parchment paper–lined baking sheet and brush the tops with the lightly beaten egg white.

Bake until very light golden, about 22 to 25 minutes. Cool on racks.

MAKES ABOUT 21

Taralli Dolci ai Fichi

RING-SHAPED
SPICY FIG COOKIES

Spicy fig-filled *taralli*, the Italian equivalent of the best imaginable Fig Newtons, come from Puglia. I added fresh orange zest to the cookie dough; now in a pinch, you can make the little rings without any fig filling at all.

FILLING
1 cup red wine
2 cloves
1 teaspoon cinnamon
¾ teaspoon vanilla extract
9 ounces dried figs, preferably
  Calmyrna, stems removed

DOUGH
3 cups (420 grams) unbleached all-
  purpose flour
½ cup plus 2 teaspoons (80 grams)
  whole-wheat flour
1¼ teaspoons baking powder
¾ teaspoon sea salt
¼ cup plus 2 tablespoons sugar
7 tablespoons olive oil
¾ cup dry white wine
½ teaspoon cinnamon
1½ teaspoons vanilla extract
Grated zest of 1 orange (optional)

GLAZE
1 egg white, beaten

Heat the red wine with the spices and vanilla. Add the figs and simmer until they are very soft and most of the wine has been absorbed, 15 to 20 minutes. Remove the cloves and with the steel blade in place, grind the figs to a paste in a food processor.

Preheat the oven to 350°F.

In a large bowl, sift together the flours, baking powder, salt, and sugar. Pour in the olive oil and white wine, and stir in the cinnamon, vanilla, and orange zest, if you are using it. Mix with a wooden spoon or with the paddle of a heavy-duty mixer until the ingredients are completely incorporated and the dough begins to hold together. Turn the dough onto a lightly floured surface and knead only until smooth. Do not knead too much or the dough will be hard to roll and the taralli will be tough.

Divide both the dough and the filling in half. On a lightly floured board, roll one piece of dough out to form a 16- × 7-inch rectangle with the edges considerably thinner than the center. Turn the dough over so the unfloured side is down. Spoon half of the fig filling evenly in a mound down the center of the dough, leaving the last inch at the ends free of filling. Fold over one side of the dough so it just covers the filling. Moisten the opposite edge with water, and fold that side over to the far edge. Turn the roll seam side down and press lightly to even and flatten it. Trim the ends and press them together to seal. Glaze the top with some of the egg white and prick it with a fork every inch or so. Repeat with the remaining dough and filling.

Bake on parchment-lined baking sheets for about 40 to 45 minutes, until lightly golden. Cool on a rack before cutting into 1-inch bars.

VARIATION

To make taralli without filling, prepare the dough with the orange zest. Pinch off pieces of dough the size of a walnut. Roll each one between your palms to form a 5- to 5½-inch-long rope, and connect the ends to make a ring. Set them on greased or parchment paper–lined baking sheets and brush with the egg white. Bake at 350°F for 20 to 22 minutes, until golden. Makes about 36.

MAKES 24

Amaretti al Caffè

COFFEE-FLAVORED AMARETTI

*I*nspired by irresistible cookies at a caffè bar in Altamura, these coffee-flavored amaretti are chewy and slightly soft inside. I ate a plateful, then bought more to slip into my pocket to nibble on as I went next door to the great medieval cathedral, with its two fierce lions guarding the portals.

7 ounces soft almond paste
1 egg white
1 tablespoon plus 1 teaspoon
  brewed espresso coffee
1 tablespoon ground Italian-roast
  espresso beans

*P*reheat the oven to 300°F.

Place the almond paste in a food processor outfitted with the steel blade, and mix until smooth, about 1 minute. Blend in the egg white, brewed espresso, and ground beans until smooth.

Spoon the mixture into a pastry bag outfitted with a ½-inch tip. Pipe 1½-inch-wide mounds 1½ inches apart on parchment-lined or buttered baking sheets. Bake for 25 to 30 minutes, until lightly browned at the edges. Cool on racks.

VARIATION

Make crunchy amaretti by using only the ground coffee beans.

MAKES 15

Pan dei Vini

SPICY WINE-FLAVORED
CHOCOLATE COOKIES

Here's a wildly enthusiastic endorsement for these deep, rich Venetian cookies that are bursting with spices, crunchy nuts, currants, candied orange peel, and a generous addition of chocolate. Simply blend the ingredients, shape into fat balls, roll them in a coating of pine nuts, and bake for about 20 minutes. Slice, serve, and watch them disappear!

About 1¼ cups (165 grams)
   unbleached all-purpose flour
2 teaspoons baking powder
1¼ teaspoons cinnamon
¾ teaspoon sea salt
1 egg yolk, room temperature
⅓ cup cream Marsala or sweet
   white wine
½ cup currants
½ cup raw almonds, toasted and
   roughly chopped
3 ounces candied orange peel,
   chopped
3½ ounces semisweet baking
   chocolate, in chunks
2 to 3 tablespoons apricot jam

TOPPING
1¼ ounces pine nuts
1 egg, beaten

Preheat the oven to 250°F.

Set the flour, baking powder, cinnamon, and salt in a large mixing bowl. Beat in the egg yolk and sweet wine. Combine the currants, almonds, orange peel, and chocolate in another bowl and add to the flour mixture. Stir in the jam to bind the mixture; then knead on a lightly floured work surface until the dough holds its shape. You may need a little extra flour just to bring it together.

Spread the pine nuts on a dinner plate. Divide the dough into six pieces, and roll each into a ball. Brush them with the beaten egg, and then roll them in the nuts until completely covered. Place them on a buttered and floured or parchment paper–lined baking sheet.

Bake for 12 minutes. Then raise the oven temperature to 400°F and continue baking for 8 minutes, until the tops are slightly glossy and very lightly browned. Cool on a rack, then cut into ¾-inch slices and serve.

MAKES ABOUT 36

Ciambellotto

RAISIN-FILLED WREATH CAKE

No wonder children in Le Marche once looked forward to coming home to their mothers and grandmothers after school: this cake with its plump raisins and its haunting cinnamon flavor was a real reward. People in Le Marche grow nostalgic whenever they talk about it, and everyone who tastes it in this country can hardly wait for seconds. This wreath-shaped cake is wonderful at breakfast, at teatime, and at dessert—try it with a little crème anglaise. It is perfect also for dipping in a glass of vin santo. I sometimes serve it with fresh berries and let the natural juices mingle with the cake.

¾ cup currants
¾ cup raisins
6 tablespoons dark rum
12 tablespoons (1½ sticks) unsalted butter, room temperature
¾ cup sugar
4 egg yolks
2 eggs
Grated zest of 2 lemons
1 teaspoon vanilla extract
3¾ cups (500 grams) unbleached all-purpose flour, or 1 cup (125 grams) cake flour and 2¾ cups (375 grams) unbleached all-purpose flour
½ teaspoon baking soda
½ teaspoon baking power
1 teaspoon cream of tartar
1 teaspoon salt
¾ teaspoon cinnamon

GLAZE
1 egg, beaten
Turbinado sugar

Soak the currants and raisins in 2 tablespoons of the rum for 15 minutes.

Cream the butter and sugar until light and fluffy, beating with a hand mixer or with the paddle attachment of a heavy-duty mixer for 4 to 5 minutes. Beat in the egg yolks and eggs, one by one, being sure each is well incorporated before adding the next. Add the lemon zest, vanilla, and the remaining 4 tablespoons rum.

Sift together the flour, baking soda, baking powder, cream of tartar, salt, and cinnamon. Sift the flour mixture over the egg mixture and fold it in gently with a rubber spatula. Drain the raisins and currants and incorporate them gently in the dough.

Preheat the oven to 375°F.

Set the dough on a work surface sprinkled with flour. Very gently roll the dough into a log shape about 18 inches long and move it to a buttered or parchment paper–lined baking sheet. Connect the two ends of the log to form a wreath shape, pinching them together well to close the ring. Pat the top flat, brush with the beaten egg, and sprinkle with turbinado sugar.

Bake the ciambellotto for about 30 minutes, until the top is lightly golden. Cool on a rack and serve warm or at room temperature.

SERVES 8

Salame Dolce

CHOCOLATE SALAME

This simple chocolate dessert makes everyone happy: it tastes wonderful, requires no cooking, and can be made a day or two ahead. In fact, it only gets better that way. Serve it in thin slices—just like a salame.

1 cup raisins
⅓ cup Marsala
11 tablespoons (1 stick plus 3 tablespoons) unsalted butter, room temperature
½ cup sugar
2½ cups leftover butter cookies, spice cookies, or Marie biscuits, whirled into fine crumbs in a processor
2 tablespoons pine nuts
2 teaspoons apricot jam
2 tablespoons unsweetened cocoa powder

Soak the raisins in the Marsala for 30 minutes; drain, squeezing out any extra moisture. Reserve the Marsala.

Cream the butter and sugar in a mixing bowl until light and fluffy, about 5 minutes by hand or 3 to 4 minutes by mixer at high speed. Add the raisins, cookie crumbs, pine nuts, jam, and cocoa and mix well to form a firm dough. If too dry, add more Marsala, 1 tablespoon at a time.

Roll the dough up in the shape of a salame on a piece of aluminum foil, wrap with plastic wrap or aluminum foil, and refrigerate for at least 3 to 4 hours, until it is well set. It keeps nicely for a week.

SERVES 8 TO 10

Ciambella

WALNUT AND RAISIN COFFEE CAKE

This sublime coffee cake, spiked with a little Marsala or rum, is real comfort food. It is even more delicious accompanied by a glass of wine.

½ cup raisins
6 tablespoons Marsala or rum
10 tablespoons plus 2 teaspoons
    unsalted butter, room temperature
¾ cup sugar
4 large eggs, separated
⅓ cup milk
1½ teaspoons vanilla extract
2 cups plus 2 tablespoons (300 grams)
    unbleached all-purpose flour
¼ teaspoon salt
1 tablespoon baking powder
½ cup plus 1 tablespoon walnuts or
    blanched almonds, toasted and
    roughly chopped
1½ tablespoons turbinado sugar

Soak the raisins in the Marsala or rum for 30 minutes. Drain, reserving the liquid.

Preheat the oven to 350°F.

Cream the butter and sugar together well. Add the egg yolks, one at a time, incorporating each one well before adding the next. Mix together the milk, reserved Marsala or rum, and vanilla. Sift together the flour, salt, and baking powder. Using a rubber spatula, beat the milk mixture into the butter mixture in three additions alternating with the dry ingredients.

Beat the egg whites to stiff peaks. With the rubber spatula, stir one quarter of them into the batter to lighten it, then fold in the rest along with the nuts and raisins.

Turn the batter into a buttered and lightly floured angel food pan or ring mold, sprinkle the top with the turbinado sugar, and bake for about 45 minutes, until the top is golden and a tester comes out clean. If you prefer to use a 9- × 5-inch loaf pan, bake for 1 hour and 10 minutes. Cool the cake in the pan for 5 to 10 minutes, then invert onto a rack, and cool to room temperature.

VARIATION

Ciambella al Anice Use 1 tablespoon anise seeds instead of the raisins and nuts. Substitute Sambuca for the Marsala or rum, or omit it altogether and increase the milk to ½ cup.

SERVES 8

Miascia

BREAD PUDDING WITH FRUIT

Sublime comfort food from Lake Como, this dessert is so delicious that it disappears in a hurry. If grapes aren't available, use more currants. Don't worry if the idea of rosemary sounds strange; it gives just the right twist of flavor to this superb, simple dessert.

4 ounces stale bread, crusts removed, cubed

¾ cup milk

1 tablespoon currants

½ cup seedless red grapes

1 apple, peeled and sliced

1 pear, peeled and sliced

Grated zest of 1 lemon

¼ cup sugar

1 tablespoon unbleached all-purpose flour

1 tablespoon cornmeal

1 egg, room temperature

½ teaspoon vanilla extract

2 tablespoons unsalted butter

1½ tablespoons turbinado sugar

1 teaspoon freshly chopped rosemary leaves

An hour before you are ready to cook, set the bread in a bowl, pour the milk over it, and leave to soak for 1 hour. Soften the currants in warm water to cover for 30 minutes.

Preheat the oven to 350°F.

Move the bread to a mixing bowl, and add the grapes, apple and pear slices, lemon zest, sugar, flour, and cornmeal. Drain the currants and add them to the bowl. Beat the egg and vanilla together and mix them in.

Oil or butter a 9½-inch round baking dish and pour in the mixture. Scatter flakes of the butter over the top, sprinkle with the turbinado sugar and rosemary, and bake for about 1 hour, until the fruit is tender and the top is light golden. Serve at room temperature.

SERVES 4 TO 6

Torta di Pere e Pane Nero

PEAR CRISP WITH
WHOLE-WHEAT CRUMBS

This pear crisp was once a popular *merenda* in the mountainous Garfagnana area of northern Tuscany, but it appears to be just a memory now. I can't imagine why, since it's both delicious and healthy. I poach the pears in wine and use the concentrated syrup to moisten the entire mixture—my own *fantasia*—instead of layering them uncooked. Don't worry if you don't have candied orange peel; it will still taste delicious.

1½ cups red wine

¾ cup sugar

1 teaspoon cinnamon

2 cloves

2 strips lemon zest

1½ pounds medium-size cooking pears, peeled, cored, and sliced (weighed after peeling and coring)

½ cup raisins

About 3 cups, 4 thick slices, fresh whole-wheat bread crumbs (Casareccio with walnuts, page 214, is particularly delicious in this recipe; trim the crusts to make the crumbs)

3 tablespoons candied orange peel, diced

3 to 4 tablespoons unsalted butter

Heat the red wine, sugar, cinnamon, cloves, and lemon zest to a boil in a medium-size enameled saucepan. Gently boil for 10 to 15 minutes, until slightly concentrated. Stir in the sliced pears and cook until tender, stirring occasionally, about 15 to 20 minutes. While the pears are cooking, set the raisins to plump in warm water to cover. Strain the pears; discard the cloves and lemon zest, but reserve the cooking liquid. Drain the raisins.

Preheat the oven to 350°F.

Butter a 1-quart charlotte mold and cover the bottom with ¼ cup of the bread crumbs. On top of it arrange one third of the poached pear slices, a handful of raisins, and one third of the candied orange. Then spread another ¼ cup of the crumbs and continue layering until you have used all the ingredients. Finish with bread crumbs. Pour the reserved cooking liquid over the top and sprinkle with flakes of the butter.

Bake until the crumbs are crisp, about 45 minutes. Serve warm.

SERVES 4 TO 6

Torta di Riso

CUSTARDY RICE PUDDING TORTE

*F*orget everything you know about rice desserts, because this rice pudding torte is in a class of its own—a thin layer of cooked rice covered with a wide swath of creamy citrus-flavored custard. A simple dessert made by mothers and grandmothers, the torta di riso is real comfort food to the people of Massa and Carrara, who are, however, in violent disagreement as to which community it really calls home. While it matters deeply to them, the rest of us can just plunge our spoons into its luscious depths. I've found that even people who don't like rice pudding can't get enough of this one.

4 cups water
½ cup Italian short-grain rice,
    preferably Arborio
7 eggs, room temperature
1 cup sugar
¼ cup rum
Zest of 2 lemons
Zest of 2 oranges
1½ teaspoons vanilla extract
Pinch salt
2 cups plus 2 tablespoons milk

*H*eat the water and rice to a simmer in a medium-size heavy saucepan. Simmer for 10 minutes; then drain, set aside, and leave to cool to room temperature.

Preheat the oven to 350°F.

Beat the eggs well with the sugar until very pale, about 5 to 7 minutes in an electric mixer. Add the rum, lemon and orange zests, vanilla, and salt and mix well. Whisk in the milk.

Butter an 8- or 9-inch baking dish, preferably one with a removable bottom. Spread the rice on the bottom and then pour the creamy mixture on top.

Bake for 45 minutes, until the top is a deep golden color.

Unmold and serve warm.

SERVES 8

Torta di Verdure

SWEET VEGETABLE TART

W hat can I say to convince people that spinach and chard make a sensational dessert tart? This is *the* dessert of Lucca, one that people have been eating for centuries, continually entranced by the combination of greens lightened with a little rice and sweetened with the same Tuscan spices that make panforte so good. Light and healthy, it seems a perfect way to end a meal.

I tasted many torte di verdure in my search for the finest, but I could not persuade Yvonne Mei, the baker of my favorite version, to divulge her secrets. She admits that the cayenne pepper is her own touch and grudgingly allows that the mixture of spices is pure Tuscan, but that was as much as I could learn. This is my best effort at reproducing the wonderful taste of her torta.

DOUGH

2 cups plus 2 tablespoons (300 grams)
   unbleached all-purpose flour

1/3 cup sugar

Pinch salt

14 tablespoons (1¾ sticks) unsalted
   butter, cool room temperature
   (cold for the processor)

1 egg yolk

1 egg

½ teaspoon vanilla extract

1 teaspoon fresh lemon juice, or
   grated zest of 1 lemon

P lace the flour, sugar, and salt in a medium-size bowl or in a food processor; mix or process to combine. Cut the butter into ½-inch pieces, and cut it into the flour mixture with a pastry blender or two knives, or pulse it in the processor, until the mixture resembles coarse meal. Add the egg yolk, egg, vanilla, and lemon juice or zest, mixing with a fork or pulsing until a dough forms. Gather the dough together and knead it very briefly on a lightly floured work surface, just until it is smooth. Form the dough into a ½-inch-thick disc, wrap it with plastic wrap, and chill for 2 hours. (You can also wrap and refrigerate the dough overnight or freeze it for up to 1 month.)

FILLING

Salt

2 tablespoons Italian short-grain rice, such as Arborio

1 pound Swiss chard

1½ pounds spinach, stemmed

3 eggs, beaten

1 slice country-style bread, crusts removed, torn roughly, moistened in 1 tablespoon milk and squeezed dry

2 tablespoons grated Parmigiano-Reggiano cheese

Big pinch cayenne pepper

¼ teaspoon cinnamon

⅛ teaspoon ground cloves

⅛ teaspoon freshly grated nutmeg

⅛ teaspoon ground coriander

¾ cup sugar

Pinch salt

½ cup tightly packed currants

⅔ cup candied orange peel, diced

1 cup pine nuts, chopped

GLAZE

1 egg, beaten

Bring a large amount of salted water to a boil, add the rice, and simmer until tender, about 15 to 18 minutes. Drain and cool to room temperature.

Wash the chard and spinach very well. Remove the white ribs from the chard and cook the leaves in salted boiling water to cover until tender, about 7 to 8 minutes. Set the spinach in a large pot with only the water clinging to the leaves and a little salt. Cover and cook over low heat until tender, about 5 minutes. Drain, squeeze dry, and chop the chard and the spinach. Let the greens cool slightly.

Set the chard and spinach in a large mixing bowl. Stir in the beaten eggs, bread, rice, cheese, cayenne pepper, spices, sugar, salt, currants, orange peel, and pine nuts and mix well. Drain again if there is any extra liquid.

Preheat the oven to 350°F.

Take the dough from the refrigerator, and divide it into two pieces, one twice the size of the other. Press each piece firmly into a ball. On a lightly floured work surface, roll the larger one out to form a 13-inch circle and the second a 9-inch circle. Butter or oil a 2-inch-deep 9-inch springform pan or quiche pan with a removable bottom. Line the pan with the larger circle of dough so that it covers the bottom and overlaps the sides. Spread the vegetable filling evenly over the dough and cover with the second circle of dough. Fold the edge of the bottom crust over the top one, trim any excess, and crimp the edges together decoratively, sealing them well. Brush the top with the beaten egg and prick the crust to allow steam to escape.

Bake on the middle rack of the oven until the crust is golden, 45 to 55 minutes. Cool in the pan to room temperature before removing the sides of the pan. Serve warm or at room temperature.

SERVES 8

Necci

RICOTTA-FILLED CHESTNUT CREPES

Tuscan friends of mine grow nostalgic when they remember stopping on their way home from school for these crepes. Made in little villages near Pontremoli, Massa-Carrara, and Lucca, this rich, nutty-tasting wintertime *merenda* was cooked and filled while they waited. In the countryside necci are still made inside *testi*, iron discs with long tong-like handles. Spoonfuls of the batter are alternated with chestnut leaves, the tongs are closed, and then the disc is thrust into the hot embers to cook. Necci are a traditional treat when friends get together in the late afternoon over a glass of wine. It is very important to have fresh chestnut flour; if the flour is at all stale, the necci will taste bitter.

CREPES

1 cup plus 2 tablespoons (125 grams)
   fresh sweet chestnut flour
1 cup minus 1 tablespoon (125 grams)
   unbleached all-purpose flour
1/8 teaspoon sea salt
1/4 cup sugar
1 1/2 cups plus 1 tablespoon cold water
2 tablespoons olive oil

FILLING

1/2 cup plus 1 tablespoon freshest
   possible ricotta cheese
1/3 cup confectioners' sugar
1/2 teaspoon vanilla extract
Candied orange peel with orange
   syrup or berry preserves (optional)

Sift the two flours with the salt and sugar into a bowl, and then whisk in the cold water and 1 tablespoon of the olive oil to make a smooth liquid batter.

Warm a nonstick 6-inch skillet, and swirl the remaining tablespoon olive oil in it over the heat. Pour off the oil, and film the bottom of the skillet with enough batter to cover it in a thin layer. Cook one side until lightly browned, then flip and cook briefly on the other side. Repeat, cooking 16 crepes and keeping them warm, wrapped in foil, in the oven.

Whirl the ricotta in a food processor outfitted with the steel blade, or press it through a sieve. Sift in the confectioners' sugar, add the vanilla, and mix well. Spread a small mound of the filling down the center of each crepe, roll it up, and serve with a little candied orange or berry preserves on the side.

SERVES 8

Mosto Cotto

FRESH GRAPE SYRUP

Think of *mosto cotto* as honey—a natural sweetener with a flavor of its own. Mosto cotto was originally made by collecting must, the free-running juices of freshly pressed grapes, during the time of the harvest and then cooking it down to the consistency of jelly. It becomes *sapa* when it is cooked down to an even more concentrated syrupy consistency, and *vin cotto* when an equal amount of wine is added and it is allowed to ferment. Mothers once made a *merenda* for their children by spreading sapa on a slice of homemade bread or by thickening it slightly, pouring it on a plate, letting it harden, and cutting it in little lozenges to eat like caramels. People in Abruzzo and Puglia made a delicious granita by pouring sapa over freshly fallen snow. To this day country people may share a communal plate as they sit down in front of a glowing golden circle of steaming hot polenta, claim a small portion for themselves, and flavor it with sapa poured into a hollow.

Sapa comes from *sapore*, the Italian word for flavor, while *mosto cotto* simply means cooked grape juice. Whatever name you choose, use it to flavor fruits (Pere al Mosto, page 266), Fig Salame (page 41), or sorbets.

2 pounds 2 ounces (8 cups) ripe
   red grapes
1 inch cinnamon stick (optional)
4 cloves (optional)
Zest of ½ lemon (optional)

Wash the grapes, remove their stems, and then either mash them in a bowl with a pestle or press them through a food processor using the shredding disc. Drain and press through a sieve, saving the liquid in a large saucepan. You will have about 5 cups liquid. Add the cinnamon stick, cloves, and lemon zest if you are using them. Set over low heat and very slowly simmer for about 1 hour to concentrate the flavor. Stir from time to time and remove any froth that surfaces. Then bring to a vigorous boil and cook down to a semiliquid thick syrup, about 1⅔ cups. Remove the cinnamon, cloves, and lemon zest and set aside to cool. Mosto can be preserved in sterilized jars or frozen.

MAKES ABOUT 1⅔ CUPS

Pere al Mosto

PEARS BAKED IN MOSTO COTTO

A wonderful and simple homey dessert that was once popular during grape season. Reminiscent of pears baked in wine, it should be served with a scoop of ice cream and with biscotti or polenta cookies on the side.

2 cooking pears
1 cup Mosto Cotto (page 265)
½ teaspoon cinnamon

Peel, core, and slice the pears. Bring the mosto to a low simmer in a medium-size saucepan, stir in the cinnamon, and add the pears. Simmer, uncovered, over low heat until the pears are easily pierced with a knife, about 15 minutes. If the liquid becomes too thick, add a little water. Serve at room temperature.

SERVES 2

Sgroppino

LEMON SORBET AND
PROSECCO DESSERT

As cooling as lemon sorbet on a hot summer afternoon and as thirst-quenching as a sparkling citrus-flavored spritzer, *sgroppino* is a refreshing Venetian dessert served in a tall glass. The first time I saw sgroppino, I thought it was a glass of milk. But how could a wonderful meal of savory Venetian cicchetti come to an end with a substance no Italian would dream of drinking? Only when I tasted it was the mystery revealed: I was drinking lemon sorbet whipped with Prosecco, the sparkling white wine of the Veneto. You must whisk the Prosecco in by hand, because a machine will melt the ingredients. Serve sgroppino in a glass and be sure to make enough. Everyone always wants more.

2 lemons
⅔ cup sugar
Substantial freshly grated nutmeg
1½ cups half-and-half
1¼ cups sparkling white wine,
    preferably Prosecco

Scrub and dry the lemons. Grate the lemon zest, the peel without any white pith, into a bowl. Squeeze the lemon juice into a bowl, strain it, and mix it with the zest. Add the sugar and nutmeg, and leave for 5 minutes. Then stir in the half-and-half.

If you have an ice-cream machine, pour the mixture into it and freeze according to the manufacturer's instructions. Otherwise pour the mixture into a shallow metal bowl and freeze it for 2 to 3 hours, or until the mixture is mushy and about half frozen. Remove it from the freezer and whirl it in a food processor with the metal blade, or in an electric mixer, or simply beat it with a whisk (but watch out for the splashes). Return it to the freezer for at least 1½ hours or until you are ready to serve it.

Transfer the sorbet to a bowl and chop it up with a spoon. Whisk in the Prosecco by hand, beating to form a foamy mixture, and pour into tall glasses. Serve immediately.

SERVES 4 TO 6

Barbagliata

ESPRESSO AND COCOA

*I*n the 1930s, when elegant Milanese women paused in the midafternoon in one of the city's fine pastry shops, they drank this special combination of coffee, cocoa, and milk. Serve it hot with whipped cream in the winter or chilled in the summer. Or be unconventional and freeze the entire mixture into a delicious rich sorbet.

¾ cup water

2 teaspoons unsweetened cocoa powder

2 tablespoons sugar

¾ cup regular milk

¾ cup brewed espresso coffee

*P*our the water into a mixing bowl, whisk in the cocoa and sugar, and stir continuously until the sugar dissolves. Transfer to a small saucepan, add the milk and espresso, and set over medium heat. Whisk continually until a white frothy foam forms on the top, about 10 to 12 minutes. Serve hot with vanilla-flavored whipped cream, or chill the mixture and serve it as a rich variation on iced coffee.

VARIATION

Barbagliata Sorbetto To prepare as a sorbet, pour the mixture into a shallow metal bowl—an ice tray would be ideal—and set it in the freezer for 2 to 3 hours, until the mixture is mushy and half frozen. Remove it from the freezer, transfer it to a food processor outfitted with the metal blade or to an electric mixer and whirl until soft. Pour it back into the metal bowl, spread it out evenly, and return it to the freezer for another hour or two. Remove the sorbet from the freezer and allow it to sit at room temperature for 10 to 15 minutes before you plan to serve it.

SERVES 4

Ficatolla del Chianti

SWEET FIG FOCACCIA

Here's a *merenda* from those sweet summer and autumn months when Italy is full of figs—green figs, black figs, fat figs, figs with moist sugary interiors. So numerous are the figs in Chianti that there are enough to eat with prosciutto and salame, to cook in fruit tarts, and still have plenty with which to make this wonderful sweet bread. Like many rustic country treats, it begins with ordinary bread dough that is enriched with eggs and butter. But when fig season arrives, it is covered with a layer of ripe sugary figs. And if there are no fresh figs? Soak dried figs in warm water to bring out their flavor and sprinkle them with abandon over the top.

SPONGE

2 teaspoons active dry yeast

3 tablespoons sugar

1 cup warm water (105° to 115°F)

2 large eggs, room temperature

1¾ cups plus 2 tablespoons (250 grams) unbleached all-purpose flour

DOUGH

1¾ cups (250 grams) unbleached all-purpose flour

1 teaspoon sea salt

6 tablespoons unsalted butter, room temperature

Stir the yeast and sugar into the warm water in a large mixing or mixer bowl; let stand until foamy, 5 to 10 minutes. Beat in the eggs with a wooden spoon or mixer paddle, and stir in the flour in two or three additions by hand or all at once in the mixer. Cover tightly with plastic wrap and let stand until bubbly, about 30 minutes.

Stir the flour and salt into the sponge. Then beat in the butter, 1 tablespoon at a time, by hand or all at once with the mixer paddle. Knead the dough by hand for 6 to 7 minutes on a lightly floured surface or for 3 minutes with the dough hook of the mixer. The dough should be sturdy enough to hold a peak if you pinch it.

First rise. Place the dough in an oiled bowl, cover it well with plastic wrap, and let it rise until doubled, about 1½ hours.

(continued)

TOPPING
1 pound sliced fresh or dried figs
⅓ cup plus 1 tablespoon turbinado
  sugar

If you are using dried figs, cover them with warm water and soak them for 30 minutes. Drain and pat them dry before using.

Shaping and second rise. Stretch the soft, slightly sticky dough out to fit a 10½- × 15½-inch oiled baking sheet. Cover it with a towel, and let it relax for 10 minutes. Then stretch it again so that it truly covers the sheet. Strew the top with the figs and the turbinado sugar, cover with a towel, and leave to rise until not entirely doubled, about 1 hour.

Baking. Preheat the oven to 400°F. If you are using baking stones, preheat them for 30 minutes. Bake the focaccia for 15 minutes. Reduce the temperature to 375°F and continue baking for another 15 minutes, until the top is golden. Cool for a few minutes in the pan, then remove and cool on a rack.

SERVES 8 TO 10

Focaccia All'Uva

RAISIN FOCACCIA

*I*magine a juicy focaccia that is absolutely bursting with raisins and you'll understand why this sweet always makes a hit. How many raisins fill its interior is up to you; if you feel daring, you could add another cupful, but be very gentle when stretching the dough to cover the baking sheet. Is this popular? I've seen Italians eat it for breakfast, at midmorning, and during an afternoon break.

2 cups raisins
1¼ teaspoons active dry yeast
2 tablespoons sugar
Raisin water
1 tablespoon olive oil
3¾ cups (500 grams) unbleached all-purpose flour, plus 2 tablespoons for the tossing with the raisins
1 teaspoon sea salt
3 tablespoons turbinado sugar

*C*over the raisins with at least 2 cups water, and let them soak for 30 minutes. Drain them, reserving the water. Warm 1¼ cups plus 3 tablespoons of the raisin water to 105° to 115°F. Reserve the remaining raisin water.

Whisk the yeast and sugar into the warmed raisin water and let stand until foamy, about 10 minutes. Stir in the olive oil. Stir the 3¾ cups flour and the salt into the yeast mixture, 2 cups at a time if you are working by hand, or all at once in a heavy-duty mixer with the paddle attachment. Mix until a dough is formed. Knead the dough by hand on a lightly floured surface for 4 to 5 minutes; or change to the dough hook and knead for 2 minutes at low speed, 2 at medium. The dough should be velvety, elastic, and slightly moist.

First rise. Set the dough in a lightly oiled bowl, cover with plastic wrap, and let rise until doubled, about 1½ hours.

Shaping and second rise. Turn the dough out onto a lightly floured work surface and pat it into a 12-inch square. The dough will be slightly sticky and very malleable. Pat the raisins dry and toss them with the 2 tablespoons flour. Cover the top of the dough with the raisins, leaving a 1½-inch margin all around. Turn in the sides. Fold the dough in thirds, as if it were a business letter. Set it seam side down on a 10½- × 15½-inch oiled baking sheet. Stretch and press the dough outward, and flatten it with the palms of your hands. Leave it to rest for 10 minutes. Then stretch it again, trying to cover the entire baking sheet. Cover with a towel and let rest until well puffed but not doubled, about 1½ hours.

Baking. Preheat the oven to 400°F. If you are using baking stones, preheat them for 30 minutes. Just before baking, paint the top of the focaccia with some of the remaining raisin water and sprinkle it with the turbinado sugar. Bake for 20 to 25 minutes, until the top is golden. Cool for a few minutes in the pan, then remove and cool on a rack.

SERVES 8 TO 10

Panesiglio Aversano

LEMON CURRANT BUNS

What did aristocratic Neapolitans eat for a midafternoon *merenda* before the 1950s? My friend Franco Santasilia, who gave me this recipe, remembers looking forward to these delicate lemon currant buns when he came home from school. Please notice that 6 hours before the real baking begins, you will need to set the lemon zest in milk to enable its flavor to permeate the liquid.

Zest of ½ lemon, all pith removed
¾ cup milk

SPONGE
2½ teaspoons (1 package, 7 grams)
   active dry yeast
1 tablespoon sugar
Reserved milk
¾ cup (100 grams) unbleached all-
   purpose flour

Six hours before you plan to bake these little sweet breads, cut the lemon zest in half and score the surface. Set the zest in the milk. After it has soaked for 6 hours, drain the lemon zest, reserving the milk. Finely chop the zest.

Warm the lemon-flavored milk to tepid (105° to 115°F). Stir the yeast and the sugar into the warmed milk in a heavy-duty mixer or a large mixing bowl; let it stand until foamy, about 10 minutes. Whisk in the flour and stir until smooth. Cover with plastic wrap and let rise until doubled, about 30 to 45 minutes.

(continued)

DOUGH

½ cup plus 1 tablespoon sugar

3 eggs, room temperature

1 egg yolk, room temperature

About 3 cups minus 1 tablespoon
(400 grams) unbleached all-
purpose flour

¾ teaspoon sea salt

9 tablespoons unsalted butter,
room temperature

1¾ cups currants

2 to 3 tablespoons unbleached all-
purpose flour

¼ cup candied citron or lemon
peel

GLAZE

1 egg white

Stir the sugar, eggs, egg yolk, and reserved lemon zest into the sponge. Mix in
the flour and the salt and stir until
smooth, using the paddle if you are working with an electric mixer. Beat in the butter, 2 tablespoons at a time, and mix
thoroughly until the dough is smooth and
velvety. If you are making the dough by
hand, knead it on a lightly floured work
surface for about 8 to 10 minutes; using a
mixer, change to the dough hook and
knead for 4 minutes. The dough should be
velvety, smooth, and soft.

First rise. Transfer the dough to a buttered bowl, cover well with plastic wrap,
and let rise until doubled, about 1¾ to 2
hours. Thirty minutes before you plan to
shape the dough, set the currants in tepid
water to soak.

Filling and second rise. Drain the currants well, pat them dry,
and toss them with the 2 to 3 tablespoons flour. Flatten the dough on
a lightly floured work surface and spread the currants and candied fruit
over it, leaving a 1-inch margin all around. Tuck in the sides and roll
up the dough lengthwise. Let it recuperate for about 5 minutes. Cut
the dough into 12 to 14 equal pieces and shape each into a ball. Place
on a lightly buttered or parchment-lined baking sheet, cover with a
towel, and let rise until puffy and half doubled, 45 minutes to 1 hour.

Preheat the oven to 400°F. When you are ready to bake, brush the
tops of the rolls with the egg white. Bake the rolls on the middle level
of the oven until they are golden, about 18 to 22 minutes.

MAKES 12 TO 14

Buccellato di Lucca

WREATH-SHAPED SWEET BREAD
FROM LUCCA

Every time I make a buccellato, it disappears so quickly that I wonder why I didn't make two. It seems that no one can resist a bread that is crammed with raisins and fragrant with orange and anise.

No upstart is this sweet bread—it has a real place in history. The name dates from Roman times, and by the Middle Ages it was the accepted gift from vassals to their overlords. Aware that the people loved their buccellato at all costs, the rulers of Lucca even imposed a tax on it to replenish the city treasury. How wonderful that this delicacy should have helped to finance local government!

Buccellato may be the source of the biscotti we know today, for its name comes from the Latin *buccella*, meaning military bread, or *biscotto*. It is certainly sold sliced and toasted in bakeries all over town. The bread keeps a long time, getting firmer as it ages, and the pieces are often dipped into wine or Vin Santo, like biscotti. Some people dip slices into Vin Santo, sprinkle them with sugar, and then cover them with fresh strawberries to make a delicious dessert.

Lucca's traditional buccellato contains lemon essence, anise, and raisins that are so chewy and full of seeds that they resemble figs. This version is one that I've eaten in a variety of places just outside Lucca. It differs in that it has the subtle taste of orange and candied orange, lots of raisins, and a hailstorm of sugar sprinkled on top.

SPONGE
2½ teaspoons (1 package) active dry yeast
1 tablespoon sugar
⅓ cup warm water (105° to 115°F)
½ cup (70 grams) unbleached all-purpose flour

Whisk the yeast and the sugar into the warm water in a large bowl, and leave until foamy, about 10 minutes. Whisk in the flour and stir until smooth. Cover well with plastic wrap and leave until doubled, about 30 minutes.

(continued)

DOUGH

3 tablespoons Marsala

2 eggs, room temperature

½ cup plus 2 tablespoons milk, room
temperature

Grated zest of 1 lemon or 1 orange

½ teaspoon lemon extract

¾ cup sugar

4 tablespoons unsalted butter, room
temperature

3½ cups plus 5 tablespoons (470
grams) unbleached all-purpose flour

2 teaspoons anise seeds, slightly
crushed

⅛ teaspoon sea salt

GLAZE

1 egg white

1 to 1½ tablespoons turbinado sugar

Stir the Marsala, eggs, milk, lemon or orange zest, lemon extract, and sugar into the sponge and mix well. Add the butter in two additions. Stir in the flour, anise seeds, and salt in two additions, if by hand, or all at once with the paddle in a heavy-duty mixer; mix for about 3 minutes. Knead by hand on a floured work surface for 8 to 10 minutes, or in the mixer with the dough hook for 3 to 4 minutes, until the dough is sticky, elastic, and velvety. It will not come away from the sides of the bowl; finish kneading by hand with a very little flour on a work surface and a tiny amount of flour on top of the dough, and it will come together well.

First rise. Place the dough in a lightly oiled bowl, cover it with plastic wrap, and let it rise until doubled, about 3 to 3 ½ hours.

FILLING

1¾ cups raisins

2 tablespoons unbleached all-purpose
flour

3 tablespoons candied orange or
lemon peel (optional)

At least 30 minutes before the end of the first rise, soak the raisins in cool water to cover. Drain and pat dry.

Shaping and second rise. Roll the dough out on a lightly floured work surface to form a 16-inch circle. Toss the raisins with the 2 tablespoons flour. Sprinkle the raisins and the candied orange or lemon peel over the dough, tuck the edges in, roll the dough up into a log, and pinch the ends closed. Move it to a parchment paper–lined baking sheet, and connect the ends to make a ring about 10 inches in diameter; press them together firmly so the wreath holds its shape. Try to keep the central opening as wide as you can. Cover the ring with a towel and let it rise until not fully doubled, about 1 hour.

(continued)

Baking. Preheat the oven to 400°F. Just before you are ready to bake, beat the reserved egg white and brush it over the dough. Sprinkle with the turbinado sugar.

Bake for 25 to 30 minutes, until the top is golden and a tester comes out clean. If the buccellato looks very brown after 20 minutes, cover it with foil and continue baking for the full time. Cool on a rack.

SERVES 8 TO 10

Ramerino all'Olio

ROSEMARY RAISIN BUNS

These plump buns are the classical *merenda* of Arezzo, the after-school treat of generations of hungry students. If you've ever eaten their city cousin, the hot cross bun made in Florence especially for Easter week, you'll recognize the resemblance; they are typically Tuscan in mixing the sweetness of raisins with the barely perceptible bite of rosemary. Should you want to make these plump buns sweeter, save the raisin water and dissolve the yeast in it.

¾ cup plus 1½ tablespoons raisins

1¼ cups warm water (105° to 115°F)

3½ teaspoons active dry yeast

¼ cup sugar

¼ cup olive oil

3¾ cups (500 grams) unbleached all-purpose flour

1 teaspoon sea salt

2 teaspoons chopped fresh rosemary leaves

Plump the raisins in warm water for 20 minutes; drain, saving the water if you want to use it, and squeeze the raisins dry.

For a sweeter bun, warm 1¼ cups of the raisin soaking water to 105° to 115°F; otherwise use regular water. Stir the yeast into the warm water in a large mixing bowl and leave until creamy, about 10 minutes. Whisk in the sugar and 2 tablespoons of the olive oil. If you are making these by hand, stir in the flour and salt, a cup at a time, and mix until the dough is no longer sticky—it will be a raggedy mass. Knead by hand on a lightly floured surface until smooth and elastic, 6 to 8 minutes. If you are making them in a heavy-duty electric mixer, add the flour and salt all at once and mix with the paddle attachment until the dough pulls away from the sides of the bowl. Change to the dough hook and knead for 2 minutes on low speed and 2 minutes on medium. The dough should be smooth and elastic.

First rise. Place the dough in a lightly oiled bowl, cover tightly with plastic wrap, and let rise until doubled, about 1 hour.

Shaping and second rise. While the dough is rising, drain the raisins and very briefly sauté them with the rosemary in the remaining 2 tablespoons olive oil. Let the oil cool to room temperature.

Flatten the dough on a lightly floured work surface and pat it into a large circle. Sprinkle the rosemary, oil, and raisins over the dough, turn the edges in, and roll it up. Leave it to rest under a towel for 5 to 10 minutes.

Divide the dough into 14 pieces and roll each one into a ball. Set them on parchment-lined or lightly oiled baking sheets, cover with a towel, and let rise until doubled, about 1 hour.

Baking. Preheat the oven to 400°F. If you are using baking stones, preheat them for 30 minutes.

If the buns have slumped during the second rise, gently reshape them. Just before baking, flatten each bun very lightly with the palm of your hand, and using a razor, cut a shallow cross on top. Let them recover from this by resting under a towel for 10 to 15 minutes. To give the rolls a slight gloss, paint them with some of the remaining raisin water. Bake for 15 to 20 minutes, until golden. Cool on racks.

MAKES 14

Maritozzi delle Marche

LEMONY SWEET BUNS

How did I get the secret for baking these little sweet buns that are as delicate as brioche yet contain absolutely no butter? It wasn't easy. I had to promise Leila, the baker in San Lorenzo in Campo, that I would never publish the recipe in Italy and certainly wouldn't divulge it to anyone in the region. Maritozzi were once sold mostly by ambulatory vendors at festivals and country fairs in the Marches, but now they are all the rage at breakfast with cappuccino or in the midafternoon with a glass of white wine.

(continued)

SPONGE

3¾ teaspoons active dry yeast

¾ cup milk, warmed to 105° to 115°F

½ cup (70 grams) unbleached all-purpose flour

DOUGH

Scant 3 cups (410 grams) unbleached all-purpose flour

½ cup plus 2 tablespoons sugar

1 teaspoon sea salt

7 tablespoons olive oil

2 eggs, room temperature

Grated zest of 1 lemon

1 teaspoon vanilla extract

¾ teaspoon lemon extract

GLAZE

1 egg white, beaten

Stir the yeast into the warm milk in a small bowl; let stand until creamy, about 10 minutes. Add the flour and stir until smooth. Cover well with plastic wrap and let rise until doubled, about 15 to 20 minutes.

Place the flour, sugar, and salt in a large mixing bowl. With a wooden spoon or the paddle of a heavy-duty mixer, stir in the sponge, olive oil, eggs, lemon zest, and vanilla and lemon extracts. If the dough seems dry, immediately add an additional 1 to 2 tablespoons water. Knead on a lightly floured board until velvety and smooth, about 8 to 10 minutes by hand, 3 minutes with the dough hook at medium speed. Don't be surprised if the dough never pulls away from the bottom of the mixer bowl.

First rise. Place the dough in a lightly oiled bowl, cover with plastic wrap, and let rise until doubled, about 1¾ to 2 hours.

Second rise. Turn the dough out onto a lightly floured work surface and cut it into 22 to 24 pieces, each about the size of a lime. Roll each into a ball. Place the rolls on lightly oiled or parchment paper–lined baking sheets. Cover them with a towel and leave them to rise until doubled, about 1 to 1¼ hours.

Baking. Preheat the oven to 375°F. Brush the buns with the beaten egg white. Bake on the middle shelf of the oven for about 10 minutes, until golden. Watch them carefully to make sure they don't brown too much on the bottom. Cool on racks.

MAKES 22 TO 24

Source Guide

Ingredients

Arrowhead Mills
P.O. Box 866
Hereford, TX 79045
(713) 364-0730
An excellent selection of flours, including durum, corn flour and polenta, organic stone-ground whole wheat, and unbleached all-purpose white.

Balducci's
424 Sixth Ave.
New York, NY 10011
(212) 673-2600
A huge selection of Italian specialties and imports including grains, beans, chestnut flour, and cheeses. They will ship all ingredients in the store.

Brumwell Flour Mill
South Amana, IA 52333
(319) 622-3455

Chestnut Hill Orchards
3300 Bee Cave Rd., Suite 650
Austin, TX 78746
(512) 327-4107 or (800) 745-3279;
    fax (512) 477-3020
Outstanding fresh organic chestnut flour, fresh frozen chestnuts, frozen chestnut purée.

Corti Bros.
5771 Freeport Blvd.
Sacramento, CA 94822
(916) 391-0300
Many of the best of Italian products, including anchovy paste, dried beans, olive oils, tomato paste, olive paste, and dried mushrooms.

Dean and DeLuca
121 Prince St.
New York, NY 10012
(212) 254-8776
Excellent selection of Italian products, including herbs, spices, olive paste and olive oils, olives, dried porcini mushrooms, cheeses, beans, grains, flours, and rices.

Giusto's
241 East Harris Ave.
South San Francisco, CA 94080
(415) 873-6566
Outstanding organically grown whole grain flours.

Kavanaugh Hill Spice Shop
1921 S. West Ave.
Waukesha, WI 53186
(414) 258-7727
Excellent spices.

King Arthur Flour
The Baker's Catalogue
RR 2, Box 56
Norwich, VT 05055
(800) 827-6836
Flours, grains, extensive ingredients and equipment for the home baker.

Manicaretti
299 Lawrence Ave.
South San Francisco, CA 94080
(415) 589-1120; fax (415) 589-5766
Rolando Beramendi has brought a panoply of outstanding Italian products to his pantry: aged balsamic vinegars, extra-virgin olive oils, Ascolane olives, olive pastes, anchovies, capers in sea salt, polentas, sun-dried tomatoes, organic rice. If you send a fax, he will let you know which shops in your area carry those products.

Mozzarella Company
2944 Elm St.
Dallas, TX 75226
(214) 741-4072; fax (214) 741-4076
Paula Lambert makes her own sheep's-
    milk caciotta and pecorino as well as
    taleggio, fresh and smoked mozzarella,
    ricotta, crescenza, and scamorza.

Paprikas Weiss
1572 Second Ave.
New York, NY 10028
(212) 288-6117
Huge supply includes spices and cheeses.
    One of the best sources for mail-order
    beans.

Phipps Ranch
P.O. Box 349
Pescadero, CA 94060
(415) 879-0787
An outstanding source of beans, includ-
    ing fava beans.

G. B. Ratto, International Grocers
821 Washington St.
Oakland, CA 94607
(510) 832-6503
Excellent collection of grains, dried
    beans, olive oils, meals and flours.
    They will ship.

Royal Pacific Foods
100 Park Place, Suite 125
San Ramon, CA 94583
(510) 831-9263; fax (510) 831-9163
Excellent candied lemon and orange
    peel.

Todaro Bros.
557 Second Ave.
New York, NY 10016
(212) 679-7766
A huge selection of Italian ingredients,
    including dried porcini, cheeses, ol-
    ives, and oils. They will ship them
    all.

Vivande
2125 Fillmore St.
San Francisco, CA 94115
(415) 346-3430
The shop is devoted to and will ship its
    Italian products, including durum
    flour, Ascolane olives, olive pastes,
    extra-virgin oils, capers in sea salt,
    and sun-dried tomatoes.

Williams-Sonoma
P.O. Box 7456
San Francisco, CA 94120-7456
(415) 421-4242;
catalogue (800) 541-2233
Excellent quality candied orange and
    lemon peel, vanilla beans, sun-dried
    tomatoes, chocolate, polenta, corn
    and durum flours, tomato paste, Per-
    nigotti cocoa. Some available
    through their catalogue, others
    through writing to the store.

Zingerman's
422 Detroit Street
Ann Arbor, MI 48104
(313) 663-0974
The shop will ship its numerous Italian
    products.

Equipment

Maid of Scandinavia
3244 Raleigh Ave.
Minneapolis, MN 55416
(612) 927-7966 or (800) 328-6722
An excellent source of baking ingredi-
    ents and equipment.

Salday Products
7533 Lindberg Dr.
Gaithersburg, MD 20879
(301) 330-9012; fax (301) 330-0602
Bakers' peels, tiles, hot bricks.

Sassafras Enterprises Inc.
1622 West Carroll Ave.
Chicago, IL 60612
(312) 226-2000
(800) 537-4941; fax (312) 226-0873
The source of baking stones, pizza peels,
    and pizza pans.

Von Snedaker
12021 Wilshire Blvd., Suite 213
Los Angeles, CA 90025
(310) 395-6365; fax (310) 454-2188
Importers of reusable nonstick baking
    sheets, a great alternative to parch-
    ment paper.

Williams-Sonoma
(see above)
Electric mixers, instant bread thermom-
    eters, pizza stones, scales, and many
    other pieces of equipment.

Selected Bibliography

Balsdon, J. P.V.D. *Life and Leisure in Ancient Rome*. McGraw-Hill Book Company, 1969.

Behr, Edward. "Pizza in Naples" in *The Art of Eating*, Spring 1992.

Bergonzini, Renato. *A Tavola con i Cibi Tradizionali della Nostra Montagna*, edito a cura del Comune di Pavullo e della Comunità Montana di Frignano.

Boni, Ada. *La Cucina Romana*. Rome: Newton Compton Editori, 1983.

Camporesi, Piero. *Alimentazione, Folclore, Società*. Parma: Practiche Editrice, no date.

Carcopinto, Jerome. *Daily Life in Ancient Rome*. New Haven: Yale University Press, 1940.

Castelvetro, Giacomo. *The Fruit, Herbs and Vegetables of Italy*, translated with and introduction by Gillian Riley. New York: Viking Press, 1989.

Cucina, magazine of the Gruppo Ristoratori Italiani, 1990–1993.

Del Conte, Anna. *Gastronomy of Italy*. New York: Prentice Hall Press, 1987.

D'Errico, Lucia Gaballo. *Il Salento a Tavola: Guida alla cucina leccese*. Lecce: Congedo Editore, 1990.

di Schino, June. "Pasta Eating in the Streets of Naples," Public Eating, Proceedings of the Oxford Symposium. Prospect Books, 1991.

Dosi, Antonietta and Schnell, Francois. *A tavola con i Romani Antichi*. Rome: Edizioni Quasar, 1984.

Falassi, Alessandro, di Corato, Riccardo, and Stiaccini, Pierluigi. *Pan che canti, vin che salti*. Editrice I Torchi Chiantigiani, 1979.

Ferrante, Maria Pignatelli. *La Cucina della Murge*. Padua: Franco Muzzio Editore, 1991.

Foscarini, Antonio Edoardo. *La cucina leccese: Tradizioni, curiosita e ricette della cucina salentina*, Volume 1. Lecce: Edizioni del Grifo, 1987.

Goria, Giovanni. *La cucina del Piemonte*. Padua: Franco Muzzio Editore, 1990.

Gotti, Marco Guarnaschelli. *Grande enciclopedia illustrata della gastronomia*. Milan: Selezione dal Reader's Digest, 1990.

Gray, Patience. *Honey from a Weed*. London: Prospect Books, 1986.

Incontri Lotteringhi della Stufa, Maria Luisa. *Pranzi e conviti*. Florence: Editoriale Olimpia, 1965.

Jannattoni, Livio. *Il Ghiottone Romano*. Milan: Bramante Editrice, 1965.

Kummer, Corby. "Real Olives," *The Atlantic*, June 1993.

Martelli, Angelo. *La cucina povera in Emilia–Romagna*. Marino Solfanelli Editore, 1989.

May, Tony. *Italian Cuisine*. New York: Italian Wine and Food Institute, 1990.

Monelli, Paolo. *Il Ghiottone Errante*. Milan: S.A. Fratelli Treves Editori, 1935.

Petroni, Paolo. *Cucina Toscana*, Vols. 1 and 2. Firenze: Gruppo Editoriale Fiorentino and Paolo Petroni, 1990.

Pianigiani, Ottorino. *Vocabulario Etimologico*. Fratelli Melita Editore, no date.

Piccinardi, Antonio. *Il Libro della Vera Cucina Milanese*. Milan: Bonechi, 1989.

Porresi, Nicola Mazzara. *La cucina marchigiana*. Edizione Fratelli Aniballi, 1978.

Revel, Jean-Francois. *Culture and Cuisine*. New York: Doubleday, 1982.

Riley, Gillian. "Giovedi gnocchi, sabato trippa." Proceedings of the Oxford Symposium, Prospect Books, 1990.

Sada, Luigi. *La Cucina della Terra di Bari*. Padua: Franco Muzzio Editore, 1991.

———. *Cucina pugliese all poverella*. Foggia: I Quaderini del Rosone, Edizioni del Rosone, 1991.

———. *Dolci Boccone di Puglia*. Bari: Edizioni del Centro Librario, 1981.

———. *Puglia*. Milan: Edizioni Sipiel, 1989.

Salvatori de Zuliani, Mariu. *La Cucina di Versilia e Garfagnana*. Milan: Franco Angeli Editore, 1983.

Salza-Prina Ricotti, Eugenia. *Il Convito nell'Antica Roma*. Rome: "L'Erma" di Bretschneider, 1983.

Simeti, Mary Taylor. *Pomp and Sustenance*. New York: Alfred A. Knopf, 1989.

Tannahill, Reay. *Food in History*. New York: Stein and Day, 1973.

Willinger, Faith Heller. *Eating in Italy*. New York: Hearst Books, 1989.

Wolfert, Paula. *Paula Wolfert's World of Food*. New York: Harper and Row, 1988.

Index